Invisible Children in the Society and Its Schools

Sociocultural, Political, and Historical Studies in Education

Joel Spring, Editor

Spring • The Cultural Transformation of a Native American Family and Its Tribe

Reagan • Non-Western Educational Traditions: Alternative Approaches to Educational Thought and Practice

Peshkin • Places of Memory: Whiteman's Schools and Native American Communities

Spring • Political Agendas for Education: From the Christian Coalition to the Green Party

Nespor • Tangled Up in School: Politics, Space, Bodies, and Signs in the Educational Process

Weinberg • Asian-American Education: Historical Background and Cultural Realities

Books • Invisible Children in the Society and Its Schools

Benham/Heck • Culture and Educational Policy in Hawaii: The Silencing of Native Voices

Lipka/Mohat/Ciulistet Group • Transforming the Culture of Schools: Yup'ik Eskimo Examples

Shapiro/Purpel, Eds. • Critical Social Issues in American Education: Second Edition

Invisible Children in the Society and Its Schools

Edited by

Sue Books
State University of New York at New Paltz

LEA LAWRENCE ERLBAUM ASSOCIATES, PUBLISHERS
1998 Mahwah, New Jersey   London

Lawrence Erlbaum Associates, Inc., Publishers
10 Industrial Avenue
Mahwah, New Jersey 07430

Library of Congress Cataloging-in-Publication-Data

Invisible children in the society and its schools / edited by Sue
Books.
     p. cm.
   Includes bibliographical references and index.
   ISBN 0-8058-2368-9 (pbk.)
   1. Socially handicapped children—United States. 2.
Socially handicapped children—Education—United
States. 3. Socially handicapped teenagers—United
States. 4. Socially handicapped teenagers—Educa-
tion—United States. 5. Educational sociology—United
States. 6. Marginality, Social—United States. I. Books,
Sue.
   HV741.I7 1998   98–33966
   362.7—dc21   CIP

Books published by Lawrence Erlbaum Associates are printed
on acid-free paper, and their bindings are chosen for strength
and durability.

Printed in the United States of America
10 9 8 7 6 5 4 3

For my wise and gentle daughter, Cora Mae

Contents

✿ • ✿

Foreword   ix
  David E. Purpel

Preface   xv

Introduction: An Invitation to Listen and Learn   xix
  Sue Books

I: YOUNG AND INVISIBLE   1

1. Homeless Children and Their Families: The Discards   3
     of the Postmodern 1990s
       Valerie Polakow

2. Living with Violence: White Working-Class   23
     Girls and Women Talk
       Lois Weis and Julia Marusza

3. The Crisis Within the Crisis: The Growing Epidemic   47
     of AIDS Orphans
       Shelley Geballe and Janice Gruendel

4. Immigrant Children: Art as a Second Language   67
       Cristina Igoa

5. Urban Appalachian Children: An "Invisible Minority"   89
in City Schools
   Kathleen Bennett deMarrais

6. Traditional Stories of Female Students in an Alternative School   111
   Linda Steet

7. "Before Their Time": Social Age, Sexuality,   121
and School-Aged Mothers
   Nancy Lesko

8. Heterosexism, Homophobia, and the Culture of Schooling   137
   Richard A. Friend

II: THE BROADER CONTEXT OF INVISIBILITY   167

9. Where Have All the Children Gone? The Transformation   169
of Children Into Dollars in Public Law 104-193
   Barbara Finkelstein, Reem Mourad, and Elyssa Doner

10. Speaking of and Against Youth   183
   Sue Books

Author Index   201

Subject Index   207

About the Authors   211

Foreword

❈ • ❈

David E. Purpel
University of North Carolina at Greensboro

This book is at once disturbing and reassuring—disturbing in that it reveals the ugly face of hostility and cruelty, and reassuring in that it reminds us that we as a species can continue to recognize and be aware of this ugliness. Sue Books and her colleagues affirm a tradition that must be regarded as miraculous by virtue of its continung capacity to engender sorrow and outrage over human suffering. The time when we can neither feel compassion for human suffering nor accept responsibility for it is a time when we will know beyond any doubt that we are living in hell.

Let me deal first with the disturbances. At the most basic level, the authors add further poignancy to the tragic history of unnecessary human suffering and to the human capacity to violate our own solemn commitments. That the weakest and most vulnerable among us bear so much of this suffering only adds to the heartbreak of these chapters, especially when one considers that caring for the weak and downtrodden is or ought to be at the core of our culture's moral vision. However, in many if not most cases, the suffering is magnified when we add to the insult of creating the vulnerability in the first place, the injury of punishing those we have stigmatized.

How is it that teenage mothers, AIDS orphans, immigrant children, Appalachian children, and others come to be "invisible" when paradoxically their visibility marks them for stigmatization? Sadly, responsibility for this lies not with the unseen, for it takes a conscious effort by the beholder to render vibrant and palpable beings into an immaterial state, an act of metaphysical virtuosity and moral degeneracy. And if, as I have suggested, invisibility is indeed in the eyes of the beholder, how and why does one learn this ability? What kind of culture fosters the development of such distorted skills and what kind of psychology allows this syndrome to be nameless?

The tendency to stigmatize and exclude is at the heart of the tragedy of division and hatred that so vividly marks the human condition and threatens our aspirations to transcend our basest instincts for survival and domination. I believe very strongly that our schools, even as they struggle to encourage us to be civil and respectful, nevertheless also feed the impulse to exclude and to dominate. The rhetoric about schools is saturated with concern for achievement and success and with the ethic of competition. "Good" students are those who achieve and "bad" students are those who do not achieve as much. Honor is awarded to those with "good" grades. Work is graded and with the implicit notion that what is also being graded is the worker. In a word, human worth becomes contingent on performance. How strikingly different from the discourse of our many moral, spiritual, and political traditions that proclaim the inherent equality and dignity of all people!

Schools are one of those places where dignity is rationed and affirmation has to be earned everyday, where students have to struggle to be accepted and valued, and where teachers and administrators dole out varying degrees of love, acceptance, and approval. Underneath all these negotiations and transactions is the fundamental message, however unspoken, that some people are better than others and that it is proper to devise ways to determine who is better and what the consequences are to be. Schools are saturated with practices of discrimination, privilege, and hierarchy, marketed as modes of promoting excellence and as effective motivational devices. If some people are to graduate with honor, it seems logical to conclude that other people can graduate without honor, never mind what those who do not graduate at all must be like. If one of the perks of teachers is to be assigned to classes of bright students, it is at least possible for the not-so-bright to consider themselves as something less than desirable.

These school practices mimic, reflect, and help to legitimate a broader meritocratic culture in which people are said to deserve their role and status based on their abilities and competencies. Status, we tell ourselves, is no longer a function of birth or riches. However, hierarchy is hierarchy whatever its origin and justification. In the context of school, it is permissible, nay it is required, to make distinctions among human beings for purposes of allocating differentiated rewards. However, the rules require that the competition be fair (a "level playing ground") and that the criteria for success relate only to merit and not to matters of race, gender, class, and the like. This enables the rule makers to believe they are objective and impartial, for if one loses in this competition, it is because of flaws in oneself, not in the system. This adds up to culturally approved and legitimated discrimination and to an officially sanctioned system of privilege for the few, the powerful, and the able.

What are we to make of those who do not measure up? Under the rules we can respect them (if they work hard and play by the rules), provide opportunities appropriate to their abilities, and urge them to have a nice day. For those who do not enter into the fray as good sports, we have bewilderment, contempt, and resentment, unsure about whether such people are sick, lazy, or subhuman.

The losers in this deadly game are not the only ones to suffer from the competition. What also gets lost (becomes invisible) is our common humanity and commitment to regard each other as divine sparks, not bundles of useful and acceptable skills wrapped in human form. The distance from this latter vantage point to the area where people are humiliated and punished for being young, sick, gay, non-White, or hungry is not all that great. Somehow, we have learned to be tough-minded, indifferent, even callous, to those who are not good enough to qualify even for the bronze.

And yet, as this volume powerfully reminds us, there is hope in these stories of pain and heartbreak. There is hope in the resilience, courage, and perseverance of victims of human callousness as they struggle for survival and dignity. There is hope in the kindness, sensitivity, and concern of those strong enough to be tender and wise enough to be responsive. And there is hope in the reality that these narratives disturb and pain us as they remind us of some of our most cherished commitments and our most profound responsibilities.

This book of witnessing itself is witness to the human impulse to challenge and ruffle the semiconspiratorial denial that constitutes our current era of "good feeling." We have a new politics of smugness and complacency where the biggest worry seems to be how long the bull stock market will last. The homeless have been banned from public consciousness and political discourse, the poor chastised for being poor, and immigrants vilified for believing that the United States is the land of opportunity.

This book is just the right kind of pin, one sharpened with honesty and compassion, to deflate this flabby and distorted balloon. The authors have not been duped into the Reaganesque and Clintonesque myths of a happy and harmonious America working hard to make room in the middle class for everyone. Neither are these authors paralyzed by a rhetoric of despair that suggests our melting pot will turn into a melting furnace as we lurch toward fratricide and chaos. They temper their suspicion with data, their revulsion with compassion, and their sorrow with admiration.

This capacity and intention to seek truth in the name of justice represents the kind of education and research that is truly liberatory. As a people, as well as individually, we need to be liberated from our deeply rooted suspicions and dreads and from our propensity to create and sustain enemies. This task cannot be left only to schools and certainly will not be eradicated by special courses, improved curricula, or even by sophisticated analyses. As we know, it "takes a village" to stigmatize a child.

For that reason, I hope this book is widely read not only within the profession but also by the lay public. We all ought to know about the indignities and cruelties it documents and about the gratuitous pain these indignities and cruelties inflict on both the unlucky and the unwanted. We also ought to be reminded of the redemptive work that needs to be done. The chapters in this book provide information, set an agenda, and point the way toward what must be done to reduce, if not eliminate, the suffering.

However, this book is more than an exercise in research, documentation, and dissemination. It is more significant than a useful catalogue of serious social problems. And it does something much more profound than increase our awareness. Ultimately, the most shocking aspect of this book is its painful and tragic *familiarity*. Although the book certainly provides the reader with valuable details, the documentation of victimization, suffering, and cruelty is perhaps the oldest story line of human existence. As Andre Gide once said, it is true that everything has already been said, but it is also true that nobody was listening. For that reason, it all must be said again.

Does anyone doubt that at some deep level we already know about the magnitude of unnecessary human suffering? Surely and ironically the well-educated people who run the engines of our social and economic system know in great and specific detail about the extent of social injustice. Is it not time to finally give up on one of our most cherished beliefs—namely, that the truth (defined as knowledge and critical insight) will make us free? The most powerful message of this book for me, paradoxically, is that knowing about all this cruelty and injustice is certainly necessary and certainly insufficient.

However, as I have tried to emphasize, the old story line of victimization, suffering, and cruelty includes the human yearning to overcome the ugly desire to inflict pain and the twisted impulse to benefit at the expense of others. We have long and rich cultural traditions with images and myths that testify to our ambivalence toward selfishness and oppression. One of the most haunting and compelling, and to me, most convincing of these stories is the one that teaches that it is not sophisticated knowledge but rather dispassionate love that can conquer these desires and impulses.

Beyond information and analysis, this book offers some important teachings—namely, that any education directed at human liberation must be deeply grounded in a commitment to creating communities of justice and love. This vocation surely requires knowledge and criticality, but these must be informed by the passions of moral outrage and tempered by the quest for forgiveness and reconciliation. Central to such an education is the need to nourish not the pursuit of excellence, not critical consciousness, not multiple interpretations (valuable as they all are), but rather the capacity to love, or at least respect, *everybody*.

I realize how trite and corny this may sound and how remote the possibility of creating such a consciousness is, given the present political context and our history as a people. (It is well to remember that the traditional project of nourishing a critical consciousness is not without its romantic aspiration, and accomplishing it is not exactly a piece of cake.) At the same time, it is important to remember that the idea of unconditional love not only has surfaced in human consciousness, but has persisted across time and space with as much tenacity as the commitment to critical rationality. Surely it is not an either–or issue. However, the authors of this harrowing and redemptive book have moved me closer to believing that we may have made a tragic mistake in putting so many of our eggs in the critical rationality basket.

If this reasoning is valid, our task becomes much more difficult and complex for it means that we have to challenge the very roots of our faith in the redemptive powers of Enlightenment rationality. It will certainly be difficult for us to shift our allegiances from Socrates to Jesus, from the deconstructionists to the Prophets, and from the relentless pursuit of critical insight to the restless struggle for human affirmation. However, when I think of the victims described in this book, I am quite sure they would have been better off if they were living among more loving rather than among more knowledgeable people.

Preface

❡ ◆ ❡

The pages that follow offer a series of reports on how various groups of children and young people are faring in our society and its schools—homeless children and their families, "the discards of the postmodern 1990s"; White working-class girls who experience domestic violence as part of the daily fabric of life; AIDS orphans and other children profoundly affected by HIV disease; immigrant children, too often suffering silently in a lonely world; Appalachian children living in urban areas where they are regarded by many, including some teachers, as cultureless, valueless hillbillies; adjudicated girls who talk as if they are in full control of their sexual lives but who remain dangerously vulnerable to repeated abuse; school-aged mothers, regarded by many, including some teachers, as social deviants and developmental oddities; and gay, lesbian, bisexual, and transgendered young people who are subjected, still, to harassment and denigration in a homophobic society and its schools. The pages that follow also affirm the capacity of many children and young people to survive and even flourish despite the painful and sometimes desperate circumstances of their lives, and to teach those who want to learn some of what we need to know to help create a world in which fewer children will suffer and in which all can be educated well.

Several concerns and commitments led to the conceptualization and development of this book. First, I wanted to bring together a collective outcry against the mean-spirited sensibility that runs through so much of the popular writing about education. All too often, children, especially "misfits" who challenge popular assumptions about children and youth, are portrayed as burdens to their schools; and public schools, in turn, are portrayed as burdens to the broader society. Secondly, I wanted to compile and share with others—particularly teacher-education students and foundations scholars—important information about groups of young people whose lives and insights have received little attention either from the educational establishment or from the broader society.

Finally, I wanted to put together a book reflective of a particular way of thinking about the social foundations of education—namely, the idea that what is foundational to education varies with the times, and that the task of foundational inquiry is therefore to interpret the times and, from that vantage point, to provide insight into how the stresses, strains, fractures, and wounds of the broader society bear upon the lives of young people, including their educational experience.[1] Today, as the various chapters in this book attest, we cannot ignore the social realities of disease, death, poverty, and violence (in and outside the home), layered over our anxiety-ridden diversity and often disorienting mobility and rootlessness.

Because those of us who aim to write meaningfully about education cannot ignore these truly awesome realities, we also, I believe, cannot ignore the need for the kind of scholarship included in this book. In terms of research methodology, the chapters differ considerably. Nancy Lesko, for example, offers a sharp conceptual analysis of how particular notions of time and development have shaped perceptions of school-aged mothers, whereas Cristina Igoa shares her reflections derived from many years of teaching immigrant children, and Lois Weis and Julia Maruszo report on ethnographic studies they conducted in working-class communities.

As a whole, however, the book reflects what I would call foundational reporting. As in all good journalism, the authors get the facts straight and set them in a meaningful context. And as in all good foundational inquiry, the authors refuse to sever their concerns with issues of schooling and education from their own moral and political commitments, from their outrage about all that weighs so heavily on some of the youngest and most vulnerable among us, or from the need to affirm and celebrate the capacity of many children to survive, thrive, and model better ways of being, despite a frightening social callousness and a desire to hear only "the good news."

ACKNOWLEDGMENTS

I would like to acknowledge the support that many people offered me as I developed this collection. First, I want to thank the authors, none of whom

---

[1] I trace this understanding of foundational inquiry to George Counts' (1934) *The Social Foundations of Education*.

knew me personally, for their willingness to work on the project. I also thank Diana Beck, Rose Rudnitski, Diane Goodman, Judy Dorney, Lee Bell, and other friends and colleagues for helping me conceptualize the book and for their continued interest in its progress. I thank my former mentor, David Purpel, for encouraging me years ago to write about (and only about) what I truly cared about and knew was important. And I especially thank my editor, Naomi Silverman, for her enthusiasm, for her considerable trust, and for her wise and practical guidance (always just the right amount, it seemed) as I pulled the book together. I also want to thank the reviewers for Lawrence Erlbaum Associates, Inc., whose supportive, insightful, and helpful comments contributed to the final form and content of this book—W. Thomas Jamison, Appalachian State University; Peter McLaren, University of California, Los Angeles; Nel Noddings, Stanford University; and Daniel A. Solarzano, University of California, Los Angeles.

Introduction:
An Invitation to Listen and Learn

❄ ◆ ❄

Sue Books
State University of New York at New Paltz

It hurts to be invisible. "I felt hidden in the second grade because whenever anyone said something to me, I just couldn't answer a thing," recalls an immigrant child from Afghanistan (p. 67). "When I went to my new school, no one talked to me. It was like I didn't exist," says another child, an immigrant from the Philippines (p. 67). "They think 'cos I haven't got no home that I haven't got nothing inside of me—they won't play with me—they won't be a buddy when we go on trips and no kids will be my friends," says 9-year-old Tim, who has been subjected to repeated episodes of homelessness (pp. 14–15). "Sometimes, I feel like a spirit ... like I can be seen but not heard ... Like a spirit, I'm always there but people don't notice the things I do!" says a 10-year-old living with AIDS in her family (p. 47).

It also can hurt to be visible. "Last time he [my mother's boyfriend] smacked me, I had a red hand on my face," says 12-year-old Elizabeth. "I walked around with a red hand on my face, only I wouldn't let anybody see it ... I skipped school and the [community] center for like 3 days so no one would ask me about it ... I hid in my closet until you could barely see it.

Then when I went back to school, I stayed real quiet because I didn't want people to look at me, notice the hand on my face" (p. 37).

The authors in this book use the metaphor of invisibility to explore the situation of many children and young people in the United States. What is it like for children to grow up today, especially those unseen or unheard? What would these children tell us or teach us if we were willing to listen? Such questions run through the book's chapters.

The language of invisibility has a long history. African-American writers have used it to describe the experience of being Black in a racist world. As Ralph Ellison's (1947/1980) invisible man explained:

> I am invisible, understand, simply because people refuse to see me. Like the bodiless heads you see sometimes in circus sideshows, it is as though I have been surrounded by mirrors of hard, distorting glass. When they approach me they see only my surroundings, themselves, or figments of their imagination—indeed, everything and anything except me. (p. 3)

Gay, lesbian, bisexual, and transgendered young people and adults have described their social situation as akin to being "in the closet"—and so, hidden and unseen in their full humanity and complexity. In his influential book, *The Other America*, Michael Harrington (1962) urged all who would listen to recognize the degree to which poverty and the poor have been rendered invisible—or distortedly visible—in a land of affluence and prosperity.

The chapters in this book draw on these traditions of social criticism and extend the metaphor of invisibility (in very different ways) to explore the social situation of many children and young people who are unseen in their complexity, humanity, strength, vulnerability, or destitution. These are children who are socially devalued in the sense that alleviating the often difficult conditions of their lives is not a social priority; children subjected to derogatory stereotypes that construe them as something other than what they are, full human beings rich in promise (Swadener & Lubeck, 1995); children educationally neglected in the sense that schools generally respond inadequately, if at all, to their needs; or children who, as a group, have received little attention either from scholars in the field of education or from writers in the popular press.

Valerie Polakow describes "the existential reality—the 'nuts and bolts' of daily survival" of homeless children and their families—and situates the often invisible terror, suffering, and shame they endure in the context of poverty and destitution in the United States. Lois Weis and Julia Marusza report on the pervasiveness of domestic violence in the lives of White working-class girls and women, a violence that is invisible in the sense that the literature on schooling has not taken into account "what it means to come to school with a broken spirit or in physical pain because of family violence." Shelley Geballe and Janice Gruendel document the increasing number of children and youth affected by AIDS, a population whose losses—often accompanied by grief, poverty, and chaos in their lives—have been largely ignored in the broader society. Cristina Igoa writes of her work with immigrant children who are becoming able, through art, to tell their stories and to share their previously invisible inner worlds. Kathleen Bennett deMarrais describes the cultural invisibility of young people who have moved with their families from Appalachia to northern cities. Linda Steet shares her observations about adjudicated girls in an alternative high school, girls who appear to be in control of their sexual lives but who in fact are routinely controlled and abused by older boys and men. Nancy Lesko critiques the popular view of school-aged mothers as deviant and destructive, a view that eclipses the hope and possibility in their particular life paths. Richard Friend describes the practices of denigration and reductionism to which gay, lesbian, bisexual, and transgendered young people are subjected—practices to which many are responding, however, with the energy and vision of social leaders modeling community responsibility.

THE SOCIAL MOMENT: A FRACTURED TIME

To speak of "children in the United States today" is, of course, to speak of young people growing up in fractured times. Profound incongruity marks this final decade of the 20th century; misery and hardship amidst comfort and prosperity. Even as, statistically, the national economy flourishes, poverty and homelessness are increasing, especially among families with children, the fastest growing population of homeless people in the United States (Children's Defense Fund, 1995). Even as children in the most affluent families in our nation enjoy more prosperity than children in any of 18 other Western industrialized countries, children in the poorest families in the United States are among the poorest in these countries (Bradsher, 1996). In 1995, as the gap between the richest Americans and everyone else grew wider than at any time since the end of World War II (Holmes, 1996), CEOs at the largest 500 companies earned an average of more than $4 million, which amounted to 197 times as much as the average worker (Greenhouse, 1996).

Even as researchers and policymakers gain an increasingly sophisticated understanding of environmental threats to children's health, millions of young people in the United States suffer from lead poisoning, tooth decay, and other easily preventable diseases and health problems. As Kozol (1995) points out,

> [M]any children in poor neighborhoods such as Mott Haven [in the South Bronx] have been neurologically impaired, some because of low-weight prematurity at birth, some because of drug ingestion while in utero, and many from lead poison in their homes and also, shockingly enough, within their schools. Although New York officially banned the use of lead in residential paint in 1960 ... notes the *Times*, the city "continued to apply 'industrial grade' lead paint" in public classrooms until 1980. (pp. 155–156)

We now know enough about lead poisoning to eradicate it; nevertheless, more than one-half of all poor children of color suffer from abnormalities due to lead poisoning (King, 1993, p. 160). Tuberculosis, a preventable disease bred in cramped living quarters, is on the rise again in some parts of the country after several decades of decline (Griffin, 1993).

As always, our public schools reflect the stresses, strains, contradictions, and injustices of the broader society. "To put it baldly, America now has some of the finest, highest-achieving schools in the world—and some of the most miserable, threatened, underfunded educational travesties" (Berliner & Biddle, 1995, p. 58).

> *Huge* differences persist in the level of support given to public schools in this country—differences that are far greater than those found in other advanced countries. ... America's wealthy suburbs have some of the world's best schools, while appallingly bad schools appear in our urban ghettoes. ... Within the worst states (Texas, for example) schools in a rich community may receive more than *five* times as much per-student funding as schools in a poor community. (Berliner & Biddle, 1995, p. 264)

Even as some students receive a world-class education, others are ghettoized and forgotten in rundown, markedly segregated, and often dangerous and overcrowded schools (Berliner & Biddle, 1995; Kozol, 1991). New York City public schools, for example, opened in the fall of 1996 "to the worst overcrowding in decades." With 91,000 students more than the system could comfortably accommodate, classrooms were "crammed into closets, cordoned off in auditoriums and plunked into locker rooms" (Belluck, 1996, p. A1). The buildings themselves were in such a state of disrepair that, according to a Board of Education report, "one in five … pose[d] a hazard to students and teachers" (Sullivan, 1996, p. B5).

Observing some of the nation's poorest schools, Jonathan Kozol (1991, 1995) found children sitting idly in overcrowded, dilapidated buildings; teachers demoralized and often uncertified; and administrators planning ahead for large numbers of dropouts and pushouts for whom there would be no room were they to stay in school. What becomes of these young people is not clear. School officials in Washington, D.C., acknowledged that although students who are expelled generally can petition for readmission after a year, "many never come back, and no one knows what happens to them" (Shear & Wilgoren, 1994, p. B1). Following the postschool lives of 1,436 ninth graders at a high school in the Bronx, a City University of New York professor found that, 6 years later, 87% had been discharged and that 80% had not graduated from any other school (Kozol, 1995).

Although a certain amount of what Jack White (1996) has called "genteel race mixing" can be found within the few public and private schools that are both committed to maintaining a racially and ethnically diverse student body and financially able to do so, U.S. public schools overall are now almost as segregated as they were in 1970—before court-ordered busing began (Kunen, 1996). Nationally, a third of all Black students in public schools attend schools where the enrollment is 90% to 100% young people of color. Meanwhile, a Supreme Court ruling in 1995 laid the legal groundwork for cities across the nation to undo desegregation mandates (Kunen, 1996).

Even as this happens and as affirmative action policies are discarded, the pursuit of privilege and advantage continues unabated. College counselors sell their services to the precollegiate cream of the crop seeking to "position themselves well" in the admissions process (Weber, 1996). Grade-school parents, well aware of its social significance, go to war over the gifted-and-talented label. For the sons and daughters of affluent parents looking to enroll them in prestigious nursery schools, the positioning starts even earlier. The admissions process, with "the usual stories about letters of recommendation written by famous people for 3-year-olds and high-powered mothers in tears because their toddlers are on the waiting list," is fraught with anxiety not only for parents, but also for admissions directors seeking to realize a full and gender-balanced "yield" from the applicant pool. "I don't sleep regularly during admissions season," said the director of the highly selective 92nd Street Y Nursery School in New York City. "I've had years when I needed a 4-year-old boy, and there wasn't one" (quoted in Bumiller, 1996, p. A21). With tuitions that range from $4,000 to $11,000 a year, "no shows" wreak havoc with the school budget.

AIMS OF THE BOOK

This book is being written at a time when educators and schools in general are being encouraged not to try to respond meaningfully to the wounds and fractures of our times, but rather to narrow their spheres of concern and to focus on the basics (whether the Democrats' new ones or the Republicans' old ones) and on the bottom line of achievement scores (Purpel & Shapiro, 1995). Much of the educational discourse is focused on how best to "fix" children regarded as problems or aberrations from the norm, with too few questions about the broader social world in which so many children have come to be seen as problems or aberrations.

We aim to speak in a different voice. As a counterproject to decontextualized problem solving, we aim not to simplify the socially induced suffering or socially imposed invisibility of children, not to redefine the massive social problems and injustices their lives reflect in ways that affirm the prevailing wisdom of the day (such as the now popular belief that lectures on personal responsibility constitute a meaningful response), and not to lose sight of the real lives of real children. Rather, we aim to report on, describe, and contextualize the life worlds of many children growing up today. As an insightful teacher quoted in Valerie Polakow's chapter observes, "Sometimes, it's easier to look away from a situation than to see it up close—real close" (p.18). We aim to resist this temptation.

ORGANIZATION OF THE BOOK

The first part of the book focuses on groups of young people whose needs are largely invisible and whose voices are largely unheard in the broader society—homeless children, White working-class girls living with domestic violence, AIDS orphans and other children affected by HIV disease, immigrant children, and Appalachian youths living in urban areas—as well as young people whose lives are visible but perceived in hurtful, distorting, or reductionistic ways—adjudicated girls, school-aged mothers, and sexual minority youth. The second part of the volume then explores the broader context of invisibility—specifically, the welfare "reform" legislation of 1996 and the denigration and caricature to which young people are subjected by the popular press.

In chapter 1, Valerie Polakow decries the tragedy of homelessness "in a society of mansions and second homes and condos," and warns:

> For our homeless children, who have become post-modern "street rats," the lifelong consequences are deep and scarring. ... Many homeless children attempt to hide the fact that they are homeless, and are traumatized by the ensuing losses ... The shift from a housed to an unhoused world frequently entails not only a loss of friends, neighborhood networks, and school changes, but a profound sense of shame and fear of being identified as "a shelter kid." (pp. 15, 19–20)

In the wake of the nation's repeal in August 1996 of its main federal welfare program, "we now confront the increasing pauperization of almost 16 million children and an alarming rise in the number of homeless families" (p. 3). Homelessness among families now exists on a scale unknown since the Great Depression. Families comprise 36.5% of the homeless population, and one in four homeless persons is now younger than 18 years.

Not surprisingly, homeless children face multiple problems in school, if they attend at all: irregular attendance, low achievement, inappropriate placement, lack of services, and, all too often, reinforcement of the shame they quickly learn to feel outside school walls. Although schools cannot "fix" the broader society in which so many children are denied both homes and dignity, Polakow argues, they "should never become autonomous landscapes of condemnation" (pp. 16–17). Poor and homeless children are often subjected to "threats, coercive teaching methods, humiliation, and indifference" (p. 17), which serve only to exacerbate the desperation they already know. "Yet good schools and good teachers," Polakow notes (with examples), "can and do make a significant difference in children's stressed and desperate lives, creating a refuge where a child may experience sensitive and supportive interventions from teachers and principals and other support staff" (p. 17).

In chapter 2, Lois Weis and Julia Marusza report on ethnographic studies they conducted in White working-class communities in the Northeast. Tales of domestic violence dominated their conversations with girls and women. Of the women interviewed, 92% shared stories of abuse. Yet, Weis and Marusza found that a sense of resignation and acceptance hung in the air. From the perspective of 11-year-old Rosie, "About 95% of the world is angry. ... It's just the way it is" (p. 35). Although domestic violence "is deeply etched into how generations of females in poor and working-class White communities construct a sense of self" (p. 39) and although this abuse affects children profoundly and has serious educational implications, very little in the literature on schooling addresses this. Instead, a professional discourse strangely quiet about the significance of domestic violence reflects and affirms a dangerous "culture of concealment" (p. 38).

Weis and Marusza urge educators to help raise awareness about "the depth, the pervasiveness, the very tedious typicality of domestic violence" (p. 42). We can no longer presume this violence is "something that happens to few—and that those few will speak up when it does" (p. 42). Although this stance may assuage collective anxieties, it protects the "structured silence" around the reality of abuse. Domestic violence must be deprivatized, Weis and Marusza argue, and seen for what it is—commonplace and pervasive, not rare and hidden.

In chapter 3, Shelley Geballe and Janice Gruendel provide information on HIV disease, describe its effects on children and young people, and comment on implications for educators and others interested in how best to respond to the social, emotional, and often economic needs of AIDS orphans and other children living in families with HIV disease. By the year 2000, it is expected that 150,000 children in the United States will have lost a mother and thousands more will have lost a father, sibling, or other family member to AIDS in what has become "the most significant plague of the 20th century" (p. 48). However, although more children in the United States will lose a parent to AIDS than to any other single cause of death, the society in general has been slow to come to terms with the significance of AIDS in the lives of children and young people. Given the social stigmatization of the disease, families affected by AIDS often conceal this "secret," and children consequently go without the social supports they need to cope with the enormous stresses and uncertainties in their lives.

Keenly aware of the multiple barriers to responding adequately to AIDS-affected children, Geballe and Gruendel call for a collective commitment to treating these children as compassionately as children whose parents die from other causes. We also need more advocacy, research, and training about the unique needs of AIDS-affected children, they argue, and more support for children and their "second families."

In chapter 4, Cristina Igoa, an immigrant child herself, shares her insights, derived from many years of teaching immigrant children, about the lonely and emotionally painful struggle of young people who have been uprooted and brought to a strange place where they are often regarded with fear and suspicion. Using art "as a second language," Igoa offers her students a vocabulary and a sheltered environment—"a nest"—in which to share their inner worlds. The children's artwork stands as powerful testimony to the expressive abilities of children "grown strong by kindness." As the children gain confidence in their artistry and in their ability to speak of themselves and of the worlds they know, others come to see their inner richness and to respect their knowledge. Not surprisingly, children's abilities across the curriculum improve in this climate of understanding and respect:

> In the development of artistic competence, the children learned how to focus and concentrate, how to observe and compare. They discovered the importance of attention to detail and patience; they internalized the concept of completing steps in order to complete a task. These skills were transferred to other academic subjects. ... Art also gave the children a framework to sharpen their imaginations and to identify their thoughts and feelings, making it easier to articulate themselves in speech and writing. (p. 80)

Whereas at the beginning of the school year, three-quarters of Igoa's students could not read a fifth/sixth grade novel in English, by the end of the year, most of the children (85%) could comprehend the book and answer in-depth questions about it in writing. And all the students strengthened their literacy skills significantly.

What immigrant children need, Igoa says, is patience, to feel welcome and liked, to be understood and helped to communicate, and to be given, in the words of a child from the Philippines, "things that they can do and not things that they cannot do" (p. 75). These are small requests, grounded in shared human need and sensible educational practice.

In chapter 5, Kathleen Bennett deMarrais describes the sociocultural situation and schooling experience of urban Appalachian children, young people who have moved with their families from the Appalachian region of the United States to northern cities and become culturally invisible in that context. "The people of Appalachia share a rich cultural heritage that includes a strong sense of kinship, a love of the land, a rich oral tradition, and a commitment to personal freedom and self-reliance," Bennett deMarrais notes, as well as "a long history of poverty, economic exploitation, and inadequate schooling" (p. 90). Among Appalachians in northern inner cities, "half of the adults ... have no more than a high school education, school dropout rates are as high as 75%, and youth unemployment is a serious problem (Obermiller & Maloney, 1994, cited p. 97).

Stereotyped and ridiculed as backward "hillbillies" by school people as well as by the broader society, "this particular group of inner-city children continues to lag far behind mainstream European American students on all measures of educational attainment" (p. 108). Not respecting or even recognizing the unique cultural background of urban Appalachian students, schools generally have made little effort to "fit" themselves into the students' culture and community. As a first step toward developing schools better able to meet the needs of these students, Bennett deMarrais urges educators to recognize urban Appalachian ethnicity and to learn something about the history and culture urban Appalachian children bring to school. Her chapter provides a starting point.

Uncomfortably aware of the relations of power reproduced in the act of speaking for and about other people, Linda Steet, in chapter 6, attempts to peel away some of the multiple layers of invisibility in the lives of the girls she taught in an alternative public high school for adjudicated teens. Steet notes that the role that men and older boys play in these girls' lives remains largely invisible in educational discussions about female juvenile delinquency, as scholars and educators still have not "figured out how to process and respond to what boys and men do to girls" (p. 112). The girls' lives are invisible also in the sense that many of them have learned essentially to be—or to perform—someone else. In this way, they deny their own experience, which often includes horrifying episodes of sexual abuse and coercion. Steet comments:

> Sex is so much a part of these girls' lives because they don't control it. Others make decisions concerning sex for them. Others have always made these decisions: when and where they will have sex, what sex acts they will do, and if it will be protected sex. None of the girls know sex as something that gives them direct physical pleasure. (p. 116)

Instead, the girls know sex as something they do "for guys," with or without their ostensible consent.

Steet urges us to move beyond the popular "rail[ing] about wild girls, children having children, girls in gangs, and so on" (p. 113); to own up to the role that both sexual abuse and miseducation about sexual matters play in the lives of many girls who "get in trouble" and to respond to their unmet needs—"needs that have long been identified and long shared by an ever increasing number of girls and by ever younger girls" (p. 119).

Nancy Lesko, in chapter 7, argues that although school-aged mothers have been visible in the public discourse, largely as chronological aberrations or social deviants, they have remained marginal (essentially invisible) in the literature on curriculum, school reform, and pedagogy. Seeing these young women differently—that is, as figures of change and hope— would require coming to terms with their sexuality, recognizing the contingency of "social age," and owning up to the political dimensions of a view of school-aged mothers as developmental oddities and threats to the broader society. Rendering young mothers "differently visible" would require adopting a critical perspective on taken-for-granted ideas about development and recognizing the reproductive rights of all women. To do otherwise is to continue to encourage young women not to take themselves, including their sexuality, seriously, and so to encourage the impulsive and unthinking behavior that often leads to unplanned pregnancy.

Richard Friend, in chapter 8, offers an analysis of how the heterosexism and homophobia of the broader culture are institutionalized into the culture of schooling. Through the twin processes of systematic exclusion and systematic inclusion—whereby positive role models, messages, and images of sexual minorities are publicly erased (exclusion) while homosexuality is sexualized and linked with pathology and danger (inclusion)—gay, lesbian, bisexual, and transgendered youth are rendered invisible in their strength, power, and human complexity. Violence against and harassment of these young people flourish in a culture shaped by discursive practices that oppress and distort. Not surprisingly, sexual minority youth drop out of school, run away, and attempt or complete suicide in wildly disproportionate numbers. Nevertheless, many of these young people respond to homophobia and heterosexism with strength and fortitude:

> Undaunted by oppressive forces, these youth work individually and collectively to transform their worlds. They fight back politically, legally, physically, intellectually, and spiritually. These are kids working on the street to create social change, organizing self-defense classes, running for public office, and constantly educating those around them. They are the youth who are moving from surviving to thriving. (p. 155)

Friend challenges educators and others to work to understand the social and emotional worlds in which sexual minority young people live; to provide resources for overcoming and dismantling the systems that oppress them; and to learn, from the examples of community responsibility and leadership many of these young people provide themselves, how to create a climate in which no one is rendered invisible or distortedly visible.

In chapter 9, Barbara Finkelstein, Reem Mourad, and Elyssa Doner offer their commentary on the Personal Responsibility and Work Opportunity Reconciliation Act of 1996. Unlike so much of the legislation that came before it, Public Law 104-193 brings poor children into view not as an economically bereft, educationally vulnerable, dependent class of victimized young people, but as the progeny of a morally profligate class of unmarried, undeserving, sexually promiscuous men and women in need of moral reclamation, social reconstruction, publicly administered discipline, and paid work. (p. 172)

These authors argue that when welfare is defined as a form of family planning, moral reconstruction, and deficit reduction, rather than as an approach to child protection, social welfare, or income support, children disappear as objects of national concern.

In the concluding chapter, I critique the politically popular but morally abhorrent practice of youth bashing in the popular press. Young single mothers and young men deemed violent have been particularly vulnerable as scapegoats for vast social problems. The older generation, I argue, owes the young something much different and much better than this: "not only the social supports they need to grow and to prosper, but also inspiring visions in which they themselves figure prominently as bearers of hope and creators of an always new and always potentially better world" (p. 197).

Let me next say a word about what this book is not—inclusive. To provide one example is always not to provide another; to highlight one thing is always to obscure another. The social invisibility of children of color, girls in general, arguably those legions of children regarded as "average"—each might have been discussed, but is not. This book is neither inclusive nor designed to stand as a model of how best to categorize social invisibility. Race, for example, is unquestionably a major factor in social invisibility, and children of color are disproportionately represented in many of the groups described—homeless children, children affected by AIDS, and school-aged mothers, for example. Nevertheless, these groups are diverse and cut across racial categories. Whereas race ought not be discounted in any exploration of social invisibility, social invisibility also ought not be reduced to race; hence my decision to conceptualize social invisibility in very broad terms and not to use race as a organizing principle for the book.

Children and young people carry in their hearts and wear on their bodies the social wounds of these fractured times. Many of these wounds, such as the terror and desperation of homelessness, are traceable to the sort of blatant injustices I described earlier. Others—the scars of harassment, violence, denigration, ostracism, and chronic misunderstanding—reflect the often unnamed or misnamed fears and anxieties of the times. Although the authors in this book do not try to speak for some of those who bear much of the weight of these harsh times, they do attempt to speak boldly and clearly of these times in which many children and young people suffer. They attempt to share the insights of those affected most directly, and in so doing, to deprivatize the social "secrets" they harbor.

In these times when education has become so explicitly politicized around issues of funding, control of the curriculum, assessment, deregulation, and so on, I hope this book offers readers an opportunity to step back and think about what it means to teach, what it means to teach children, and what it means to teach children today. As always, the question hangs heavy: How can we best respond as educators, but also as friends, parents, or neighbors of children and young people who need and deserve not only to be fed, housed, and physically protected, but also to be listened to, heard, and respectfully educated? What would those who bear much of the brunt of the social dysfunction of these times tell us if we would listen?

We need to listen to and learn from the young not only for our own edification, but also to free them from the need to harbor and conceal who they are and what they know. Rarely ever, I suspect, has there been so much good work waiting and needing to be done by so many people.

REFERENCES

Belluck, P. (1996, September 5). Classes open in New York City in closets, hallways, cafeterias. *The New York Times*, p. A1.

Berliner, D. C., & Biddle, B. J. (1995). *The manufactured crisis: Myths, fraud, and the attack on America's public schools*. Reading, MA: Addison-Wesley.

Bradsher, K. (1996, August 14). Low ranking for poor American children. *The New York Times*, p. A9.

Bumiller, E. (1996, April 7). Sifting sandbox aptitude tests. *The New York Times*, p. A21.

Children's Defense Fund. (1995). *The state of America's children: Yearbook*. Washington, DC: Author.

Ellison, R. (1980). *Invisible man*. New York: Random House. (Original work published 1947)

Greenhouse, S. (1996, June 16). The maximum wage. *The New York Times*, p. E6.

Griffin, M. L. (1993). *Health and health care profile of New York City's new school admissions, 1990-1991*. (Working paper). New York: Community Service Society.

Harrington, M. (1962). *The other America: Poverty in the United States*. New York: Macmillan.

Holmes, S. A. (1996, June 20). Income disparity between poorest and richest rises. *The New York Times*, p. A1.

King, C. R. (1993). *Children's health in America: a history*. New York: Twayne Publishers.

Kozol, J. (1991). *Savage inequalities: Children in America's schools*. New York: Crown.

Kozol, J. (1995). *Amazing grace: The lives of children and the conscience of a nation*. New York: Crown.

Kunen, J. S. (1996, April 29). The end of integration. *Time, 147*(18), 39–45.

Purpel, D. E., & Shapiro, S. (1995). *Beyond liberation and excellence: Reconstructing the public discourse on education.* Westport, CT: Bergin & Garvey.

Shear, M., & Wilgoren, D. (1994, July 10). Expulsions rise as schools get tough on violence. *The Washington Post,* p. B1.

Sullivan, J. (1996, November 19). Hazards seen at one-fifth of schools. *The New York Times,* p. B5.

Swadener, B. B., & Lubeck, S. (Eds.). (1995). *Children and families "at promise": Deconstructing the discourse of risk.* Albany: SUNY Press.

Weber, B. (1996, April 28). Inside the meritocracy machine. *The New York Times Magazine,* 44–49, 56–58, 68.

White, J. E. (1996, April 29). Why we need to raise hell. *Time, 147*(18), 46.

I

YOUNG AND INVISIBLE

1

Homeless Children and Their Families: The Discards of the Postmodern 1990s

❃ ◆ ❃

Valerie Polakow
Eastern Michigan University

It was a hard world, but are we less hard now?... For certain religious sensibilities, such children fulfilled the ineffable aims of God. For the modern folk, Mr. Darwin was cited, and the design was Nature's. So the flower girl Mary, and the newsies and the rest of these child beggars who lived among us, were losses society could tolerate. Like Nature, our city was spendthrift and produced enough wealth to take heavy losses without noticeable damage. It was all a cost of doing business while the selection of the species went relentlessly forward...

—Doctorow (1994, pp. 66–67)

In *The Waterworks*, E. L. Doctorow's narrator describes the world of the "street rats," the destitute children of New York City in the late 1800s, before the advent of the Progressive era and 50 years prior to the New Deal and the signing of the Social Security Act, which guaranteed legal entitlement to public assistance for all poor children. As we approach the end of the 20th century, we might well ask, what are the losses that we are prepared to tolerate? In 1997, we now confront the increasing pauperization of almost 16 million children and an alarming rise in the number of homeless families as the already flimsy social safety net continues to shred. What does it mean to be a destitute American child groping for handouts in the shadows of privilege and affluence? What does it mean to be a homeless American child, whose "heavy losses" and "noticeable damage" are largely made invisible as corporate wealthfare and the savage politics of distribution conceal the pillaging of the public economy and the repeal of public entitlements for poor children in the name of "personal responsibility" and the "opportunity society"—a Swiftian irony indeed for those whose young lives have been gutted by recent welfare "reform" policies.

In order to understand the existential reality—the "nuts and bolts" of daily survival—confronting homeless children and their families, it is important to contextualize homelessness within the larger landscape of poverty and destitution that currently imperils the lives of millions of families in the United States.

THE NEW FACES OF CHRONIC POVERTY
AND HOMELESSNESS

Chronic poverty has become an endemic feature of the landscape of the other America; the largest constituency of poor Americans is young children, and the younger in age, the higher the destitution. Whereas 21% of children under 18 are classified as living in poverty, 25% of children under 6 and 27% under three years old live in poverty (Children's Defense Fund, 1996), the majority of whom reside in poor single-mother households. Hence, while children account for 27% of the U.S. population, they represent 40% of all poor people (U.S. Bureau of the Census, 1996). It is clear that the increasing economic vulnerability of the single-mother family represents a child welfare crisis of growing magnitude that has been further exacerbated by recent welfare "reform" legislation. The failure of public policy to address the daily survival needs of economically vulnerable single mothers also threatens their children's basic physical, social, and developmental needs. The term *feminization of poverty* has been widely used since the late 1970s to describe the particular plight of women who, as single mothers, are disproportionately poor and who face an alarming array of obstacles that threaten their family stability (Ehrenreich & Piven, 1984; Goldberg & Kremen, 1990; Gordon, 1990; Pearce, 1978; Polakow, 1993, 1994), so that by the late 1980s women and their children had become a significant majority of America's poor (U.S. Bureau of the Census, 1989). A widespread lack of affordable housing, health care, and child care fre-

quently coalesce to form a triple crisis confronting single mothers, who as
both providers and nurturers of their children, cannot sustain family viabil-
ity when they are low-wage earners. Hence, it is not surprising that many
single-mother families who are living on the edge plunge into homelessness—and that they now comprise 70% to 90% of homeless families nationwide (Bassuk, 1990; Steinbock, 1995). It is also estimated that more than
half of such famlies become homeless because the mother flees domestic
violence (National Clearinghouse for the Defense of Battered Women,
1994).

It was during the 1980s that family homelessness first emerged as a major
social problem, of a magnitude not seen since the Great Depression. It is
now estimated that families comprise 36.5% of the overall homeless population (Bassuk, 1996; U.S. Conference of Mayors, 1995), and that one in
four homeless persons is now a child younger than 18 years old (National
Law Center on Homelessness and Poverty, 1993). Despite the dismal record
of the United States in failing to develop public policies that provide for the
basic shelter, health, and daily living needs of its most vulnerable citizens—poor mothers and their children—female and child poverty is still
cast as a "moral" problem, tied to public rhetoric about "family values" and
"family breakdown," which, in turn, is used to rationalize further cuts in
public assistance. Drastic federal budget cuts for subsidized housing during
the Reagan years shaped the current national housing crisis so that by 1993,
households with worst-case housing scenarios had reached an all-time high
of 5.3 million households, where families with children made up 43% of
these households (National Coalition for the Homeless, 1996a; U.S. Department of Housing and Urban Development, 1996). At present, only one
third of households eligible for federal housing assistance actually receive it
(Lazere, 1995), and 3.8 million households with children pay more than
50% of their income on rent, whereas over 2.2 million households with
children pay more than 70% of their income on rent (Kaufman, 1996). In
45 states and in the District of Columbia, it is estimated that families would
need to earn at least double the minimum wage in order to afford a
two-bedroom apartment at Fair Market Rent (National Low Income Housing Coalition, 1996). Furthermore, 1 in 5 homeless persons is actually
employed in full or part-time work (U.S. Conference of Mayors, 1995).
Despite this, many working poor adults can no longer find affordable shelter.

The severe shortage of affordable housing for families has been made even
more acute by severe Congressional funding cuts. Cuts totaling $297 million
to the HUD Homeless Assistance programs, $30 million to the Emergency

Food and Shelter Program, and $5.8 million to the Education for Homeless Children and Youth Program were all made in fiscal year [FY] 1996. Although $2 million was restored to the latter program in FY 1997, all other programs were frozen at FY 1996 levels. In addition, the Emergency Community Services Grant, which during FY 1995 was funded at $19.7 million, was eliminated. When all homeless assistance programs are considered, the funding cuts from FY 1995 to FY 1997 involved a 26% loss of overall funding. And these cuts merely exacerbate what was already a critical situation nationwide, leaving millions of families with children unable to find permanent shelter (National Coalition for the Homeless, 1996b).

However, a minimal and inadequate public-assistance safety net still existed until August 1996. That, too, has now been eliminated. The new welfare law that passed the House and Senate with bipartisan support, and that was signed into law by President Clinton on August 22, 1996 repealed the main federal welfare program, Aid to Families with Dependent Children, mandated by Title IVa of the Social Security Act of 1935, thereby reversing a decades-long federal commitment to provide public assistance to poor children. In the following section, the impact of the new welfare law is discussed.

DISMANTLING WELFARE: THE IMPACT OF PUBLIC LAW 104–193

According to The Center on Budget and Policy Priorities, the impact of the new law is far reaching (see Super, Parrot, Steinmetz, & Mann, 1996), cutting $55 billion of support to low-income programs. Aid to Families with Dependent Children (AFDC), Job Opportunities and Basic Skills (JOBS), and Emergency Assistance (EA) programs are all eliminated under this legislation. Instead, states will receive block grants of money, known as TANF (Temporary Assistance to Needy Families) grants based on 1994 levels without regard to subsequent changes in the level of need in a state. These TANF grants will be disbursed to families in need on a first-come, first-served basis. Being a poor child no longer automatically qualifies you for assistance. If a single-parent family becomes eligible for state assistance, mother and children will be limited to 2 years of support if the mother does not comply with stringent work requirements. After a maximum of 2 years (and states may choose to provide less than the maximum), all benefits will be cut. If no jobs are available and the 2-year limit is up, mother and children will be left with no safety net other than private charity. Furthermore, there is a lifetime limit of 5 years on public assistance, with states given the option of choosing to set stricter limits. Although hardship exemptions will be available to 20% of families, it is anticipated that during either high periods of unemployment or during a recession, larger and larger pools of destitute families will emerge and become homeless.

In addition, there are sweeping cuts of services to legal immigrants, their children, and their aging parents, as well as to thousands of disabled poor children who will lose their SSI payments due to far more stringent eligibility requirements. Food stamps will be cut $27.7 billion over the next 6 years, and denied to all legal immigrants and to single unemployed adults after 3 months in any 3-year period. The Center on Budget and Policy Priorities estimates that in an average month 1 million jobless individuals unable to find work will be denied food stamps under this provision. While there are no funds for job creation in the new welfare law, neither are there sufficient viable jobs available in poor urban and rural communities (Wilson, 1996). The National Coalition for the Homeless points out that the relationship between TANF grants and the new work requirements will actually provide states with an incentive to reduce the number of recipients on welfare by redefining eligibility criteria, rather than paying for work programs:

> While the ostensible goal is to encourage people to work, the likely result will simply be rules that eliminate people from the welfare rolls faster, denying them needed resources and pushing them into homelessness... In many cases needy families will have to choose between housing and food. (National Coalition for the Homeless, 1996c, p.1)

The Urban Institute estimates that the immediate effect of the new law will be to throw 1.1 million more children into poverty and predicts the further destitution of those already impoverished. Over the next 6 years it is anticipated that approximately 3 million more children will fall into poverty (Super, Parrot, Steinmetz, & Mann, 1996).

Given the grim record—and a worsening record to come—how do children and teens who plunge from destitution to homelessness fare? In the following section, the actual lives of individual children and youth are profiled and discussed: What happens to them as they experience the trauma of an unsheltered existence, struggling to survive in schools and communities in which they have become postmodern "street rats"?

LIVING ON THE OUTSIDE[1]

Michael's Story

Michael is a bright, articulate 8-year-old who has experienced four episodes of home-lessness in his young life. He was born into homelessness after his mother, 8 months pregnant, fled to Michigan to escape his father's violence. During the latest episode of homelessness, when the family fled from drug and gang violence at a public housing site, Michael was so traumatized, that as we drove to a shelter, he lay on the floor of the car, screaming and clutching his pillow as he cried: "I hate this life—why can't I live in a place like other kids—it's not fair—I won't have friends no more at school—it's the worst thing in the world when you don't got no home. I never never want to go in that shelter..." Michael lay crying on the floor, curled up in a fetal position, and refused to leave the car to set foot in the shelter. An hour later, after being coaxed inside, he sat on the stairway, angrily shouting about his mother, "Why does she do this to us—why can't we have a regular home like other kids—I can't go to school no more 'cos my friends will find out I'm in a shelter—I hate her, I hate her—I'm gonna run away from here..."

During the 3 months that Michael spent alternating between the shelter and a "welfare motel" he experienced terrible nightmares, became very fearful, and lashed out aggressively at classmates in school. He ran away from school twice in the middle of the day and was punished by suspension. After the family was rehoused, Michael witnessed renewed threats of violence against his mother, by his father who had tracked her down in Michigan. At that point Michael snapped. One afternoon, the school janitor found him trying to crawl into the furnace, saying he wanted to die. Soon after, he was hospitalized for 14 days at a children's psychiatric unit. When I visited him in the hospital he told me, "I don't got no reason to live."

Michael is not yet 9 years old, yet his story of despair, terror, and desperation as his young life and fragile supports crumble around him is not unusual. James Garbarino (1992) argues that "In America being poor is deadly" (p. 227) and if you are living in one of the housing projects designed for those who live in the other America, there is no sense of daily stability, but rather a pervasive sense of fear and powerlessness. Garbarino claims this mirrors the experience of living in a war zone, which produces posttraumatic stress syndrome. In Garbarino's Chicago studies, interviews with public housing tenants reveal that shootings, gangs, elevators, and darkness are the most serious daily dangers that single mothers and their children confront, and that "100% of the children 5 years old and under had direct contact with shooting" (Dubrow & Garbarino, 1989, p. 11).

---

[1]The stories of Michael and Monika were documented by the author during 1996 and 1997.

Michael's experience of near destitution and dangerous daily living in his neighborhood was already a fearful existence, which came to a head when his mother fled with the family, after Michael's teenage sister had been attacked by gang members. Yet for Michael at 8 years old, that fearful but "housed" existence was still preferable to the terror of homelessness, and the painful loss of his kitten, another casualty of their homelessness. Michael's mother, whose life had literally been one of staggering odds (raped at 16 by a stepfather and fleeing to another state, an adult victim and survivor of domestic violence, emotionally destabilized by constant daily dangers), also told a story that not surprisingly echoes the stories of thousands of other women who eventually become homeless families with children. Nationwide, 50% of all homeless women and children become homeless because of domestic violence (*Women and Violence*, 1990). Bassuk's recent study of a community in Worcester, Massachusetts indicates that 63.3% of homeless mothers experienced severe physical violence by adult intimate partners and that during their own childhoods, more than 40% of homeless mothers were victims of sexual molestation, and two thirds had been assaulted by severe physical violence on the part of their adult caretakers or by other household members (Bassuk, 1996). Hence, the links between homelessness and domestic violence, stretching from childhood through adulthood, are starkly apparent.

Michael at 8 years old was forced to endure both the trauma of homelessness and the terror of violence against his mother; yet during these months, he did not receive any intervention services from either of the two schools he attended. When he and his family lived at the welfare motel, his mother was forced to use a cab to get him to school—despite the McKinney Homeless Act provisions—resulting in many absences from school and a rapid drain on her limited resources. When the family was rehoused in a different area, Michael had to change schools, losing friends and a former classroom teacher who had been supportive. When his episodes of aggressive and unmanageable behavior began at his new school, there were persistent reports of misbehavior to his mother, followed by school suspensions. Until Michael became suicidal and was hospitalized, there had been no psychological or educational interventions available to support him, yet he had exhibited clear signs of posttraumatic stress disorder. Rather, he was a burden, one of "them," a kid who did not fit, whose destitution and continuous family upheaval disrupted the classroom. What future do such children have? In many ways, Michael serves as a poster child for the Other America—one of many discards along the path of invisibility.

Monika's Story

Monika is a 17-year-old homeless adolescent; a bright, soft-spoken, and fearful girl with a desperate longing to find a stable home and to stay in school, where, despite her traumatic existence, she has managed to maintain a 4.0 grade point average. I first met her when she sought help from the educational coordinator of a homeless assistance program in Michigan. Monika describes her childhood as one involving constant moves and multiple school changes: "I've never been at one school for more than 2 years in a row, because I lived with my mom and dad at different times and I had to go back and forth between them, because neither of them wanted me ... I guess."

Monika had been living with her mother and stepfather when her mother died after a long illness. Soon after her mother's death, she found herself homeless: "My stepdad kicked me out last month after my mom died—and my real dad (shrugs) ... who knows where he is—and now it's real hard to keep contact with my two half-brothers and sister because you have no actual address and no home ... I've been having a lot of problems, because after that I went to my aunt and she kicked me out and then I was living with my friend's grandmother and she kicked me out this week and I was trying to register for school but they wouldn't accept me because I didn't have a guardian ..."

After Monika, acting on her own initiative, sought help from the county's homeless assistance program, the educational coordinator helped her register for school—but in a new school district, as she had no transportation to her old school. At present, she has moved into a temporary and unstable living situation. She describes the past week: "I had no one to turn to—I was going from day to day never knowing where I'd be that night ... It's tough when you never know what's going to happen and then moving from one place to the next ... and it's tough never knowing how you're going to get to school ... and then if I couldn't get there I had no adult to make an excused absence for me ... and then you think there's no other place for you to go and I thought the next day I can be on the street with nowhere to go, but then my friend said I could live with him and his mom until I find a place... "

Despite the nightmare of the past weeks, Monika is determined to complete her senior year: "I don't care what happens to me—I'm going to graduate—I'm going to college. I know what I want to be ... I want to be a teacher ... I just need help. I want to know that I'll have a stable place to live where I won't get kicked out and where I can get a job and go to school ... It makes me very scared because now I don't know what will happen to me." Monika's total resources stood at $10 as she waited to hear whether she would be accepted into a teen group home, and whether she would be eligible to receive any public assistance payments.

Ironically, Monika is one of the more "privileged" homeless students —academically successful and strongly motivated to graduate—for as the educational coordinator bluntly states in an interview (December 12, 1996):

Teachers like kids who look like Oliver Twist. She's white and she's female and she gets good grades. Every once in a while I get a kid like her who endears herself to adults and that's one of the strongest things going for them ... but there's just not a chance for the tough kids ... I will run into a high school kid who's been homeless, who's dropped out, and I'll tell the school, "This kid needs to be re-enrolled now," and I'll be told, "Do you know who this kid's brothers and sisters are? Do you know what this kid did when he was here before?" Really the bottom line is they don't want these kids in their schools.

SCHOOLING "THESE KIDS"

The McKinney Act: Educational Rights and Barriers

The U.S. Department of Education estimates that nationally there are 750,000 school-age children who are homeless (National Law Center on Homelessness and Poverty, 1995), and approximately 23% do not attend school during their periods of homelessness. In 1987, Congress passed the Stewart B. McKinney Act designed to provide emergency assistance, programs, and benefits to homeless people. Title VII(B) of the Act—Education for Homeless Children and Youth—requires states to remove barriers that impede the education of homeless children and to provide protections for their educational needs (National Law Center on Homelessness and Poverty, 1995; Rafferty, 1995). Congress reauthorized Title VII(B) of the McKinney Act in 1990 and in 1994, directing states to improve coordination of services for homeless children and expanding the programs to include preschool children. The McKinney Act mandates that children should be integrated into existing public school education programs and states are now required to develop programs that ensure that homeless children and youth have the same access to public education and services that all other resident children receive (Chapter 1, Head Start, Individuals with Disabilities Education Act). In addition, the law requires that residency requirements be revised so that homeless children may either continue to attend their schools of origin through the end of the school year or transfer to the school of the attendance area where the child is sheltered, "whichever is in the child's best interest" (McKinney Act 722(e)(3)A; cited in Rafferty, 1995, p. 40). McKinney also mandates the speedy transfer of immunization records, birth certificates, special service evaluations, and guardianship records, and requires that comparable services, such as transportation and school meals, be offered to homeless students.

The McKinney Amendments strengthen the rights of homeless students by directing that states review and revise all laws, regulations, and policies that "may act as a barrier to the enrollment, attendance, or success in school of homeless children and youth" (721(2); cited in Rafferty, 1995, p. 41). Whereas the original Act focused exclusively on residency laws as an access barrier, the Amendments went further and focused on the need for services once children were enrolled in school. The Amendments require states to develop and implement professional training programs for school staff to enable them to respond to the needs of homeless children, to gather data on the number and geographical location of homeless children, and to demonstrate that state and local education agencies have developed policies to remove barriers to access and retention and to ensure "that homeless children are not isolated or stigmatized" (Rafferty, 1995, p. 41).

Although the McKinney Act clearly laid out a platform of educational and legal rights for homeless children and youth, in many areas it remains an unfunded mandate, subject to Congressional funding cuts and to noncompliance by states. In 1990, the National Law Center on Homelessness and Poverty surveyed homeless service providers in 20 states and found that 75% of the providers identified transportation as a barrier, 70% listed transfer of school records, and 60% cited residency requirements as barriers to educational access for children (National Law Center on Homelessness and Poverty, 1995). In 1995 the National Law Center conducted a nationwide review of the McKinney Program and found that 40% of family shelter service providers continued to cite birth certificates, transfer of school records, and transportation as the most significant barriers still confronting homeless children; and 74% reported that transportation still constituted a major barrier for homeless children whose school of origin was in another district, with more than half of the children transferring to a school in the shelter's attendance area. In addition, 45% of survey respondents indicated that homeless children had problems obtaining tutoring services or evaluations for special education, and less than half of all preschool-age children attended early childhood programs.

In order to receive McKinney funds, states are required to submit plans to the U.S. Department of Education reporting on measures they have taken to ensure that children who are homeless have access to public education. However, under the recently implemented Improving America's Schools

Act, states are now permitted to combine plans from several other educational programs into a single consolidated plan. In 1995, concerned about the impact of consolidated plans on the specific goals of the McKinney Act, the National Law Center reviewed the state plans. The Center found that only 9 states had submitted individual plans and that six of the nine plans adequately addressed homeless children's needs. However, in the 41 states that adopted consolidated plans, there was a widespread failure to address the specific educational needs of homeless children or to provide detailed measures for meeting their needs. The Center concluded that although the McKinney Act succeeded in reducing barriers to education, so that homeless children now have "a foot in the schoolhouse door," large cuts in program funding as well as noncompliance threaten to shut that door, reversing gains already made (National Law Center on Homelessness and Poverty, 1995).

A Foot in the Schoolhouse Door

The myriad problems confronting homeless children, when they do manage to squeeze one foot in the schoolhouse door, have been extensively documented; attendance, academic failure and poor achievement, and inappropriate placement or lack of special services. Once homeless children are enrolled in school, school attendance continues to constitute a major obstacle for their families. A national study of families seeking assistance from Traveler's Aid found that 43% of school-age homeless children were not attending school (Maza & Hall, 1990). Children who are homeless either consistently fail or perform at below-average levels in contrast to their housed peers (see Rafferty, 1995; McChesney, 1993; Rafferty & Rollins, 1989; Bassuk & Rosenberg, 1988). They are more likely to score poorly on standardized tests and less likely to be promoted at the end of the school year, and the need for remediation and tutoring is one of the most frequently cited needs by state education agencies (Rafferty, 1995).

Rafferty, who has written extensively and comprehensively about the psychological, educational, and legal rights of homeless children (see Rafferty, 1995; Rafferty & Rollins, 1989; Rafferty & Shin, 1991), points out that once access barriers are solved, placement in appropriate educational settings frequently does not occur, particularly when a period of homelessness means a move to a new school district. She cited each of the 22 education coordinators for homeless children in New York City reporting delays in the transfer of records, which impedes their ability to place homeless children in appropriate programs. And because children who are homeless are often transient, educational needs are not identified in a timely fashion and special education evaluations may never be completed (Rafferty, 1991, 1995).

Residential instability frequently means family breakups—mothers who become homeless risk the loss of their children to protective services, as foster care policies characterize homelessness as neglect (Steinbock, 1995), and adolescents who become homeless with their families are frequently unable to stay with them. A recent national survey conducted by Jacobs, Little, and Almeida (1992) found that 40% of shelters had operating policies that excluded adolescent boys. Residential instability also leads to high rates of school mobility, which in turn is associated with a loss of educational services, diminished rates of attendance, and academic failure (Rafferty, 1995). This is particularly disruptive for high school students who frequently find themselves facing grade retention and loss of credits. Berck (1992) quotes a high school student: "Between all the school changing, my credits were messed up and they said I might have to stay back another year. I didn't know what was going on, so I dropped out and started working full-time" (p. 82). In Monika's situation, described earlier, it was clear that her struggle to stay in school and complete her senior year was contingent on where she would sleep the following night and how much longer she could remain resilient in the face of all the psychological stress she endured. If she were not an academically successful student, it is unlikely that she would have remained in school after her repeated episodes of homelessness.

Shame, Stigma, and Discrimination

> I just don't have time for these kids on top of my teaching—they transfer in and out and we're meant to educate them too—it's just too much of a burden, and their mothers move them from place to place—they don't have proper records and Tim's the third one of them I've had in the past 2 years. (Third-grade teacher quoted in Polakow, 1993, p.145)

Tim, one of "them," was a 9-year-old boy whom I met when he transferred to his fourth school after repeated episodes of homelessness with his young mother and baby sister. His teacher saw him as a burden who had no place in her classroom, and his classmates followed her example, isolating and taunting Tim about his appearance. Tim, angry and hurt, tells me: "They think 'cos I haven't got no home that I haven't got nothing inside of me—they won't play with me—they won't be a buddy when we go on trips and no kids will be my friends" (Polakow, 1993, p. 145).

Tim, like many thousands of homeless children, experiences shame and isolation due to his placelessness. Many homeless children attempt to hide the fact that they are homeless, and are traumatized by the ensuing losses, as we saw earlier in the case of 8-year-old Michael. The shift from a housed to an unhoused world frequently entails not only a loss of friends, neighborhood networks, and school changes, but also a profound sense of shame and fear of being identified as "a shelter kid." One staff member at a family shelter in Michigan reported that they had painted the shelter's logo on a brand new van, but removed the logo after they realized the children did not want to be dropped off near the school. The staff member remarked, "If they don't know what it means to be a shelter kid, be assured that the other kids at school will let them know" (Dohoney & Reiling, 1996, p. 13). Although school-age children and adolescents are particularly sensitive to peer perceptions, the attitudes of school personnel from secretaries to teachers to principals frequently mirror the negative discourse of the media, congressional welfare rhetoric, and the public at large, all of which constructs poor families as mired in their own behavioral pathologies—where poverty and homelessness become one's personal responsibility. My own ethnographic classroom observations of poor children in public school classrooms in Michigan document widespread discrimination and prejudice on the part of teachers and school personnel toward destitute children and their families—where classroom environments for poor children, particularly difficult and angry children, become landscapes of condemnation that reveal shared experiences of exclusion, humiliation, and indifference (Polakow, 1993).

One homeless education coordinator in Michigan illustrates the problem as she describes a situation involving a fourth-grade child whom she picks up from school and takes to an after-school tutoring program (interview, January 12, 1997):

> The child was placed in a resource room at the school. They felt she needed to be placed there pretty intensively … So the first time I go to pick her up out of her classroom, the teacher says, "This child can never remember anything—she forgets everything—I can't even imagine her knowing to wait for you in the office when you come get her—what is her mom on drugs or something? She needs to have constant attention!" Now this is not the child I know. She tries hard, she knows how to read and write. She misspells words, but she's only a fourth grader and she's been through such a lot in her life and she's homeless … But the teacher's attitude is: These kids are causing me a whole lot of stress and I don't

want to have to deal with it ... There's definitely a stigma attached to my kids and they feel it. By the time they are teenagers they've got a record and then people look at them and say: You made this problem, you contributed to your situation—you're responsible. It's your own fault ... Thank God the McKinney Act protects these kids because otherwise they'd have nothing!

CONFRONTING INVISIBILITY: ADVOCACY FOR HOMELESS CHILDREN

As we consider the plight of homeless children in the United States, it is clear that their lives are emblematic of the widespread indifference to destitute children and their families now embedded in pernicious public policies that construct homelessness. Recent attempts to build nonpartisan bridging networks to advocate for children only serve to further conceal the destructive assaults on poor children and their mothers initiated by the Republican's Contract with America, which, with complicit acquiescence from Democrats, destroyed the last vestiges of a federal safety net for families through the passage of the welfare repeal law. The legacy of the 104th Congress and of President Clinton's first term of office is a shameful one; the deliberate impoverishment of millions of children who, together with their families, have already begun the precipitous fall into homelessness. This invisibility of terror, of suffering, and of despair is well concealed by the personal responsibility discourse—the new rhetorical coinage that serves to mask deeply embedded racist, misogynistic, and class attacks on poor women, poor children, and poor people. The acceptance of staggering income inequalities—the richest 1% of households now control about 40% of the nation's wealth ("The Rich," 1995, p. A14)—and diminishing public investment and supports consigned millions of American families to lives on the edge. There are high costs to homelessness—its terrors, its continuing instability, the shame and humiliation, the hunger, the lack of any sense of stability or belonging, and as Steven Banks, director of the Homeless Family Rights Project, puts it, "We are creating a lost generation of children who simply do not know what it is like to be in stable housing" (Herbert, 1996, p. A11).

Schools that Serve as Advocacy Models

Although schools cannot change the destructive public policies afflicting poor families that are now in place, schools should never become autonomous landscapes of condemnation. Threats, coercive teaching methods, humiliation, and indifference only serve to exacerbate the desperate worlds that children are attempting to cope with as part of their daily experience. Homeless children often manifest their problems by acting out, exhibiting aggression, depression, regressive behavior (especially younger children), inattentiveness, hyperactivity, and chronic tiredness and anxiety (Linehan, 1992). Yet good schools and good teachers can and do make a significant difference in children's stressed and desperate lives, creating a refuge where a child may experience sensitive and supportive interventions from teachers, principals and other support staff. As Haberman (1994) points out, it is necessary to develop forms of "gentle teaching" that address the multiple stresses of children growing up in poverty, in violent neighborhoods, and by extension those who are homeless.

There are instructive local examples of schools that specifically cater to homeless students. The Thomas J. Pappas Regional Education Center in the Phoenix area serves children K–8 who are homeless, doubled up, or in contingent living situations, attempting to provide a supportive temporary schooling experience for all uprooted and dislocated children. A Pappas teacher and principal describe their situation:

> The teachers and staff are aware that every student comes from an uncertain environment each day, which may result in extremely non-traditional behaviors … The lives of students away from school are fragmented and frightening. Yet, because of the extensive outreach to area shelters and the community network of support, the school thrives, and so do the students. (Woods & Harrison, 1994, p. 125)

Impressive support services characterize Pappas, a magnet school, which transports students from all over Phoenix. Case-by-case individualized teaching accommodates students' diverse emotional and cognitive needs, with the same teachers and aides dealing with the students each day. As the staff points out, "Each teacher's lesson plans reflect the knowledge that each day stands alone. Each lesson must open and close on the same day because a child may not return" (Woods & Harrison, 1994, p. 124). Breakfast, lunch, and snacks are provided and there are supplies of clothing, shoes, and personal items (shampoo, deodorant, etc.) available for students, as well as food boxes that can be taken to their families after school. A medical clinic staffed by a full-time nurse and volunteer pediatricians also attends to the health needs of homeless children and provides a place for students to rest or nap if they have been wandering the streets at night, or unable to sleep at a shelter.

The Benjamin Franklin Day Elementary School in Seattle is another inspiring example. Here, a committed school principal courageously confronted a two-tiered urban school with exclusionary practices, and rebuilt it as a model of a full-service school with strong parent/teacher/community relationships. Quint (1994) quotes Principal Carole Williams:

> As the principal of B. F. Day I choose not to be concerned with the established societal standards and bureaucratic dictates of "doing things right." Rather, I choose to illuminate a compelling direction of "doing the right thing." I want teachers who are willing to go the 22 yards when it comes to letting children know we will never give up on them. If that translates into hugging and holding a psychologically beaten child, if it means walking down the street and buying him a hamburger, or washing that child's face and combing his hair—whatever—I expect it. (p. 33)

In discussing how staff learned to deal with homeless students, one teacher insightfully remarked:

> The greatest challenge was trying not to blame the kids or their families for having fallen through the cracks of society … In many ways we refused to acknowledge our own prejudices and bias regarding the homeless population. We had little understanding of their plight. Sometimes, it's easier to look away from a situation than to see it up close—real close. (pp. 34–35)

Teachers were encouraged by their principal to visit their students in emergency shelters, and to develop a heightened awareness and sensitivity to the destitute lives that many children and their families led. Students, in turn, were to be educated and sensitized about the difficulties experienced by those who were homeless; and teachers recollected how in the early days of the school's rebuilding, homeless children were often taunted and called "shelter rats" or "garbage" by their housed peers. A model program, KOOL–IS (Kids Organized On Learning In School), was implemented, where students and their parents were invited to talk about their daily lives and problems to staff after 3 p.m. The program also provided funding as well as human and material resources to deal with the myriad problems confronting families. Because there was a powerful parent/school/community connection in place, the school became a space of acceptance not only for homeless children, but for their mothers as well, and for all the destitute families whose children attended the school. Quint (1994) points out that

> Although B. F. Day is a "work in the making," it is a valuable demonstration of how … one school and one community share in a vision of how life might be

different for its children ... The work at this one site—now expanding to encompass many of the schools in the state of Washington—is rich with implica- tions for the future of all our schools and for the increasing proportion of at-risk children they serve. (pp. 126, 133)

Although Quint concludes her qualitative study of B. F. Day on this rather optimistic note, I wonder whether, in the current political and economic climate, that optimism about the future is warranted. Both B .F. Day and Pappas are unique creations, developed by remarkable individual adminis- trators with strong commitments to destitute and homeless children. Prior to August 1996, all of these families were eligible to receive the now defunct AFDC (Aid to Families with Dependent Children) assistance. Clearly the Pappas and B. F. Day schools are impressive examples of successful local advocacy at work, but the broader social and economic conditions that make their existence necessary should never be accepted as the natural order of things.

Local commitment, dedication, volunteerism, educational advocacy, and community involvement are vital to enable disenfranchised and disempow- ered families to survive, but that should not obscure the fundamental responsibility of our own government to protect its citizenry and residents against homelessness, hunger, destitution, and lack of health care. Afford- able subsidized housing, not emergency shelters and dangerous, drug-in- fested housing projects; a living wage, not minimum wages that keep 18% of full-time workers under the poverty line; universal health care, not 40 million Americans without any health care insurance; subsidized universal public child care that makes it possible for mothers to work, not the unaffordable stratified system of care that exists now, where cheap unsafe and unlicensed child care exclusively serves poor children. These are neither impossible nor utopian dreams. They exist effectively in most of Western and Northern Europe—in countries with strong public benefits and income transfers. The rate of child poverty in the United States is currently higher than in 18 other Western industrialized nations and 6 to 7 times higher than in Denmark, Sweden, and Finland (Children's Defense Fund, 1996) where family and child social supports are strongest. Public income transfers do work. So do higher taxes. Both are anathema to our current private responsibility discourses, which promote privatization, profits, and the pillaging of the public economy at an enormous social cost.

Homelessness is an outrage in a society of mansions and second homes and condos. It is also a searing tragedy for all who are unsheltered. For our homeless children, who have become postmodern "street rats," the lifelong consequences are deep and scarring. And as Ellison's narrator prophetically warns us, "There's a stench in the air ... What else but try to tell you what was really happening when your eyes were looking through?" (1972, p. 438–439) .

Invisibility, concealment, the savage act of "looking through"—all require confrontation of the growing "stench" in our society and a clear recognition that the human rights of homeless families have long been signed away. For those of us who are privileged and housed, advocacy requires making visible the overwhelming stench of rights denied, and of children discarded.

REFERENCES

Bassuk, E. L. (1990). Who are the homeless families? Characteristics of sheltered mothers and children. *Community Mental Health Journal, 26,* 425–434.

Bassuk, E. L., & Rosenberg, L. (1988). Why does family homelessness occur? A case control study. *American Journal of Public Health, 78*(7), 783–788.

Bassuk, E. L., Weinreb, L. F., Buckner, J. C., Browne, A., Salomon, A., & Bassuk, S. S. (1996). The characteristics and needs of sheltered homeless and low-income housed mothers. *Journal of the American Medical Association, 276*(8), 640–646.

Berck, J. (1992). *No place to be: Voices of homeless children.* Boston: Houghton Mifflin.

Children's Defense Fund. (1995). *The state of America's children: Yearbook.* Washington, DC: Author.

Children's Defense Fund. (1996). *The state of America's children: Yearbook.* Washington, DC: Author.

Doctorow, E. L. (1994). *The waterworks.* New York: Random House.

Dohoney, J. M., & Reiling, D. (1996). *Homeless in Michigan: Voices of the children.* Lansing, MI: Kids Count in Michigan.

Dubrow, N., & Garbarino, J. (1989). Living in the war zone: Mothers and young children in a public housing project. *Child Welfare, 68*(1), 3–20.

Ehrenreich, B., & Piven, F. F. (1984, Summer). The feminization of poverty: When the family wage system breaks down. *Dissent, 31,* 162–168.

Ellison, R. (1972). *Invisible man.* New York: Vintage.

Garbarino, J. (1992). The meaning of poverty in the world of children. *American Behavioral Scientist, 35*(3), 220–237.

Goldberg, G. S., & Kremen, E. (1990). *The feminization of poverty: Only in America?* New York: Greenwood Press.

Gordon, L. (Ed.). (1990). *Women, the state, and welfare.* Madison: University of Wisconsin Press.

Haberman, M. (1994). Gentle teaching in a violent society. *Educational Horizons, 172,* 131–135.

Herbert, B. (1996, September 23). Families on the edge. *The New York Times,* p.A11.

Jacobs, F. H., Little, P., & Almeida, C. (1992). *Supporting family life: A survey of homeless shelters.* Unpublished manuscript, Tufts University, Department of Urban and Environmental Policy, Medford, MA.

Kaufman, T. (1996). *Housing America's future: Children at risk.* Washington, DC: National Low Income Housing Coalition.

Lazere, E. (1995). *In short supply: The growing affordable housing gap.* Washington, DC: Center on Budget and Policy Priorities.

Linehan, M. F. (1992). Children who are homeless: Educational strategies for school personnel. *Phi Delta Kappan, 74*(1), 61–65.

Maza, J. A., & Hall, P. L (1990). No fixed address: The effects of homelessness on families and children. *Child and Youth Services, 14*(1), 35–47.

McChesney, K. Y. (1993). Homeless families since 1980: Implications for education. *Education and Urban Society, 25*(4), 361–380.

National Clearinghouse for the Defense of Battered Women (1994, February). *Statistics Packet: (3rd ed.).* Philadelphia, PA: Author.

National Coalition for the Homeless. (1996a, October). *Facts about homeless families and children in America.* Washington, DC: Author.

National Coalition for the Homeless. (1996b). *FY 95–FY97 funding for homeless assistance programs.* Washington, DC: Author.

National Coalition for the Homeless. (1996c). *Welfare repeal: Moving Americans off welfare into homelessness.* Washington, DC: Author.

National Law Center on Homelessness and Poverty. (1993). *No way out.* Washington, DC: Author.

National Law Center on Homelessness and Poverty. (1995). *A foot in the schoolhouse door.* Washington, DC: Author

National Low Income Housing Coalition, (1996). *Out of reach: Can America pay the rent?* Washington, DC: Author.

Pearce, D. (1978). The feminization of poverty: Women, work and welfare. *The Urban and Social Change Review, 11*(1 & 2), 28–36.

Polakow, V. (1993). *Lives on the edge: Single mothers and their children in the other America.* Chicago: University of Chicago Press.

Polakow, V. (1994). Savage distributions: Welfare myths and daily lives. *Sage Race Relations Abstracts, 19*(4), 3–29.

Quint, S. (1994). *Schooling homeless children: A working model for America's public schools.* New York: Teachers College Press.

Rafferty, Y. (1991). *And miles to go. … Barriers to academic achievement and innovative strategies for the delivery of educational services to homeless children.* Long Island City, NY: Advocates for Children.

Rafferty, Y. (1995). The legal rights and educational problems of homeless children and youth. *Educational Foundations and Policy Analysis, 17*(1), 39–61.

Rafferty, Y., & Rollins, N. (1989). *Learning in limbo: The educational deprivation of homeless children.* Long Island City, NY: Advocates for Children. (Eric Document Reproduction No. ED 312 363).

Rafferty, Y., & Shin, M. (1991). The impact of homelessness on children. *American Psychologist, 46,* 1170–1179.

The rich get richer (1995, April 18). [Editorial]. *The New York Times,* p. A14.

Steinbock, M. (1995). Homeless female-headed families: Relationships at risk. *Marriage and Family Review, 20*(1, 2), 143–159.

Stewart B. McKinney Homeless Assistance Act of 1987, 42 U.S. §11301 *et seq.* (amended 1988).

Stewart B. McKinney Homeless Assistance Amendments Act of 1990, Pub. L. No. 101–
    645, 42 U.S.C.A. §11421–11432.
Super, D. A., Parrot, S., Steinmetz, S., & Mann, C. (1996). *The new welfare law*. Washington,
    DC: Center on Budget and Policy Priorities.
U.S. Bureau of the Census. (1989). Poverty in the United States. *Current Population Reports*
    (Series P–60, No. 163). Washington, DC: U.S. Government Printing Office.
U.S. Bureau of the Census. (1996). Income, poverty, and valuation of non-cash benefits:
    1995. *Current Population Reports* (Consumer Income Series P60–193), pp. 60–194.
    Washington, DC: U.S. Government Printing Office.
U.S. Conference of Mayors. (1995). *A status report on hunger and homelessness in America's
    cities: 1995*. Washington, DC: Author.
U.S. Department of Housing and Urban Development. (1996). *Rental housing assistance at a
    crossroads: A report to congress on worst case housing needs*. Washington, DC: Author.
Wilson, W. J. (1996, August 18). Work. *The New York Times Magazine*, pp. 26–31, 40, 48,
    52–54.
Women and violence hearings: Hearing before the Senate Judiciary Committee, 101st Cong., 2nd
    Sess. 37 (1990).
Woods, C., & Harrison, D. (1994, November/December). *The Clearing House*, 123–126.

2

Living with Violence: White Working-Class Girls and Women Talk*

❧ • ❧

Lois Weis and Julia Marusza
State University of New York at Buffalo

Yeah, I used to get to the point where I stood in between the two of them, praying that neither one of them would hurt each other, and I'd end up getting punched in the middle because I couldn't stop them … My father would come home drunk … I mean, there was blood in our house just about every day. Somebody was always whacked with something … And dinner time, to this day … I can't sit at a table and eat with my kids … Because every time we sat and ate … just as you're getting ready to eat, a fight broke out and you couldn't leave the kitchen. So you had to sit there and listen to it.

—Suzanne, 31

My mom got money from her boyfriend for my school pictures, and when they came back, he saw them as I was getting ready for school … He threw them and said that I messed up my hair. But I got up an hour early that day to fix it, I remember, only my hair just flattened, not on purpose. He got real mad and picked up a lamp and threw it at her and it hit her but I tried to block it and got hit too. It fell on the floor all in pieces. She was crying because she was hurt and because he left and I was crying because I knew she would let him come back. So we were both crying picking up the glass. Then I walked to school and I didn't open up my mouth once all day because I thought I would cry if I did.

—Christina, 13

---

*This analysis was funded by generous grants from the Spencer and Carnegie foundations.

The silence surrounding domestic violence is finally being shattered. In the wake of Congressional proposals that, by cutting welfare benefits and food stamps, reify the male-headed nuclear family, we are becoming increasingly aware that all is not well with the picture-perfect family. Evidence is mounting that many women are abused in such families and many children's hopes and dreams are shattered by crushing blows delivered by their parents. This news literally explodes off the pages of the daily papers. Private family space, a man's castle, may not be quite so comfortable or safe for women and children as we once thought. Yet, the literature on schooling does not take this into account. We do not consider how these traumas are embedded within the lives of the children we teach, or what it means to come to school with a broken spirit or in physical pain because of family violence.

Within the past 15 years, some excellent work has been done on girls and women in school (Eckert, 1989; Holland & Eisenhart, 1990; Valli, 1988; Wallace, 1987). This work uncovered the ways in which schools reinforce particular cultural arrangements wherein men are considered dominant and women "other" or lesser than males (Arnot, 1982; Biklen & Pollard, 1993; Kelly & Nihlen, 1982; Wrigley, 1992). Several studies have focused specifically on the cultures that girls and women produce themselves, and on the ways in which these cultures are linked to broader structural inequalities (McRobbie, 1991). Although all such research is useful in terms of our understanding of the ways in which institutions contribute to unequal outcomes for girls and women, as well as the ways in which the cultures produced by girls and women contribute to these outcomes, the issue of violence as embedded in these arrangements remains almost wholly unexplored.

This absence contrasts sharply with the broader literature on male violence against women. This literature spans a number of areas, ranging from discussion of the battered women's shelter movement (Schechter, 1982) to manuals on how to escape violent situations (Nicarthy, 1989; White, 1985) to legal issues surrounding such violence and to empirical and theoretical explorations of domestic violence (Dobash & Dobash, 1979; Steinmetz & Strauss, 1974; Hoff, 1990; Walker, 1984). Although it is widely argued that violence in the home appears across social classes, it is now generally acknowledged that there is more such abuse among poor and working-class families.

This fact renders the lack of attention to domestic violence more striking in discussions about girls and women in educational institutions serving poor and working-class communities. How is it that violence in the home has never emerged as a category around which identities were constructed in the myriad ethnographic investigations conducted in schools serving poor and working-class students (Everhart, 1983; Fine, 1991; Valli, 1988; Weis, 1990; Willis, 1977)? While Rubin (1976) touched on this issue in the mid-1970s in her now classic *Worlds of Pain*, hers is the exception rather than the rule, and school ethnographies, including Lois' (Weis, 1990), conducted in White working-class communities, never broached the subject.

Drawing from two large-scale ethnographic investigations conducted recently, we argue in this chapter that domestic violence is deeply embedded within White working-class communities and that this abuse has serious implications for what goes on in schools. To us, girls and women are quietly and in selective spaces speaking out. They are, to use Don Belton's (1995) term, "speaking their name" as they attempt to cope with the violence that rages on around them in their homes. Many of these females are living in pain—in distress, without hope. Why, then, hasn't this broken through in prior ethnographies? Why is this all so well-guarded a secret in White working-class communities? Why are White working-class girls and women so silent on this topic—so silent that the only time they will discuss it is in the spaces in which we conducted our interviews? Why didn't Lois, we ask ourselves, pick this up in the study that led to the publication of *Working Class Without Work*, a study located in a White working-class community in the northeastern United States?

Although we cannot answer these questions fully, we think abuse is so buried in White working-class communities that unless we, as investigators, specifically ask about violence, the topic simply does not come up. It broke through in the data gathered by Lois and Michelle Fine as part of a large-scale Spencer Foundation project designed to capture the narrations of low income White, Latino/Latina, and African American young adults about their lives since leaving high school. Outside the confined bounds of the school, in the private space of our interviews, narrations of abuse came pouring out. From childhood violence, to abuse by former lovers or husbands, to current stories of violence directed at their sisters, domestic violence saturated the lives of those to whom we spoke. The secret was out for us. Lois and Michelle pained over the stories and over the fact that they were previously untold to academic researchers. We felt privileged to hear these accounts, yet pierced by the agony that hung in the interviews and in our minds as we read and wrote.

Julia Marusza walked with us through much of this data. She, like Lois and Michelle, painfully wrote with the words of the women we had interviewed. So she knew, and took this into account when she gathered data among middle school girls in a community center and in a bilingual school serving a White working-class population. Knowing opened the way for Julia to learn more about this terrible secret. We pool resources in this chapter to place this issue in both our minds and our hearts. White working-class girls and women are experiencing alarming rates of domestic violence. Their story needs to be told. And so we tell it as White working-class women and girls speak their name and tell their sad tale.

Throughout this essay, our (Lois' and Julia's) authorial voice is both muted and clear. It is muted in the sense that we provide large chunks of interview data through which we encourage the reader to listen carefully to the words and worlds of our interviewees. It is clear, though, as we do not hide our outrage at the violence in this community. Women and children are being abused in White working-class homes and neighborhoods at alarming rates, and there is no scream emanating from within the community that brings this to the nation's attention. We are concerned for the safety of the women and children with whom we worked. We are concerned for the emotional well-being of the children who go to school daily surviving unspeakable horror in the home, a horror that affects their ability to learn academic material as well as to grow emotionally. So our outrage is not veiled, and our anger over government proposals that reify the sanctity of the home is well justified. As we write, President Clinton has signed a sweeping welfare reform bill which will affect the lives of women and children in profound ways. Whatever problems welfare in its current state may have, it still allows an abused woman to leave a violent home and set off on her own. By taking away that safety net, we are consigning women and children to stay in homes that may be "headed" by a man who will continue to abuse or even kill them.

URBAN WHITE WORKING-CLASS WOMEN

We first visit women who were interviewed as part of a Spencer Foundation study headed by Lois and Michelle and designed to capture the narrations of low income White, Latino/Latina, and African American men and women, ages 23 to 35, about their lives since leaving high school. In total, 150 individuals were interviewed in Jersey City, New Jersey, and Buffalo, New York. Interviews, in two segments, spanned 3 to 5 hours.

Interviewees were drawn from "meaningful urban communities" such as Head Start programs, literacy centers, churches, parenting groups in schools, and community organizations such as Hispanics United and the Urban League. In addition, extensive focus group interviews were held. For example, we held focus groups with African American mothers who bring their children to an early childhood center, African American men who are active in their church, and White working-class women who have their children enrolled in a Diocesan elementary school. All interviewees either were selected by the gatekeepers of the organizations with which we worked or were nominated by their peers. We highlight this only to suggest that all of our interviewees are connected to meaningful networks and do not represent, in all likelihood, the most alienated individuals within any given community. Many of these poor and White working-class women, however, were self-described as estranged from kin in so far as they were the one's "left behind" in communities of concentrated poverty while more fortunate siblings fled "up" and out to the suburbs. In this analysis, the 15 White women were all from Buffalo, and 11 were high school graduates. Fifty-six percent were married. Most of their husbands worked in lower level white collar positions or in blue collar positions.[1]

When we began, we did not intend to do a study on domestic violence. Indeed this was, in some sense, far from our minds. However, the reality is that 92% of the White working-class women we interviewed narrated histories or contemporary experiences of abuse. These women were severely beaten, and many were repeatedly abused by the men in their lives. Although the proportion of women being beaten is incredibly high, higher than estimates in the literature of about 70%, it is even more striking that this is a well-guarded secret in White working-class communities. "Settled living" women, to use Joseph Howell's (1972) term—women who are married and whose husbands earn an adequate living—are at great pains to keep this information secret as they go about raising their children and protecting the ideology of the "good" family life. It is only when White working-class women become "hard living"—or exit from the nuclear family arrangement—that they are consistently willing to speak loudly about abuse in this class fraction. "Settled" women spoke to us softly in the confines of our individual interviews, telling us their terrifying histories, but once we pulled them together in focus groups, silence set in. "Settled" women were no longer willing to speak about abuse even though we knew from the individual interviews that many of the women sitting with us had histories of abuse,

---

[1]The full two-city data is reported in Fine, M. & Weis, L. (1998). *The unknown city: Lives of poor and working-class young adults.* Boston: Beacon Press.

histories that they had shared only weeks earlier.

This contrasts with African American women who were willing to share their experiences in focus groups. The African American women's shared stories of abuse, compared with the White women's, were less frequent and, at the same time, more public. African American women spoke with us in focus groups about violence, sharing their experiences of pain and suffering, sharing their strength and hope. They told and retold stories to one another, with sympathetic nods all around the group. The White working-class women who revealed in individual interviews that they suffered at the hands of belligerent men, were also part of focus groups with other White working-class women. However, they would not speak openly to one another about their troubles. They shut the door to that part of their lives. They locked the rest of the world out and coped, or not, alone.

We now take you into the private worlds of three of our narrators—Suzanne, Kathy and Anna—in order to open up the whole cloth of women's pain, passion, and violence that festers beneath the surface of this raced and gendered class fraction. Suzanne, a 31-year-old White married mother of four, is unemployed and currently volunteers in a local school. She and her husband applied for public assistance but were denied funds because they fell over the income line for qualification. Alcohol abuse saturated her family of origin and all who were associated with this family:

> I grew up in an alcoholic family ... Both parents were alcoholics, so we basically were left alone a lot ... We were raised, basically, in the back room of a bar ... We didn't have a good home life as far as that goes. That's probably why I'm the opposite ... There was no, there was always degrading things said to us ... There was none of the self-esteem stuff or anything else like that. We were always called dumb and stupid and told we weren't going to amount to anything ... I have two, well, I had three sisters and one brother. One sister died of SIDS [Sudden Infant Death Syndrome] when she was 3 months old. And my brother committed suicide when he was 27 because he just couldn't handle. He, he was one of those kids that never felt like he fit in. So, he did everything, what everybody dared him to. And one kid, when he was 21, somebody dared him to jump into the creek, in the middle of winter. And he did. And he became paralyzed ... So, when he was 27 he killed himself because he couldn't handle the fact that being paralyzed and not getting married and not, you know, having anything else ... My other sister turned out to be an alcoholic because she followed my parents' steps. And my other sister is an oddity. Because they usually say if you come from an alcoholic family, you're either an alcoholic or you're totally against it. I'm totally against it [drinking]. My sister turned out to be an alcoholic, and my other sister is a social drinker [laughs]. Which they say doesn't happen.

Suzanne drew attention to the ways in which alcohol and violence were, for her, linked. According to Suzanne, many of her siblings were, in hindsight, unaware of the family's dysfunctions while they were growing up, and today are living lives filled with the same forms of abuse. Talking about her nonalcoholic sister, Suzanne said:

She lived in la la land. I always tell her, I don't know where she lived, because she didn't live in our house … You know, she's so condemning of my [alcoholic] sister. And I told her, but look at what we were raised in. And that's the first thing my other sister [the alcoholic] will say is, "Well, mom and dad did it and we're all here." But we're not all here. You know, my brother killed himself because of it. And, she actually lost her life because of it, because she's so busy drinking. She's not raising her kids either. So her kids are going through the same thing, basically, all over again. And she also, my mother, was abused by my father all the time. And my sister let men beat her up too. She used to get beat up terrible all the time. So, her kids have seen that already too. And they say that's another trend … the abuse … You try to find somebody like your father and you end up in that type of situation. And just like my brother, my brother hated to see my father beat up my mother. But at the same time, he beat the hell out of his girlfriends. So … it's a thing, after you see it, you think it's normal even though it's not … I'm against it [alcohol], because I saw my mother [who was also an alcoholic] … my father used to tell my mother, "Who would take you with four kids? What would you do [if you left me or I left you]?" And he used to call her fat and ugly, and she was beautiful and thin. You know, but it's a game they play to keep you in your place.

Suzanne commented further on how she used to defend herself from the outbreaks at home and the ways in which she is affected today by those experiences:

And with me with my father, he tried once. He used to try to, used to fondle me. And that was about it. So, and then one time he grabbed me and I smacked him. It was the only time I ever hit my father because I don't believe that you should ever hit your parents, but I swore that he was not going to do to me what he did to the rest of that family. And since that time, he never touched me because I'm bigger than him … And my mother … I used to tell my mother, why didn't you sit on him? He was so thin and so little, you could have just sat on him instead of getting beat up all the time. But my mother wouldn't. She was afraid of him. Yeah, I used to get to the point where I stood in between the two of them, praying that neither one of them would hurt each other, and I'd end up getting punched in the middle because I couldn't stop them and get them parted … My father would come home drunk. He would go out on the couch and go to sleep and my mother would wake him up and drag him off the couch. Well, you're asking for a fight, you know … I don't want him hitting her. Just like I don't want her hitting him. I mean, there was blood in our house just about every day. Somebody was always whacked with something. And dinner time, to this day, I still don't sit at the dinner table with my kids. We eat in the parlor in front of the TV, or whatever. I can't sit at a table and eat with my kids. Because every time we sat and ate, we had to sit there. And you weren't allowed to leave and just as you're getting ready to eat, a fight broke out and you couldn't leave the kitchen. So you had to sit there and listen to it. So I can't sit at the table.

Contrary to the Norman Rockwell images of the nuclear family sitting down to eat dinner, Suzanne, as a child, was entangled within a set of family relations that drowned in alcoholism and, according to her, with the violence associated with that drinking. As she stated, "The scariest thing is never knowing if you were going to wake up and have a mother and father." She recounted sleeping in her clothes every night in case she had to flee her house in the middle of the night. The fact that she now sleeps without clothes is seen and felt as an act of immense liberation. Among the women interviewed, however, Suzanne's stories are not the only examples of such abuse, and are not even necessarily the most extreme. As evidenced in the data, these White working-class women's lives were marked by concentrations of fear and violence that seem to mount from the moment they were born. Although not every White working-class household looks this way, the violence that does exist is rough and hard and has a lingering presence.

Kathy is a 24-year-old White female, currently unemployed, having worked previously as an aide to profoundly physically and mentally handicapped adolescents. Kathy has an infant son and a 5-year-old daughter, neither of whom are the children of the man with whom she is now in a relationship. Kathy received WIC benefits but has not applied for welfare. Her savings amount to $1,500, and this is what she is living off of at the moment. Kathy's life has been filled with violence from every direction. A prototype of the "hard living" woman, she was raised by an abusive father, raped when she was 12, and brutally assaulted by the father of her first child when she was 18. Kathy remembered the things that frightened her while growing up:

My father terrified me ... He had a very bad temper ... and my mother's drinking. My father would never physically hurt my mother because she would have packed us up in a heartbeat. But he mentally abused her. Nothing was ever good enough, nothing was ever right. Um, she wanted to go back to work. He kept telling her, "No, no, no. Your place is here" ... Like no matter which way she turned, he was there with a blockade, trying to stop her from being her own person, developing her own will ... She started drinking ... I don't remember when she started, but I do remember one instance very vividly. My brothers don't remember this. I was

10. We were down in Georgia, visiting my father's sister and her husband ... My mother was, had a glass and it was half full of wine, and what she kept doing was drinking it and filling it back up to half when my father was home. And I saw this, like, well, my father caught on to her. And my father was a big man, he was probably about 6 ft 1 or 6 ft 2 ... He grabbed all three of us, picked us up and threw us in the Winnebago and took off. And he was going to leave her there. And I remember screaming. We must have gone about 4 or 5 miles out and maybe even more than that. We were screaming, screaming, "We don't want to leave mama, we don't want to leave mama." He was just going to leave her down there and take us with him ... At that point I didn't care if he hit me or not. I just kept screaming and screaming and screaming. And if he hit me I was going to scream even louder. I wanted to go back, and I didn't care what he did. You know, if he slapped me for screaming, I was going to scream louder. I screamed myself hoarse and he finally turned around.

Both Kathy and Suzanne narrated lives filled with shock and shame, surrounded by hitting, crying, verbal abuse, and insecurity. The small Kathy did not know whether or not her mother would be abandoned by her father in Georgia, and Suzanne slept in clothes each night of her young life in case she had to escape for help or safety.

Anna is a 26-year-old White female. A single mother, she has one son, age 8. She is on public assistance and is unemployed at present. She has been in and out of abusive relationships throughout much of her young life. Among the "hard living" group, Anna sought therapy for the past year and said that she found it helpful in understanding her tendency to pursue and stay in abusive alcoholic relationships. She stated that she could live without a man—that her own sanity is worth living by herself if that ends up to be the case. As she reflected back upon her life through therapy, she said she was forced to confront her past:

My father worked at a place called J. H. Williams, and they made tools. He was making pretty good money. The only problem was my father was a miser ... Actually, I really couldn't say he was a miser because he would spend money, but he would spend money on himself ... He would order things out of these magazines that were junk-like. I used to get one from Spencer, one from, I don't even remember the names of these places, but he would order things that were just, one thing I can remember was a calendar where it was like a lifetime calendar. You could just change the months on it and the days. When my father passed away, I think we had about 30 of them, all the same. Coasters. There were tons of them, just stupid little things, he would buy by quantities. He would save everything from twist ties to bags to the Styrofoam packages from meats, and I can understand saving some of it, I save certain things like that ... but my father, they were in the upstairs apartment, which we could have been renting it if we could have fixed it or cleaned it up. Because when I was young, probably about one, we had a fire, and he started fixing the downstairs, but he never finished the upstairs, and all of his stuff was just up there. It was in my bedroom [she never had a bedroom because there was too much "garbage" in it—she slept in her parents' room]; it was in the pantry; it was in the … kitchen. There was just stuff everywhere, on the kitchen table, in the bathtub, just junk that he would buy or save. And he used to buy himself lots of clothes. He never bought me any clothes or my mother any clothes. My uncle used to go and get me clothes from the Goodwill.

At a later point, Anna described her family as follows:

My father's an alcoholic and my mom is mentally ill; she's schizophrenic and it was tough. My father was also abusive in some ways. He wasn't real abusive compared to what you hear about some kids going through, but he was abusive and he was also … he had a big belief that the man runs everything and the woman belongs home barefoot and pregnant. I was kind of the caretaker. I did the cooking from, I can remember 7 years old, making dinner and cleaning … It was more or less, I was to take care of my mother instead of her taking care of me.

At school, Anna explained that she was picked on by the other children due to her lack of cleanliness, a result of her father's obsessive control over the household. Anna also remembered a few instances of sexual abuse, while perhaps dismissing others from memory:

[The teacher] would call me "piggy," "smelly," "dirty," names like that, and the kids started following along with it. And I'd say by the fourth grade, I started cleaning myself out, I didn't care anymore, but my father had this thing that you were allowed to take a bath once a week. He would measure the shampoo, he would measure the soap, and if he thought somebody was using the shampoo when he said you shouldn't, you'd get a beating. But I got sick of it, and the beatings almost became to be painless when hit with a belt or punched … It almost didn't faze me any more … I figured I'd rather be clean and go to school and have friends because it hurt more to not have friends than to be hit by my father … I know that we all slept in the same bed, which was another thing. I didn't have my own bedroom. My bedroom was filled with garbage, and I remember when I started developing, my father would put his arm around me and touch me on my breasts, and I always wondered; he would make it look like he was sleeping, but sometimes I thought that he was awake because I would move his hand, and it would go back up. But I don't remember anything more than that. I suspect that things had happened when I was in foster homes, and that I blocked it out because I do have a lot of hard time with any intimate relationships.

Growing up in poor and working-class White homes, these women have been subjected to various forms of violence throughout their lives. Their bodies carry biographies of abuse. Suzanne, Kathy, and Anna described sexual, verbal, and physical abuse. Kathy recounted that she was beginning to suspect her father killed his first wife. Through self-reflection, she was beginning to piece together the emotional fragments of abuse in her own life and that of her half sister and is coming to believe that her father could have shoved his first wife down a flight of stairs, from which she suffered an aneurysm the next morning and died. Apparently, she did die from an aneurysm; the only question is the extent to which his beating precipitated it. Kathy could, however, imagine that it was true—that her father was such a violent man that he did this. As she approached her teens, she used to run by the railroad tracks to get away from home. There, one day, she met another sixth grader—a boy—who raped her in her secret hiding place, a private space to which she would run to escape her abusive father. He left her with a "surprise package": She was pregnant at the age of 12 and her friend's mother arranged for her to have an abortion. Kathy was lurched from one violent encounter to another, as were many of the women we interviewed. If they were not beaten as a child or now, it was their sisters who were being abused by husbands or lovers.

The hand of the male is not soft and supportive for Suzanne, Kathy, and Anna, but is instead violent and brutal—a force to be feared. Given this, one would expect that poor and working-class White women would voice some critique of men and family. The most striking point here is that they do so only rarely, and the intimacies shared in an interview do not translate into collective sharing nor do they spur a critical analysis of the cyclical patterns of violence that have programmed and continue to regulate gender relations inside some poor and working-class White families. Although White women were willing to tell us a great deal in the secret space of our interviews, they left relatively unaltered their tone of reconciled contentment in which they wrapped narratives of the family as loving, and little scratches the surface as these women attempt to raise the next generation.

WHITE GIRLS, DOMESTIC VIOLENCE, AND SCHOOL

Next, we hear the voices of 8 preteenage girls interviewed as part of an ethnographic study conducted by Julia. The poor and working-class girls interviewed live in a section of Buffalo, New York. This piece is one slice of a larger ethnographic study of the constitution of urban poor and working-class White gendered identities among a group of middle school youth attending a neighborhood community center and a bilingual school in the same neighborhood. The scope of the research spanned more than a year of participant observation and in-depth interviews with community center staff, teachers, and about 20 White youth who travel each day between both sites. Questions were asked in relation to family, community, school, and activities at the community center.

Similar to the work by Lois and Michelle on adult women, Julia did not set out to research domestic violence in the lives of girls. Instead, this theme boldly and consistently emerged in the narrations of these girls. As regular visitors to the neighborhood community center, this group probably did not represent the most disengaged youth within the neighborhood. Nevertheless, when asked to describe their community, these girls soon began to tell stories of women being abused at the hands of men. Jamie, age 12, said:

> It's a pretty good place to live ... There's lots of auto crashes, drunk people. Lots of people go to the bars on Friday and Saturday and get blasted. They're always messing with people. Some guy's always getting kicked out of the bar for fighting. Guys are mostly fighting with their girlfriends and are getting kicked out for punching so they continue to fight in the street; I see it from my bedroom window, only the girl mostly gets beat up really bad.

Christina, age 12, said:

> There's lots of violence in this neighborhood. Like there's this couple that's always fighting. When the guy gets mad he hits her. It happens ... upstairs in their house. She's thrown the coffee pot at him and the toaster; they [coffeepot and toaster] landed in the street ... I saw it while walking by ... The guy would show off all the time in front of his friends. One day when he was hitting her she just punched him back and told him she wasn't going to live with him anymore. He used to hit her hard. She used to cry but she would still go out with him. She said she loved him too much to dump him. A lot of people go back.

Lisette, age 13, said:

> It's overall, a nice neighborhood ... There's like a lot of physical and mental abuse that goes on. Just lots of yelling. I know one mother that calls her daughter a slut. She tells her, "You're not worth anything; you're a slut" ... There's one family where the mother's boyfriend sexually abused her little girl, and stuff like that. The girl was like 7, and like he's still with them. The mother didn't care ... It's like fathers and boyfriends beat on the kids. They [mothers] don't take a stand. They don't say, "Well, you know that's my daughter" or, "That's my son." It's like they don't care. They think that they're just to sit down and be home ... They just sleep all day or watch TV. Some of them drink all day and are high and spend a lot of time sleeping it off.

Rosie, age 11, said:

My neighborhood's quiet sometimes. It's a nice neighborhood, I guess. Sometimes it could be violent. There's a lot of drugs in this neighborhood … Like there was my mom's friend who came over once with bruises all over. Her boyfriend beat her up because she had a guy from downstairs come up to her house. The boyfriend got real mad and he was going to kill her because he was jealous. I didn't see the fight but I saw her. She looked like a purple people eater … There's this one girl who got beat by her boyfriend. She did drugs and had another boyfriend, and the first boyfriend found out and got jealous. Violence is pretty much common in people's lives. About 95% of the world is angry. They attack things or litter, abuse people, and do other bad things like rape or kill. It's just the way it is.

Even though the community is seen as "a pretty good place to live" and "overall, a nice neighborhood," the girls' descriptions of residency quickly devolved into stories of violence—mostly violence directed towards women by men in both public and private spaces. As Jamie watched out the window from her second-story flat, it was a normal occurrence for men to hit women in public sites, such as in a bar or on the street. As Christina walked down the street, she observed that violence also existed between men and women behind the closed doors of homes. Christina noted that women often returned to their abusive partners. Lisette distinguished between different types of abuse—physical and mental—and gave examples of abuse between mothers and boyfriends, daughters and sons. This sophisticated way of looking at abuse is striking, and is likely attributed to the extremely close relationship Lisette has with Ruby, the White middle-aged activities coordinator at the community center, who also serves as an informal counselor to area youth. Rosie, it can be argued, was so desensitized to abuse, that she humorously recalled how a badly beaten friend of her mother resembled a "purple people eater." In Rosie's view, "About 95% of the world is angry. … It's just the way it is."

Although these girls may look at abuse differently, they all were quick to recognize violence as a defining feature of their community. Missing in these arguments, however, was the recognition that men are accountable for their abusive behavior. Instead, some girls blamed women for letting males hit them and for returning to violent relationships. It was as if they believed it is acceptable or normal for males to abuse females, and that it is the women's duty to negotiate her way around this violence. Lisette, for instance, was very critical of many neighborhood mothers whom she felt were not adequately putting their children's needs first.

For these girls, abuse existed not just in public places and in the private dwellings of others. Violence also occurred in their own homes. Similar to poor and working-class White women, the girls typically contextualized violence as part of the past, as "things are better now." The younger females, though, were not as consistent in packaging such events in history. For instance, Sarah and Elizabeth shifted from present to past in describing the abuse in their homes. Many girls recalled chilling vignettes of unbridled rage that patterned their upbringing. Anne, age 11, said:

> My mom and her boyfriend constantly fight because they drink. When I was little I remember being in my bed. I was sleeping, only my other sisters came and woke me up because my mom and her boyfriend were fighting. We [Anne and sisters] started crying. I was screaming. My sisters were trying to calm me down. Our door was above the staircase and you could see the front door. I just had visions of me running out the door to get help because I was so scared. My oldest sister was like 9 or 10 and I had to go the bathroom and we only have one and it was downstairs. She sneaked me downstairs and into the kitchen and there was glasses smashed all over, there were plants under water, the phone cord was under water in the kitchen sink. It was just a wreck everywhere. But most of all, there were streams of blood mixing in with the water, on the floor, on the walls ...

Rosie, age 11, said:

> I remember one Christmas my mom and my uncle were fighting. I escaped out the window to get help for my mom. We were living on the bottom floor at the time. I didn't have time to take a coat or mittens, I just grabbed my goldfish bowl ... I think it was because I didn't want to ever go back there. I immediately ran to the [community] center but it was closed, being like 3:00 in the morning or something. So I just ran around the neighborhood and water was splashing out of my goldfish bowl, and the fish were dying, and I was freezing, and I couldn't even scream anymore.

Elizabeth, age 12, said:

> I want my mother's boyfriend to stop drinking so much. He drinks a lot. Like a sink full of beer cans because his friends come over a lot too. They bring over cases and he usually gets drunk off a 12-pack ... Like every other day he will start screaming and blaming things on my sister [age 5], me, and my mom. My mom tells him, no, it's not our fault. He forgets a lot too, like what he did with his money, or where he puts his pens and pencils. He starts screaming at us because he thinks we take them. The house has to be a certain way. If one thing is out of place, he'll hit us or lock us in the closet for awhile until my mom screams so much he lets us out ... but things are better now.

Sarah, age 11, said:

I used to think of myself as a zero, like I was nothing. I was stupid; I couldn't do anything ... I don't anymore because we're all done with the violence in my house ... I've tried to keep it out since I was a kid ... My mom and John [mother's boyfriend] will argue over the littlest things. My mom is someone who is a violent person too. Sometimes she hits us, or he does. Then she would take a shower and we would get all dressed up, and we would all go out somewhere. After something bad would happen, she would try to make it better. She's a real fun person ... We're really close. We make cookies together and breakfast together.

As these narrations indicate, domestic violence permeates the lives of these young poor and working-class White girls. In a moment of desperation Rosie sought refuge at the community center, but it was long closed for the night. Mom offered little salvation as she was often drunk, violent herself, or powerless as the man in her life is on an abusive rampage. As they escaped into the icy night or were locked in closets, these girls had little recourse from the extreme and terrifying conditions which governed their lives. In Sarah's case, her mother was also violent, yet was thought of as making up for that abuse by involving her daughter in family-style activities. Sarah learned, therefore, not to see or feel pain. Given these accounts, it is easy to conclude that the effects of domestic violence are not something that can be contained at home, and the data indicate that exposure to abuse profoundly shapes their behavior in other places, such as school.

As Elizabeth, age 12, said:

About twice a month they [mom and boyfriend] fight. But not that far apart. Last time he [boyfriend] smacked me, I had a red hand on my face. I walked around with a red hand on my face, only I wouldn't let anybody see it ... I skipped school and the [community] center for like 3 days so no one would ask me about it ... I hid in my closet until you could barely see it. Then when I went back to school, I stayed real quiet because I didn't want people to look at me, notice the hand on my face.

Christina, age 13, said:

When I had a boyfriend he [father] got so mad at me. He told me I wasn't allowed to have a boyfriend. I didn't know that because he never told me. He said that if he ever saw him again I would get my ass kicked. So one day he heard that Robbie [boyfriend] walked me to school. Well, he [father] came over that night and pulled down my pants and whipped me with his belt. I was bloody and the next day full of bruises. But I hurt more from being embarrassed to have my pants pulled down at my age. It hurt to sit all day long at school; that's all I could concentrate on. I couldn't go to the nurse because then she would find out. Nobody knew how I hurt under my clothes. I couldn't go to gym because people would find out, so I skipped. I hid in the bathroom but got picked up by the hall monitor who accused me of skipping gym to smoke. I just got so mad when I heard this, I pushed her [monitor] away from me and yelled. I was out of control with anger when they were dragging me down to the principal's. I got suspended for a week and had to talk to a school psychologist for 2 weeks about how bad smoking is for your health.

Rosie, age 11, said:

My mom got money from her boyfriend for my school pictures, and when they came back, he saw them as I was getting ready for school ... He threw them and said that I messed up my hair. But I got up an hour early that day to fix it, I remember, only my hair just flattened, not on purpose. He got real mad and picked up a lamp and threw it at her and it hit her but I tried to block it and got hit too. It fell on the floor all in pieces. She was crying because she was hurt and because he left and I was crying because I knew she would let him come back. So we were both crying picking up the glass. Then I walked to school and I didn't open up my mouth once all day because I thought I would cry if I did.

Anne, age 11, said:

Sometimes at school I just avoid teachers because they might feel sorry for me because they might see like bruises or something ... Sometimes I act bad so they won't feel sorry for me, then if they see a bruise or something they would think I deserved it. I would rather have them think that than getting the principal or nurse.

These glimpses into the lives of White girls indicate that children from violent homes are learning at a very young age how to negotiate lives that are enmeshed inside a web of overwhelming circumstances. Elizabeth spoke about how her mother's boyfriend blamed her and her mother and sister for all that was wrong, whereas Rosie was hit with a lamp while trying to protect her mother. As they devised ways to conceal their bruises, they each faced their pain alone. Elizabeth skipped school and sought shelter from the world in the same closet in which she was punished by her mother's boyfriend. Christina choked on her anger and pain and separated herself from school activity only to become embroiled in another set of problems. As Rosie quietly sat through class, her physical and mental pain rendered her completely disengaged from academic and social life at school. Anne deliberately "acted bad" to distract teachers from focusing on her scars of abuse.

These girls revealed that they direct incredible energy toward keeping their abuse a secret while in school. This culture of concealment is likely in response to a number of fears, including fear of public embarrassment, fear of further angering an abuser, and fear that families will be torn apart by authorities. While observing these girls at school, Julia noticed that, on a few occasions, some of them sustained bruises that perhaps could not be so easily hidden under long sleeves and turtlenecks. One day, for example, Christina came to school wearing an excessive amount of eye makeup, which was noticeable, considering she usually did not wear any. While talking to her outside after school, Julia realized that this was probably an attempt to conceal a blackened eye, which could clearly be seen in the harsh light of day.

Interestingly, Julia did not hear any talk of domestic violence at school, critical or otherwise. While at school, it did not seem that any of the girls sought help from their White female peers, teachers, or anyone else in coping with abuse. Instead, in the space of the school, a code of silence surrounding domestic violence prevailed, even though the girls articulate an awareness of others' abuse throughout the neighborhood. Not once did Julia hear students or teachers query others about violence or raise concern, nor was abuse even mentioned as a social problem in classes in which human behavior was discussed. Even on the day that Christina came to school attempting to camouflage a bruised eye, Julia did not observe a teacher pull her aside to talk, or hear her friends ask her if she was all right or comment on the unusual method of concealment. Dragged by their families from one violent situation to the next, it is remarkable that these girls are, for the most part, able to get through the school day, go home, and come back again tomorrow.

CONCLUSION

Domestic violence is deeply etched into how generations of females in poor and working-class White communities construct a sense of self. These two data sets indicate that from childhood, many are socialized into a code of silence that works to further encase abuse inside the communities in which they live. Also revealed in the data, this silence is maintained and hardened by most of the institutions that structure the lives of these females, including family, school, and community. Violent outbursts are not isolated instances, as an overwhelming number of men, both in the past and present, lash out toward females in the public and private corners of their lives. While males are on an abusive rampage, girls often cannot turn to their mothers or older sisters for help, as they too are pushed by violent men inside stifling and unhealthy private spaces so deeply that they often do not have any voice left at all. With the further cutting of welfare and other programs, we are condemning adult women to a life of stunted emotional growth and unspeakable horror, and are allowing their children to inherit that structured silence and pain.

We argued that there is an extraordinarily high level of domestic violence in the homes of many of the children with whom we, as educators, work. Although we focused on White working-class families, there is ample evidence that abuse in the home spans the class structure, although such violence is highly correlated with socioeconomic status, to be sure. Given that biographies of violence permeate the homes and lives of many of our students, what does this mean for our own understanding of children's behavior and resulting classroom practice? Whether or not a child is living with such abuse currently, if a parent has a history of violence, it affects the child. Our parenting practices are locked in our own biographies. Although this can certainly be unraveled through therapy and self-help groups, we know from our data that few White working-class parents have been involved in such activities. White working-class families either distrust therapy or lack the resources for such a long-term expense. Committing to therapy, Al Anon (a group for families of alcoholics), or Narcotics Anonymous (a group for families of drug addicts) also necessitates reliable transportation and money for child care. Only one woman in Lois' sample was involved in a self-help group, even though numerous females narrated histories of alcohol and drug abuse in their families of origin, and severe beatings associated with this abuse. This is a population that "goes it alone," leaving emotionally tattered women and men to be raising the next generation. Without help, the imprint of being raised in a violent situation travels through the generations. These children are in our classrooms and schools, smiling and sullen, victimized and victimizing. What do we know about the effects of violence on them? What do we know about the effects of violence on their parents?

For the past 15 years, investigators have turned their attention to the plight of battered women (Dobash & Dobash, 1979; Hoff, 1990; Steinmetz & Strauss, 1974; Walker, 1984). However, only recently have scholars begun to unravel the effects of violence on children in the home. This is a relatively new area of research and there are inconsistencies in the findings. We do know, though, that children are deeply affected by violence in the home and that this can affect the child's ability to succeed in school.

According to Elkind (1984), family problems are the main reason children at the elementary level do not attend school. Even when children from violent homes do attend, they are often unable to concentrate (Jaffe, Wolfe, & Wilson, 1990). Often children feel responsible for the abuse; they consider it their fault, just as in the case of divorce. In such instances, children either fake illness in order to stay at home and "protect" the parent, or they may actually become sick from fear and worry (Afulayan, 1993).

It is now generally acknowledged that many children in violent homes are the victims of abuse themselves (Grusznski, Brink, & Edelson, 1988). Children often become a convenient target in a violent home and they are blamed for "all that is wrong." A second reason for children being hurt in abusive homes is that thrown objects can, at times, inadvertently hit them. Children sometimes feel that they must protect their mothers, and are hurt as the father lunges out at both the mother and child. This happens more to boys than girls, because boys position themselves as protector more often than do girls (Fantuzzo et al., 1991).

According to Wagar and Rodway (1995), each child has his or her own way of coping with domestic violence. One means may be aggressive acts against those in the environment so that they may feel safer. Some children, in contrast, draw within themselves, exhibiting internalized behavioral problems such as somatic disorders, insomnia, and heightened anxiety (Hughes, 1988; Jaffe et al., 1990). Martin (1976) suggested that children living in homes with family violence feel guilt, shock, and fear because they are constantly at risk of being abused themselves. The development of psychological adjustment problems is high among youth from violent families, contended Wagar and Rodway (1995), because of parental neglect due to an intense focus on violence in such households.

Hughes and Barad (1983) measured the psychological functioning of children who came to a battered women's shelter in Arkansas. Using several standardized self-esteem and anxiety measures, they concluded that the preschool children were most disrupted by violence in terms of personality development. The self-concept of boys tended to be more negative than that of girls, who had more anxiety, worry, and oversensitivity. Additionally, boys were more aggressive than girls and acted out more than boys from nonviolent homes (Walker, 1984). There is also some evidence that boys receive the brunt of parental abuse (Jouriles & Norwood, 1995).

A wide array of studies, including our own, confirm these points. Children who grow up in violent homes are at considerable risk for developing a wide range of problems including headaches, abdominal pains, stuttering, enuresis, and sleep disturbances (Reid, Kavanaugh, & Baldwin, 1987). Other investigators reported that the most frequently noted psychological disturbances include depression, anxiety, suicidal tendencies, phobias, withdrawal, lowered self-esteem, and overt psychoses (Hughes, 1988).

Research also indicates that children who witness violence in the home exhibit more externalizing behaviors, such as aggression and conduct disorders (Fagan, Stewart, & Hansen, 1983). Such children have more academic difficulties (Westra & Martin, 1981) and lower measured levels of relationships with peers (Wolfe, Jaffe, Wilson, & Zak, 1985). As noted earlier, it is also becoming clearer that physical abuse of children in homes with spousal abuse is much higher than normal (Boker, Arbitell, & McFerron, 1988); some studies estimate it is 129% higher (Gibson & Gutierrez, 1991, as cited in Randolph & Conkle, 1993).

The evidence is clear, then, in this relatively new area for research that violence in the home affects children in profound ways. As educators, it is important that we begin to pry open this silenced space and understand what it means when so many of our students come from violent homes or are being raised by parents who were brought up in violent homes. The evidence is strong that current parents have been affected profoundly by the violence they witnessed as children and that this, in turn, affects their parenting capabilities. This is not to suggest that parents, particularly poor parents, inhibit children's progress in school. Our intention in writing this is certainly not that, and we are aware of the possible misuses of our data in this direction. Rather, it is our intention to raise awareness about the reality of the lives of many of our students and the ways in which violence affects student behavior and attachment to school. They notice that we—educators—refuse to notice.

We tell you these stories in part to discomfort, to inform you of the depth, the pervasiveness, the very tedious typicality of domestic violence. We offer no solutions to educators, researchers, or policymakers, except the caution that we cannot continue to act "as if" domestic violence or child abuse were idiosyncratic, anomalous, something that happens to few—and that those few will speak up when it does. No, indeed, such violence is broad based and we can assume it is well represented in our classrooms. The question, then, is what is our responsibility to respond?

We recognize that teachers are mandated, in most states, to learn about domestic violence, to identify and report suspected victims. Many teachers do report; yet almost all are ambivalent, fully cognizant of the terrible options that await "identified victims." Deeper, more radical responses to this issue are desperately needed. We see that domestic violence must be taught as a pervasive social problem, an aspect of gendered relations in the home and on the streets. In history, science, and English high school classrooms, there is much to be learned. Young women and men can be encouraged to serve internships in domestic violence shelters, on hot lines, in advocacy organizations so that they understand the phenomenon to be widespread. In school, youth can begin to recognize a social movement that is well developed and responsive, so that they can touch and feel and access resources if necessary.[2]

We recognize that domestic violence, like many social problems schools are asked to contend with, has no easy answers. Although we see the utility and the limits of inviting youngsters to come see the counselor; we suggest bolder responses, built into curriculum, community service, and critical engagement with social movements, so that young women and men see this problem as social and political, not merely as personal. Youth and adults must recognize the depth and pervasiveness, must realize they are "not alone," and must engage with the sense of possibility that fuels social movements against violence against women.

In the same way that girls must learn not to be victims, boys must learn not to be victimizers. Boys will not wander into the counselor's office, and few girls do, to talk about violence at home. And yet, given that all students are in history class, English, and health, and that many students enroll in conflict resolution courses today, we argue that there are ample opportunities for educators to deprivatize this deeply personal and political feature of contemporary intimate life. We have a responsibility to allow young people to imagine very different possibilities for their own lives. Seeing, working with, and advocating for shelters, hot lines, and temporary housing can be an empowering experience for any preteen or teenager, especially a youth who has endured domestic life amidst violence. Such exposure may be sufficient to interrupt the all too glib, all too assumed "cycle of violence." We say all this not to "load on" another topic of social import, not to stuff the curricular day any further, but to acknowledge that educators' and researchers' stance toward domestic violence—that it is tragic, rare, and in need of detection—may be a strategy suited only toward diminishing our anxieties.

---

[2]These ideas were developed in conjunction with Michelle Fine.

A structured silence concerning abuse blankets the institutions that comprise the poor and working-class White communities in which the females in our studies reside. Although the girls in Julia's study were conditioned at home, school, and elsewhere not to view abuse critically, they all were regular visitors to a neighborhood community center. Unlike schools, which are constricted by state guidelines, we believe spaces such as community centers, churches, activist agencies, and arts programs provide a place in which people can creatively form and sustain a sense of possibility. Although critical discourse concerning abuse is presently not raised in this community center, forums within, such as Girls Club and Boys Club, do exist in which such discussions could take place.

It is important to recognize that people are struggling with structures that seem to shut them out. The existence of the community center and its activities geared toward youth speak to this point. We feel that it is vital to understand such spaces and the potential they possess for enabling us to reimagine how politics and community life could be. Furthermore, through networking among informal sites, a vibrant voice of hope could multiply in strength. As the women and girls in this chapter indicated, their lives are being invaded by violence from all sides. It is up to us to target schools and informal spaces in which youth congregate with programmatic change and sufficient funding. Domestic violence is tragic; it is also commonplace. The children who live in abusive homes are waiting to see what we will do about it.

REFERENCES

Afulayan, J. (1993). Consequences of domestic violence on elementary school education. *Child and Family Therapy*, 15(3), 55–58.

Arnot, M. (1982). Male hegemony, social class, and women's education. *Journal of Education*, 164(1), 64–89.

Belton, D. (Ed.), (1995). *Speak my name: Black men on masculinity and the American dream*. Boston: Beacon Press.

Biklen, S., & Pollard, D. (1993). *Gender and education*. Chicago: University of Chicago Press.

Boker, L., Arbitell, M., & McFerron, J. (1988). On the relationship between wife beating and child abuse. In K. Yllo & M. Bogard (Eds.), *Feminist perspectives on wife abuse*. Newbury Park, CA: Sage.

Dobash, R., & Dobash, R. (1979). *Violence against wives*. New York: The Free Press.

Eckert, P. (1989). *Jocks & burnouts: Social categories and identity in the high school*. New York: Teachers College Press.

Elkind, P. (1984). *All grown up and no place to go*. Reading, MA: Addison Wesley.

Everhart, R. (1983). *Reading, writing, and resistance: Adolescence and labor in a junior high school*. Boston: Routledge & Kegan Paul.

Fagan, J., Stewart, J., & Hansen, K. (1983). Violent men or violent husbands. In D. Finkelhor, R. Gelles, G. Hotaling, & M. Straus (Eds.), *The dark side of families*. Beverly Hills: Sage.

Fantuzzo, J., DePaola, L., Lambert, L., Martino, T., Anderson, G., & Sutton, S. (1991). Effects of interparental violence on the psychological adjustment and competencies of young children. *Journal of Consulting and Clinical Psychology, 59*(2), 258–265.

Fine, M. (1991). *Framing dropouts: Notes on the politics of an urban public high school*. New York: State University of New York Press.

Grusznski, R., Brink, J., & Edelson, J. (1988). Support and education groups for children of battered women. *Child Welfare, 7*(5), 431–444.

Hoff, L. (1990). *Battered women as survivors*. New York: Routledge.

Holland, D., & Eisenhart, M. (1990). *Educated in romance: Women, achievement, and college culture*. Chicago: University of Chicago Press.

Howell, J. (1972). *Hard living on Clay Street: Portraits of blue collar families*. New York: Anchor Books.

Hughes, H. (1988). Psychological and behavioral correlates of family violence in child witnesses and victims. *American Journal of Orthopsychiatry, 58*, 77–90.

Hughes, H., & Barad, S. (1983). Psychological functioning of children in a battered women's shelter: A model preventive program. *Family Relations, 31*, 495–502.

Jaffe, P., Wolfe, S., & Wilson, S. (1990). *Children of battered women*. Newbury, Park: Sage.

Jouriles, E., & Norwood, W. (1995). Physical aggression toward boys and girls in families characterized by the battering of women. *Journal of Family Psychology, 9*(1), 69–78.

Kelly, G., & Nihlen, A. (1982). Schooling and the reproduction of patriarchy: Unequal workloads, unequal rewards. In M. Apple (Ed.), *Cultural and economic reproduction in education: Essays on class, ideology, and the state*. London: Routledge & Kegan Paul.

Martin, H. (1976). *The abused child*. Boston: Ballinger.

McRobbie, A. (1991). *Feminism and youth culture: From Jackie to just seventeen*. Boston: Unwin Hyman.

Nicarthy, G. (1989). From the sounds of silence to the roar of a global movement: Notes on the movement against violence against women. *Response to the Victimization of Women and Children, 12*(2), 3–10.

Randolph, M., & Conkle, L. (1993). Behavioral and emotional characteristics of children who witness parental violence. *Family Violence and Sexual Assault Bulletin, 9*(2), 23–27.

Reid, J., Kavanaugh, & Baldwin, J. (1987). Abusive parents' perception of child problem behavior: An example of paternal violence. *Journal of Abnormal Child Psychology, 15*, 451–466.

Rubin, L. (1976). *Worlds of pain: Life in the working-class family*. New York: Basic Books.

Schechter, S. (1982). *Women and male violence: The visions and struggles of the battered women's movement*. Boston: South End Press.

Steinmetz, S., & Strauss, M. (1974). *Violence in the family*. New York: Dodd Mead.

Valli, L. (1988). Gender identity and the technology of office education. In L. Weis (Ed.), *Class, race, and gender in American education*. Albany: State University of New York Press.

Wagar, J., & Rodway, M. (1995). An evaluation of a group treatment approach for children who have witnessed abuse. *Journal of Family Violence, 10*(3), 295.

Walker, L. (1984). *The battered syndrome*. New York: Springer.

Wallace, C. (1987). *For richer, for poorer: Growing up in and out of work*. New York: Tavistock.

Weis, L. (1990). *Working class without work: High school students in a de-industrializing economy*. New York: Routledge.

Westra, B., & Martin, H. (1981). Children of battered women. *Maternal Child Nursing Journal, 10*, 41–54.

White, E. (1985). The psychology of abuse. In *Chain chain change for Black women dealing with physical and emotional abuse*. Seattle: South End Press.

Willis, P. (1977). *Learning to labor*. New York: Columbia University Press.

Wolfe, D., Jaffe, P., Wilson, S., & Zak, L. (1985). Children of battered women: The relation of child behavior to family violence and maternal stress. *Journal of Consulting and Clinical Psychology, 53*, 657–665.

Wrigley, J. (Ed.), (1992). *Education and gender equality*. London: Falmer Press.

3

The Crisis Within the Crisis:
The Growing Epidemic of AIDS Orphans

Shelley Geballe and Janice Gruendel
Citizens for Connecticut's Children and Youth

Sometimes, I feel like a spirit. I feel like I can be seen but not heard. Not many people pay attention to me. Like a spirit, I'm always there, but people don't notice the things I do!

—a 10-year-old living with AIDS in her family
(Fanos & Weiner, 1994, p. S45)

My father died from it [AIDS], from using drugs ... I knew about it for a year, and it messed up my life ... I used to go to school, walk in the hallways, and I never used to go to class. [If I did] go to class, I used to just sit there and talk to the teacher back, never used to do my work.

—Eric Santiago, 13
(Gould, 1995)

Some nights we [mother and her 6-year-old daughter] talk about it. Some nights she says, "Mommy, you'll be the Nana of my children, won't you?" And I say, "I hope so." And the next night she says, "Mommy, why can't the doctors make you better?" And the next night she says, "You won't be there, will you?" And the next night she'll say, "Who will take care of me?"

—Kara, a young single mother with AIDS
(Geballe, Gruendel, & Andiman, 1995, p. 7)

47

These words of a 10-year-old, a 13-year-old, and a young mother begin to tell the story of children living in families with HIV and AIDS. Not infected with the disease themselves, these children nonetheless experience its devastating consequences. And they are not alone. In the United States, it is estimated that by the turn of the century, 150,000 children will lose a mother and thousands more will lose a father, sibling, or other member of their family as AIDS moves from its epicenter in our urban areas out into the suburbs and from coastal areas into America's heartland (Michaels & Levine, 1992). Worldwide, the epidemic of AIDS orphans is quickly reaching catastrophic proportions; it is estimated that 8.7 million children have already been orphaned by AIDS.

Although more U.S. children will lose a parent to AIDS than to any other single cause of death, we have been slow to respond specifically to their needs. Importantly, the limited research that has been done with HIV-affected children and youth suggests they are a population at extremely high risk—for developmental, behavioral, and mental health problems, for teenage pregnancy, and even for HIV infections themselves (Bauman & Wiener, 1994; Dane & Miller, 1992; Fanos & Wiener, 1994; Geballe, Gruendel, & Andiman, 1995; Levine, 1993; Levine & Stein, 1994; Roth, Siegel, & Black, 1994).

Who are these children and why have they been virtually invisible in the midst of the most significant plague of the 20th century? This chapter provides current information on the spread of HIV disease in the United States, summarizes the challenges and impact of AIDS on children of various ages, and outlines issues of import to educators and others interested in how we can help AIDS-affected children develop resilience in the face of significant odds.

THE INVISIBLE CHILDREN AND YOUTH OF AIDS

Acquired Immunodeficiency Syndrome (AIDS) was first identified in the United States in 1981. By 1994, more than 25,000 U.S. residents diagnosed as having AIDS had died, including more than 55,000 deaths in 1994 alone. In 1994, AIDS also became the leading cause of death among all Americans age 25 to 44—adults in their prime childbearing and child rearing years. Hundreds of thousands more Americans are infected now by the Human Immunodeficiency Virus (HIV), the virus that causes AIDS, and many new infections continue to occur. Each year, more than 60,000 U.S. residents are diagnosed as having AIDS (Karon et al., 1996). Although the survival of persons infected by HIV has improved since antiretroviral, protease inhibitor, and prophylactic treatments have become available, long-term prognosis remains poor (Enger, Graham, Peng, Chmiel, Kingsley, & Detels, et al., 1996).

At first predominantly a disease of White homosexual or bisexual men, AIDS now increasingly affects American women. Heterosexual contact is the most rapidly increasing category of HIV transmission among women (Centers for Disease Control and Prevention, 1994a). In 1994, 18% of the AIDS cases reported were among women, compared to only 7% in 1985 (Centers for Disease Control and Prevention, 1995). AIDS in the U.S. now disproportionately affects African-Americans and Latinos. Although there were 50 AIDS cases per 100,000 population overall in the U.S. in 1993, rates among certain minorities were substantially greater at 266 per 100,000 for African American men, 162 per 100,000 for African American women, 146 per 100,000 for Hispanic men, and 90 per 100,000 for Hispanic women (Selik, Chu, & Buehler, 1993). The AIDS rate for African American women in the U.S. is approximately 15 times greater than that for White women (Centers for Disease Control and Prevention, 1994b).

As AIDS has increased among women, perinatal (pregnant mother to child) transmission of HIV has become a major cause of illness and death among children in the United States. More than 15,000 children have become infected in this way, and more than 3,000 have died (Simons & Rogers, 1996). Fortunately, recent research suggests perinatal transmission of HIV from mother to child can be reduced from 25% to 8% with the administration of Zidovudine (AZT) during pregnancy and labor and to their newborns after delivery (Conner et al., 1994). Although this breakthrough gives great promise of curbing most new perinatal infections among children, each additional infant spared infection through AZT therapy faces the tragic certainty of becoming a motherless child.

HIV disease is also increasing among teenage populations. Because the symptom-free period in adults—the time between infection by HIV and clinical expression of the disease—extends nearly a decade in most infected men and women (Andiman, 1995), AIDS' emergence as a leading cause of death among men and women age 25 to age 44 reflects infections occurring as much as a decade earlier—between age 15 and 34. HIV seroprevalence studies among older adolescents reflect these disturbing trends. Studies of college students have shown an overall rate of infection of about 1 in 500. Among more disadvantaged populations, however, AIDS' impact is more severe. One in 40 of the 21-year-old minority applicants to the Job Corps were found by the early 1990s to be infected (St. Louis et al., 1991). A study of adolescents coming to a health clinic in Washington, DC found that 1 in 244 was infected in 1987, but 1 in 52 was infected just 5 years later (D'Angelo et al., 1994).

Who are the invisible children and youth of AIDS? They are the infected children who live in families with HIV disease. They are children born to an infected mother who escaped infection themselves. They are children born before their parent(s) contracted the virus. Some will be their family's only child; others will have several siblings. Their siblings may be healthy, or one or more may be HIV infected themselves. AIDS-affected children may live with both parents, or they may live in single-parent families or families reconstituted as the result of divorce or of the illness itself. They may live in disadvantaged economic circumstances or in apparent wealth. Whether from poverty or comfort, city or suburb, the common bond that unites these children is their invisibility as AIDS sweeps through both their families and their communities (Geballe et al., 1995).

Unique Challenges of AIDS-Related Deaths for Children and Youth

Although chronic illness or death of a parent or sibling from any cause clearly exposes children to a variety of major psychological challenges, those who work with children affected by AIDS believe the "specific constellation and intensity of problems facing families affected by HIV set this disease apart from all other contemporary health problems" (Bauman & Wiener, 1994, p. S1). A summary of the AIDS-specific challenges follows.

Disturbing Clinical Course.   AIDS' clinical course is marked by characteristics that can be enormously disturbing and disruptive to children, including marked physical changes (such as dramatic wasting and disfiguring dermatologic disorders), behavioral and cognitive changes (such as AIDS encephalopathy and AIDS dementia complex, which can result in deterioration of short-term memory, mutism, and loss of ability to walk, swallow, and void), and often severe debilitation. For many AIDS patients, these physical and behavioral problems can result in the loss of a job and income, and eventually a home. Eric, the 13-year-old whose father died from AIDS, said:

It's like when they die, you don't want to go to the funeral, 'cause you want to remember the way they were and not the way they are ... My mother took pictures of me next to him, and when she showed me the pictures, I feel scared, 'cause it don't look like him. (cited in Gould, 1995)

Matthew, a father with AIDS, described events that he and his son will inevitably face:

If I was to get sick tomorrow ... one by one I lose things. I lose my job, because I can't do it any more. I lose my income because I'm not working. I lose my insurance. I lose my home and my son loses his home with me ... He starts to lose the support of me, as his father. I start becoming too weak to give him the things he needs from a father ... So, at the end of this chain of events, you have Matthew with basically nothing [and you] have his 5-year-old son witnessing this whole, awful, terrible dilemma and being traumatized by it. (Geballe, Gruendel, & Andiman, 1995, p. 232)

Uncertainty.   There is no relief from the single current certainty of AIDS: the infected individual will eventually die. The rest of the course of AIDS is characterized by tremendous uncertainty for both the infected parent and the affected child. Periods of acute, serious illness punctuate the daily living of families in which a person has AIDS. The infected parent is in and out of the hospital. No one knows when the hospitalization will occur, how long it will last, and whether the parent will return home. During these periods, children are placed informally with neighbors or extended family, or more formally in foster care. Children often are moved to a new school with new teachers and no friends. Living with such uncertainties as these poses great challenges to the secure psychological base essential to a child's development of a healthy and functional personality (Nagler, Adnopoz, & Forsyth, 1995).

Multiple Losses.   AIDS frequently causes illness and death in more than a single family member, and often in more than a single generation of the family (Siegel & Gorey, 1994). These multiple and multigenerational deaths challenge the very integrity of the child's family in a manner akin to war (Apfel & Telingator, 1995). They will almost certainly subject children to additional losses (including changes of residence, of school, of parental figures, and separation from siblings) that may result in a "bereavement overload" (Kastenbaum, 1977), leaving children vulnerable to loss and disruption later in life (Apfel & Telingator, 1995; Fanos & Wiener, 1994).

Splitting up the sibling group after parental deaths compounds the loss of the parents, especially in families where older siblings had assumed a caregiving role to younger siblings and strong feelings of dependency and attachment had developed (Siegel & Gorey, 1994). Separation of siblings may have particularly adverse consequences for children from communities in which the sibling role has particular significance (Groce, 1995). Consider, for example, the comments and questions of Grace, a mother, grandmother, and now a foster and adoptive mother who lives with 13 children, all of whose lives have been changed by AIDS:

> One of my adopted children hasn't expressed much emotion about the baby's death. In therapy, it comes out that his death conjures up memories of her birth mother's death, and the recent death of her little friend. She's not sure how to express her feelings and I'm sadly thinking that with all of the loss she's experienced my kid should be a pro at crying. Except that overwhelming loss shuts her down. How will my kids come out of this epidemic? Will their bodies survive and their hearts die? (Geballe, Gruendel, & Andiman, 1995, p. 239)

Stigma.   AIDS remains a highly stigmatized disease, causing persons affected as well as persons infected to be victimized by discrimination (resulting in possible loss of employment, housing, health care, and health insurance) and to be ostracized by their communities and even by their own families (Geballe, 1995; Geballe et al., 1995; Lipson, 1994; Nagler et al., 1995). Joey DiPaolo, a teenager, said of his own HIV infection:

> From 1988 to 1990, I didn't want to tell anybody about it, 'cause the doctors were telling me and everyone was telling me not to tell anybody about it, because I'll have my house burned down like the Rays and I'll be run out of town like the Whites. I mean Ryan White and the Rays down in Florida. (Gould, 1995)

Similarly fearful, Kara, the young mother with AIDS, explained why she hid her face in the interview:

> I'm concerned that my child, who does not have AIDS, won't be allowed to have friends at school or visit her friends' houses or have her friends visit her house. I'm afraid she'll be called names or teased. I have to hide my face because I have a terminal illness that everybody's afraid of, and my child would pay for it ... She's been rejected by every member of my family. She's been rejected by her father. She doesn't see him at all. (Gould, 1995)

Silence and Family Secrets.   Many parents are reluctant to talk openly and honestly about their infection with their children from a sense of shame and self-reproach—both because their children might inquire about parental "risk behaviors" that occasioned the infection and also because they know they have brought harm to their children, directly (through infection) or indirectly (by leaving them behind at death) (Lipson, 1994; Nagler et al., 1995). Infected parents also resist telling children about their condition because the disclosure forces "into common awareness ... the parent's own illness and potential death" (Lipson, 1994, p. 563). As a result, the disease becomes "unnamed, unspoken, and often unspeakable to children who then have no name for what they know is happening to their loved ones and to themselves" (Nagler et al., 1995, p. 75). Often, if children are told that the parent has HIV disease, they are also told to keep the "family secret," denying them access to social support that could help buffer them from this enormous stress (Siegel & Gorey, 1994).

Disproportionate Impact in Communities of Poverty. The majority of families now living with HIV disease in the U.S. have a history of either drug dependence or exposure to drug users (Bauman & Wiener, 1994). Thus, AIDS-affected children disproportionately come from families that are already unstable, economically vulnerable, and with limited access to health care, housing, and transportation (Bauman & Wiener, 1994; Groce, 1995). Their children have been "already abandoned ... to constricted and narrow fates ... the cards unreasonably stacked against them" (Novick, 1995, p. 248). They commonly confront multiple other losses and stresses in their lives and have a range of chronic unmet educational, social, and health care needs—factors that will act synergistically with the stresses occasioned by AIDS (Siegel & Gorey, 1994).

Impact of AIDS on Affected Children and Youth

Where do children go when one or both parents die of AIDS? Data available to date strongly suggest many AIDS-affected children will live first with an extended family member, most likely a grandmother or aunt, and often without the benefit of formal permanency planning (Draimin, 1995). It is not clear that these placements become permanent for the children; there is insufficient longitudinal research to answer that question. It is clear that many grandparents who take on responsibility to raise their second families do so with great love and dedication but without adequate income, space, or community support.

Some children who do not go to live with a grandparent or other loved one are placed as wards of state child welfare departments in foster homes, group homes, or shelters. No firm numbers exist on such placements, but early research suggests that 10% to 25% of AIDS-affected children go directly into this system (Draimin, 1995). Sadly, it is not always possible for sibling groups to be placed in the same foster home and AIDS-affected children who are separated from siblings thus suffer the loss of remaining family ties.

Not surprisingly, children and youth affected by HIV disease in their families exhibit many behaviors signaling the need for mental health and social support. One small study of adolescents found that all experienced significant isolation from their peer and adult social networks, one-third exhibited frequent "acting-out" behaviors in home or at school (for example, truancy, disruptive behavior resulting in school suspension or arrest, defiance of parental rules, or running away), three-quarters reported problems in schoolwork, and of the older girls who reported having sex, four of five had been pregnant at least once (Draimin, Hudis, & Segura, 1992). In another study, the first 47 teens interviewed revealed that in the preceding 6 months nearly three-fourths had been in a serious physical fight where there was punching or hitting, 13% had been arrested and gone to court for illegal activity, and a third said they would be in more trouble if the police knew all they had done (Rotheram-Borus & Draimin, 1994).

AIDS-affected children and youth universally worry about their futures, and in particular, who will care for them during parental hospitalizations and after the parents' deaths. Their anxiety is especially acute if one parent has already died from AIDS. Among preschool children, parental depression, unpredictability, and erratic behavior can result in the child's insecure attachment to caretakers and a limited sense of self-worth. Slightly older children (4 to 6 years) often exhibit excessive dependency, oppositional behavior, and problems forming and maintaining peer relationships (Lewis, 1995). Children report fears of contagion and of their own early death (Fanos & Wiener, 1994). Children before the age of puberty often hold themselves responsible for the illness in the family (Apfel & Telingator, 1995). Children also may feel great anger with the parent at becoming infected and at infecting other family members, compromising their capacity to have a sense of positive identification with a parental figure that is so necessary to their development (Apfel & Telingator, 1995; Fanos & Wiener, 1994; Mellins & Ehrhardt, 1994).

The developmental and health needs of AIDS-affected children can go unmet, as parental attention is diverted to more pressing demands from ill siblings and from their own deteriorating health (Mellins & Ehrhardt, 1994). Some children report feeling invisible, a feeling that has "profound ramifications for identity formation" (Fanos & Wiener, 1994, p. S45). Infected parents can place heightened demands (emotional and caregiving) on the well children, reversing normal parent-child roles and leading some children and youth to resist age- and situation-appropriate outbursts of anger or disagreement, lest they become a greater strain on their parents. Among well adolescents, this relinquishment of the normal impulse toward rebellion coupled with intense feelings of ambivalence toward the ill parent can render the developmentally-normal conflicts around separation nearly impossible to resolve, resulting in "such impulsive solutions" as uncontrolled defiance, running away, and high risk sexual encounters (Fanos & Wiener, 1994; Hudis, 1995; Lewis, 1995).

Necessary support for a child's mourning can be lacking, especially when it is the child's mother who died, when the child's surviving parent is struggling with grief over losing a spouse or child to AIDS, or when well-established patterns of family secrecy about the disease thwart open communication about the child's feelings of loss (Apfel & Telingator, 1995; Fanos & Wiener, 1994; Lewis, 1995).

Fostering Resilience

Just as the literature about the psychosocial responses of children to other chronic diseases and deaths in their families provides a framework to anticipate the responses of AIDS-affected children, so too does recent research on resilience provide a model for successful intervention efforts on their behalf (Cohen, 1994; Gruendel & Anderson, 1995; Siegel & Gorey, 1994). Three factors appear to contribute to the resilience of children facing difficult psychological, familial, and environmental circumstances (e.g., Demos, 1989; Garmezy, 1993; Luthar & Zigler, 1991; Rutter, 1993; Werner & Smith, 1989). Each of these factors—the way a child approaches challenges, the child's experience within the family, and the external supports that exist for the child—is important in its own right and also operates in interaction with the others. This interaction occurs within the context of the child's developmental level, their culture, and the parent's relative state of well-being. Importantly, when one of these factors is somehow weakened, the other two must grow in strength and significance if resilience is to result (Gruendel & Anderson, 1995).

Characteristics of the child that promote resilience include an active rather than passive orientation to problems, persistence in problem resolution, access to a range of flexible strategies to respond to problems, development of a broad range of interests and goals, and skill in using peers and adults to receive support and assistance. Family characteristics that contribute to resilience include a consistent nurturing relationship between at least one parent, older sibling, or other adult and the child; consistent parental supervision tempered by predictable rules and balanced discipline; empathetic understanding of the child as a unique individual; an open system of communication in which problems and planning for the future are shared; and cohesiveness among family members (Brown & Harris, 1989; Clausen, 1991; Dunn & Plomin, 1990; Pellegrini, 1993; Quinton & Rutter; 1988; Rutter, 1993). Effective social support from outside of the family is the critical third leg of the resiliency triad. For children, effective social support means relationships with caring individuals in whom to trust and safe places to expend energies and express emotions. Such support often includes same-age and older friends, parents of friends, church leaders, teachers, and coaches (Gruendel & Anderson, 1995; Luthar & Zigler, 1991).

Applying recent research on resilience to the situation of AIDS-affected children and youth provides several initial insights concerning key elements of any resiliency-based model of care. First, the quality of care and support the child receives from whomever assumes the primary caretaker role during the parent's illness and after the parent's death is especially critical (Furman, 1974; Rutter, 1966, 1979, 1983). Early permanency planning is essential to reduce the stresses of the inevitable transition and enhance the likelihood that siblings can remain together (Geballe, 1995). The intervention also must fully and creatively support the child's "second" family or new caretaker (Ginchild & Perez-Porter, 1996; Mandelbaum, 1995; Mullen, 1996). It must involve the child, and it must ensure that the child's basic physical and emotional needs are met so that he or she feels free to mourn the losses and move on. The intervention must work concurrently with the infected parent to support that parent's relationship with the child (as well as the second family), thus helping the child to better understand, before the parent's death, the necessity for the move to the second family (Draimin, 1995).

Second, open communication about the illness and death is essential. The child affected by AIDS will need to communicate thoughts and fantasies about the death of the parent or sibling and to express feelings of anger, guilt, sadness, and loss. The child also will need to receive accurate information to dispel misconceptions, such as a young child's common fantasy that his own evil thoughts caused the death (Siegel & Gorey, 1994).

Third, children's own internal coping abilities can be strengthened, by providing them both with opportunities to distance themselves from what is going on in the immediate family and with mental health support, problem-solving skills, esteem-building experiences, positive outlets for physical energy and emotional expression, and a chance to be actively involved (in an age-appropriate way) in planning what happens to them. School and after-school programs and summer camps targeted to AIDS-affected children are good ways to provide such opportunities.

Fourth, most of these children are on trajectories of extraordinarily high risk given the multiple losses and stresses in their young lives, their own chronic unmet social, educational, and health care needs, and the sense of isolation they feel because of the continuing stigma surrounding AIDS. Promoting consistency and stability in the child's environment at every opportunity is of paramount importance. To the extent maximally possible, the amount of environmental change the child experiences, especially at the time of parental death, must be reduced so that the child can draw comfort and a sense of security from familiar surroundings and predictable routines.

Lingering Barriers to a Caring Response

Although well into the second decade of the AIDS epidemic, AIDS "orphans" remain invisible, their needs largely unmet. If we are to change this, we must identify and address the multiple reasons for their continued invisibility—genuine ignorance, still, about the disease and its impact on children and youth; the stigma of the disease and the attendant secrecy that surrounds it; a crisis-based, rather than prevention-based, focus in key social service systems; and a system of entitlements and supports that assume family needs and configurations different than those in which AIDS-affected children often live.

Most professional AIDS training to date has focused on how HIV is transmitted, the use of precautions, and, to a lesser extent, the clinical course of the disease. There has been very little training on the needs of AIDS-affected children. As a result, professionals may not consider AIDS-related stressors in a child's household as a factor that might contribute to a sudden change in behavior, a delinquent act, or a slip in grades. AIDS-affected children and youth have been similarly invisible within research communities. A 1994 literature review showed "no empirical studies of the grief reactions of AIDS orphans" and noted that "only recently have their mourning problems begun to receive attention in the clinical literature" (Siegel & Gorey, 1994, p. S66).

Given its socially sensitive modes of transmission, communicability, profoundly disturbing clinical course, and fatality, AIDS remains marked by stigma. As a result, AIDS-related illnesses often remain family secrets. Also, most state AIDS confidentiality laws—enacted to protect families from harassment and discrimination—bar disclosure, without the permission of the infected person(s), of AIDS-specific information among professionals who might assist children. As a result, traditional sources of support for children with an ill or dying parent such as churches, school, or neighbors are often unavailable to AIDS-affected youth, not necessarily because these supports are unwilling to help (although they may be), but because they simply do not know of the need.

Key systems that should be available to help AIDS-affected children—their own families, the mental health system, the child welfare system—increasingly operate with a crisis rather than a prevention focus. In a family living with AIDS, the needs of the uninfected children are often secondary as the family strains to meet the more pressing emotional and physical needs of ill family members. AIDS service organizations have also, for the most part, focused little attention on the needs of the uninfected, surviving children. Neither the child welfare nor the mental health system is currently structured or funded to reach most children before there is crisis.

Many current laws concerning guardianship and eligibility for social welfare benefit programs were adopted since the last epidemic of orphans in this country. Their goals, requirements, and incentives are responsive neither to the needs of AIDS-affected children nor to those of their new caregivers. As one commentator pointedly stated, "The system still revolves around the White nuclear family model … two young parents with only one of them working, good educations, no money problems, no addictions. Grandparents raising AIDS orphans find little sympathy from that system" (Lade, 1996). Current reform initiatives in welfare and health care exacerbate this mismatch. Three examples illustrate this.

First, many public and private health insurance systems are converting from a fee-for-service payment system to managed care. Unfortunately, the restrictions commonly placed on the amount, duration, and scope of children's mental health services covered under managed care are not responsive to AIDS-affected children, who need home-based mental health services (because their ill parents are unable to transport them to care), whose grief cannot be resolved in only six (or so) outpatient sessions (as they will need continuing mental health care as they pass each new developmental milestone and grieve the death of a parent anew), and whose grief cannot be resolved simply through antidepressant medication.

Second, recent welfare "reform" initiatives impose work requirements and time limits on assistance to try to get parents back on their feet, supporting their children. This vision of welfare conflicts with the needs of grandmothers who have assumed the care of grandchildren orphaned by AIDS and who have no legal obligation to provide for them. For these struggling kin caregivers, cash assistance may need to be long term. Also, work requirements imposed on a grandmother by welfare reform that keep her from staying home and caring for a grieving grandchild are unfair and cruel. AIDS-affected children were invisible when welfare reform was debated. Corrective legislation to exempt relative caregivers from the time limits and job requirements of welfare reform are of paramount importance.

Third, in those states in which the plight of AIDS-affected children is becoming more widely understood—states with extremely high rates of HIV infection among women—there has been some responsiveness in the law of guardianship with at least nine states creating new options, such as standby guardianships and coguardianships (Geballe, 1995; Ginchild & Perez-Porter, 1996). The law remains hostile, however, to caregivers who assume a second-family role for children orphaned by AIDS and who lack sufficient income to assume these significant new financial responsibilities. AFDC/TANF and other cash assistance programs fall short of the amount necessary to bring families above the poverty line. Generally, foster care benefits are greater, but are awarded only if the child is placed in state custody, the caregiver becomes licensed or certified, and the state maintains oversight over the household (Mandelbaum, 1995). For many relative caregivers, poverty is a better option than this loss of both family independence and security for the child. To address this problem, a number of states have adopted, or are considering, programs of subsidized guardianships that would allow second families to maintain legal custody of children in their care while receiving greater financial support (Ginchild & Perez-Porter, 1996).

In light of these multiple barriers to responding in a caring way to AIDS-affected children, we need to make a collective commitment to treating children affected by AIDS with no less compassion than children who lose parents to other causes of death. We also need more advocacy, research, and training about the unique needs of AIDS-affected children. Finally, we need more coordination and cross-training among AIDS, child welfare, and children's mental health systems, and more support for initiatives that support children and their second families if the invisible children of AIDS are to become more socially visible.

IMPLICATIONS FOR EDUCATORS

We have students who have lost one parent, both parents, siblings, grandparents, aunts, and uncles. It's very difficult to lose somebody that's close to you at any age, but to lose your support system when you're a young kid is devastating. We have kids who are hurting, and with kids who are hurting, they can't focus on their primary function of "let me make sure I'm passing all my subjects" because here's this great emotional weight that's on them. And somebody needs to hear them.

—Bonnie Long, principal, New York City Junior High School #56
(Gould, 1995)

From preschool to high school, public, private, and state-run, educational settings across America are receiving increasing numbers of students living in families with AIDS. For all children, school is the primary environment outside the family where they should be developing competence and experiencing positive growth. For children struggling with the trauma and challenge of AIDS in their families, success at school becomes essential. Yet, critical opportunities for school success may be blocked by circumstances of the family, behaviors of the child, misinformation and misunderstanding by educators, the lack of access to programs that promote health, belonging, and the safe expression of feelings and physical energy, or a lack of understanding that the school must act as part of a community team for children living with AIDS in their families.

One critical element of a child's likelihood for school success is whether he or she actually gets to school. For children living with AIDS in their families, absences from school are not uncommon. Some children as young as 8 or 9 become caregivers for the ill parent, and teenagers often become substitute parents for younger siblings. Sometimes students are absent because the parent has been hospitalized and the child is now living with another family or in state care. Students often do not explain these absences because of family secrets associated with AIDS. Current confidentiality laws also generally prohibit disclosure of the AIDS status of a parent, principally to protect the adult from discrimination (Geballe, 1995). Whereas this may be beneficial to the infected parent, it can hinder the ability of educators to understand a child's absence (or behaviors) and to respond appropriately.

As noted earlier, children living with AIDS in their families may exhibit a range of problematic behaviors in school that signal the psychological trauma they are experiencing. These behaviors vary according to the developmental level of the child and the stage of parental illness, but range from withdrawal, anxiety, and fearfulness in younger children to acting out, verbal disrespect, physical violence, and early and unprotected sex in older youth. In communities with a high rate of HIV disease, whole groups of students, who had earlier been doing well, may suddenly begin to exhibit behavior problems. Often, when mental health professionals become involved with such students, they find that many have experienced a recent death in their families and that bereavement and support groups can be extraordinarily helpful. A partnership between teachers, administrators, and mental health professionals is especially critical in these circumstances, not only to assist children struggling with death in their families but also to ensure that such children are not misdiagnosed as learning disabled.

Beyond mental health support, adolescents struggling with AIDS in their families may require other kinds of school-based programs. Because involvement in early and unprotected sex can be a common behavior of AIDS-affected youth, access to school-based health education, teen pregnancy prevention programs, and school health clinic services is essential. The right of youth to give legal consent for needed health care must be assured (Geballe, 1995). Also, students who have lost one or both parents to AIDS may be struggling to provide financial support as well as psychological parenting to younger siblings in an attempt to keep the family together. For these young people, mentoring programs and workplace training can be extraordinarily helpful. For children and youth whose family life has deteriorated through a series of parental hospitalizations, involvement in school sports and recreation programs can provide essential structure and peer support. Involvement in writing, art, and other creative activities can help them express some of the pain and uncertainty they feel daily.

The schools' role as a critical part of the early warning system for AIDS-affected children and as a source of support to them is best fulfilled when schools act as part of a community team. Schools can act as advocates for students who are missing school to care for ill family members by mobilizing community-based, in-home support services. Schools can assist AIDS-affected students who are in need of second families by helping to identify caring adults willing to open their hearts and homes to them. Schools can refer grieving students to local mental health providers and can work in partnership with them to create support groups. Establishing liaisons with local AIDS service organizations helps assure that schools maintain a current understanding of the nature of the epidemic in their communities. The AIDS organizations also can assist in providing the training about HIV disease that is often necessary for both teachers and administrators—to address concerns about how the disease is spread, to challenge any prejudices they may have, and to enable them to identify and meet the predictable needs of children who remain invisible to other parts of the human service and health systems.

THE LAST WORDS

Professor Alvin Novick (1995) of Yale University recently wrote of his fear that many affected families, including the affected children, will

> experience a "loss of the future." That is, the future may come to seem too bleak, too hopeless to plan for, too unsolvable to be real ... Many children will float day to day unless they receive wise and informed counsel and support (p. 248).

An important part of this "wise counsel and support" must come from educators in our schools.

Listen to Florence Samperi of the Henry Street Settlement House in New York City: "We not only work with the families, but we must then work with the schools. ... You have to develop hope for the future, and hope for children is school. School cannot replace a parent, but it can surely give hope" (Gould, 1995).

And, finally, listen again to the words of one 10-year-old living with AIDS in her family: "Sometimes I feel like a spirit. I feel like I can be seen but not heard. Not many people pay attention to me. Like a spirit, I'm always there, but people don't notice the things I do!" (Fanos & Wiener, 1994, p. S45).

This is the voice of one of the many invisible children living in families with HIV disease and AIDS. The infected parents will die. The affected children will live. It is up to us, however, to determine if they will truly survive. That can only happen if we finally see and hear them.

REFERENCES

Andiman, W. (1995). Medical aspects of AIDS: What do children witness? In S. Geballe, J. Gruendel, & W. Andiman (Eds.), *Forgotten children of the AIDS epidemic* (pp. 32–49). New Haven, CT: Yale University Press.

Apfel, R., & Telingator, C. (1995). What can we learn from children of war? In S. Geballe, J. Gruendel, & W. Andiman (Eds.), *Forgotten children of the AIDS epidemic* (pp. 107–121). New Haven, CT: Yale University Press.

Bauman, L., & Wiener, L. (Eds.), (1994, June). Introduction. *Journal of Developmental and Behavioral Pediatrics, 15*(3).

Brown, G., & Harris, T. (1989). *Life events and illness.* New York: Guilford.

Centers for Disease Control and Prevention. (1994a). Heterosexually acquired AIDS—U.S., 1993. *MMWR, 43,* 155–160.

Centers for Disease Control and Prevention. (1994b). AIDS among racial/ethnic minorities—U.S., 1993. *MMWR, 43,* 644–655.

Centers for Disease Control and Prevention. (1995). Update: AIDS among women—U.S., 1994. *MMWR, 44,* 81–84.

Clausen, J. (1991). Adolescent competence and the shaping of the life course. *American Journal of Sociology, 96,* 805.

Cohen, F. (1994). Research on families and pediatric human immunodeficiency virus disease: A review and needed directions. *Journal of Developmental and Behavioral Pediatrics, 15*(3), S34–S42.

Conner, E. M., Sperling, R. S., Gelber, R., Kiselev, P., Scott, G., O'Sullivan, M. J., Van Dyke, R., Bey, M., Shearer, W., Jacobson, R. L., (1994). Reduction of maternal–infant transmission of human immunodeficiency virus type 1 with Zidovudine treatment. *New England Journal of Medicine, 331,* 1173–1180.

D'Angelo, L. J. (1994). HIV infection and AIDS in adolescents. In P. A. Pizzo & C. M. Wilfert (Eds.), *Pediatric AIDS: The challenge of HIV infection in infants, children, and adolescents* (2nd ed., pp. 71–81). Baltimore: Williams & Wilkins.

Dane, B., & Miller, S. (1992). *AIDS: Intervening with hidden grievers.* Westport, CT: Auburn House.

Demos, E. V. (1989). Resiliency in infancy. In T. Dugan & M. Rutter (Eds.), *The child in our times: Studies in the development of resiliency* (pp. 3–22). New York: Brunner/Mazel.

Draimin, B. (1995). A second family? Placement and custody decisions. In S. Geballe, J. Gruendel, & W. Andiman (Eds.), *Forgotten children of the AIDS epidemic* (pp. 125–139). New Haven, CT: Yale University Press.

Draimin, B., Hudis, J., & Segura, J. (1992). *The mental health needs of well adolescents in families with AIDS.* New York: Human Resources Administration.

Dunn, J., & Plomin, R., (1990). *Separate lives: Why siblings are so different.* New York: Basic Books.

Enger, C., Graham, N., Peng, Y., Chmiel, J. S., Kingsley, L. A., Detels, R., Munoz, A., (1996). Survival from early, intermediate, and late stages of HIV infection. *JAMA, 275,* 1329–1334.

Fanos, J., & Wiener, L. (1994). Tomorrow's survivors: Siblings of human immunodeficiency virus-infected children. *Journal of Developmental and Behavioral Pediatrics, 15*(3), S43–S46.

Furman, E. (1974). *A child's parent dies: Studies in childhood bereavement.* New Haven, CT: Yale University Press.

Garmezy, N. (1993). Children in poverty: Resilience despite risk. *Psychiatry, 56,* 127–136.

Geballe, S. (1995). Toward a child-responsive legal system. In S. Geballe, J. Gruendel, & W. Andiman (Eds.), *Forgotten children of the AIDS epidemic* (pp. 140–164). New Haven, CT: Yale University Press.

Geballe, S., Gruendel, J., & Andiman, W. (Eds.). (1995). *Forgotten children of the AIDS epidemic*. New Haven, CT: Yale University Press.

Ginchild, R., & Perez-Porter, M. (1996, September). State initiatives slowly respond to kinship care. *Clearinghouse Review*, 521–530.

Gould, R. (Director/Producer). (1995). *Mommy, who'll take care of me?* [Film]. (Co-production of Connecticut Public Television, Hilltop Productions, Inc., and Rabbit Ears Productions).

Groce, N. (1995). Children and AIDS in multicultural perspective. In S. Geballe, J. Gruendel, & W. Andiman (Eds.), *Forgotten children of the AIDS epidemic* (pp. 95–106). New Haven, CT: Yale University Press.

Gruendel, J., & Anderson, G. (1995). Building child- and family-responsive support systems. In S. Geballe, J. Gruendel, & W. Andiman (Eds.), *Forgotten children of the AIDS epidemic* (pp. 165–189). New Haven, CT: Yale University Press.

Hudis, J. (1995). Adolescents living in families with AIDS. In S. Geballe, J. Gruendel, & W. Andiman (Eds.), *Forgotten children of the AIDS epidemic* (pp. 83–94). New Haven, CT: Yale University Press.

Karon, J. M., Rosenberg, P. S., McQuillan, G., Khare, M., Gwinn, M., & Petersen, L. R. (1996). Prevalence of HIV infection in the U.S., 1984 to 1992. *JAMA, 276*, 126–131.

Kastenbaum, R., Jr. (1977). Death and development through the life span. In H. Friegel (Ed.), *New meanings of life* (pp. 35–47). New York: McGraw-Hill.

Lade, D. (1996, March 17). Grandmother: In the age of AIDS, retirees such as Antonia Moyano often offer the only net between their grandkids and a free fall into the foster care system. *Sun Sentinel*.

Levine, C. (Ed.). (1993). *A death in the family: Orphans of the HIV epidemic*. New York: United Hospital Fund.

Levine, C., & Stein, G. (1994). *Orphans of the HIV epidemic: Unmet needs in six U.S. cities*. New York: United Hospital Fund.

Lewis, M. (1995). The special case of the uninfected child in the HIV-affected family: Normal developmental tasks and the child's concerns about illness and death. In S. Geballe, J. Gruendel, & W. Andiman (Eds.), *Forgotten children of the AIDS epidemic* (pp. 50–63). New Haven, CT: Yale University Press.

Lipson, M. (1994). Disclosure of diagnosis to children with human immunodeficiency virus or acquired immunodeficiency syndrome. *Journal of Developmental and Behavioral Pediatrics, 15*(3), S61–S65.

Luthar, S., & Zigler, E. (1991). Vulnerability and competence: A review of research on resilience in childhood. *American Journal of Orthopsychiatry, 61*(1), 6–22.

Mandelbaum, R. (1995). Trying to fit square pegs into round holes: The need for a new funding scheme for kinship caregivers. *Fordham Urban Law Journal, 22*, 907–935.

Mellins, C., & Ehrhardt, A. (1994). Families affected by pediatric acquired immunodeficiency syndrome: Sources of stress and coping. *Journal of Developmental and Behavioral Pediatrics 15*(3), S54–S60.

Michaels, D., & Levine, C. (1992). Estimates of the number of motherless youth orphaned by AIDS in the U.S. *JAMA, 268*, 3456–3461.

Mullen, F. (1996, September). Welcome to Procrustes' house: Welfare reform and grandparents raising grandchildren. *Clearinghouse Review*, 511–520.

Nagler, S., Adnopoz, J., & Forsyth, B. (1995). Uncertainty, stigma and secrecy: Psychological aspects of AIDS for children and adolescents. In S. Geballe, J. Gruendel, & W. Andiman

(Eds.), *Forgotten children of the AIDS epidemic* (pp. 71–82). New Haven, CT: Yale University Press.

Novick, A. (1995). Epilogue: Women and children in a time of plague in America. In S. Geballe, J. Gruendel, & W. Andiman (Eds.), *Forgotten children of the AIDS epidemic* (pp. 247–249). New Haven, CT: Yale University Press.

Quinton, D., & Rutter, M. (1988). *Parenting breakdown: The making and breaking of inter-generational links.* Aldershot, Hants, England: Avebury.

Pellegrini, D. (1994). Training in social problem solving. In M. Rutter, E. Taylor, & L. Hersov (Eds.), *Child and adolescent psychiatry: Modern approaches* (3rd ed., pp. 829–843). Oxford: Blackwell Scientific.

Roth, J., Siegel, R., & Black, S. (1994). Identifying the mental health needs of children living in families with AIDS or HIV infection. *Community Mental Health Journal, 30*(6), 581–593.

Rotheram-Borus, M. J., & Draimin, B. (1994). *Interventions for adolescents whose parents live with AIDS.* (NIMH Grant MH49958–03)

Rutter, M. (1966). *Children of sick parents.* London: Oxford University Press.

Rutter, M. (1979). Protective factors in children's responses to stress and disadvantage. In M. Kent & J. Rolf (Eds.), *Primary prevention in psychopathology: Vol. 3. Social competence in children* (pp. 49–77). Hanover, NH: University Press of New England.

Rutter, M. (1993). Resilience: Some conceptual considerations. *Journal of Adolescent Health, 14*(8), 626–31.

St. Louis, M., Conway, G. A., Hayman, C. R., Miller, C., Petersen, L. R., Dondero, T. J., (1991). Human immunodeficiency virus infection in disadvantaged adolescents: Findings from the U.S. Job Corps. *JAMA, 266*(17), 2387–2391.

Selik, R., Chu, S., &. Buehler, J. (1993). HIV infection as leading cause of death among young adults in US cities and states. *JAMA, 269*(23), 2991–2994.

Siegel, K., & Gorey, E. (1994). Childhood bereavement due to parental death from acquired immunodeficiency syndrome. *Journal of Developmental and Behavioral Pediatrics, 15*(3), S66–S70.

Simons, R., & Rogers, M. (1996). Preventing perinatal HIV infection: How far have we come? *JAMA, 275,* 1514–1515.

Werner, R., & Smith, R. (1989). *Vulnerable but invincible.* New York: Adams Bannister Cox.

4

Immigrant Children: Art as a Second Language

Cristina Igoa
Hayward Unified School District
and College of Notre Dame, Belmont

I felt hidden in the second grade because whenever anyone said something to me, I just couldn't answer a thing. When it was time for recess, I didn't have anyone to play with. The only person who played with me was my imagination.

—Child from Afghanistan

I felt very lonely when I first came here from the Philippines. When I went to my new school, no one talked to me. It was like I didn't exist.

—Child from the Philippines

"*Hidden… lonely… like I didn't exist….*" When you hear the words of immigrant children, you can begin to comprehend what it means for a child to be uprooted from his or her country of origin and confronted with a strange new world, a world whose inhabitants seem to ignore or resent those who are "different." Moreover, at the very moment they are under pressure to grasp the complexities of the new language and culture, immigrant children are reeling from a combination of losses that leave them feeling diminished and inadequate to meet the challenge.

67

I myself was an immigrant child and have worked with hundreds of immigrant children in various levels in school. Thus, the immigrant child's unique perspective on isolation is well known to me.

Nothing is more painful for a child than the feeling of nonexistence. If immigrant children are to succeed in the tasks of learning English and adapting to the United States' way of life, they must feel that their true selves can be both seen and heard. They need to feel that they are valued and understood.

The feeling of being understood is a most powerful and healing human experience. It is an immense challenge for the classroom teacher to demonstrate understanding of the inner world of the immigrant child. The teacher must find ways to draw the children out of their silence and sense of invisibility, ways to give them sheltered opportunities for self-expression, and ways to acknowledge the value of what the children have to say. When all this is accomplished, the children are given the sense of security and self-regard they need to take on the challenges of both a new language and a new life.

This article speaks directly to teachers and to those interested in the successful education of immigrant children. It attempts to bring out the emotions and struggles of the immigrant child to be authentically visible. It speaks of children who search for expression of feelings that are deeper than rational thinking but who, for lack of words to communicate to the larger society around them, often withdraw from themselves as well as from others. Ultimately, this article demonstrates how immigrant children can point the way for teachers to mediate their visibility through art.

In the process of uprooting and transition from their country to a new country, immigrant children have experienced many losses. This article initially discusses some of these; the loss of self-expression, self-identity, cultural identity, and confidence. The article then addresses the cues that immigrant children give about how to help them, and art as a second language that can move these children beyond their losses and isolation. Finally, the article outlines in detail examples of my use of art with immigrant children in the classroom and the successes that using art can achieve at turning each type of loss into strength and growth for the immigrant child.

LOSS OF SELF-EXPRESSION

Although immigrant children have access to their mother tongue and can express themselves at home and to peers and teachers at school who speak their language, their ability to express themselves as fully in English takes time. Researchers have documented that it takes more than 6 years for immigrant children to compete academically with their English speaking peers (Ada, 1993; Cummins, 1986). Are these children then to wait that long to be able to communicate fully in another language? There are those who can compete sooner, yet beneath their apparent academic achievement, many have buried thoughts and emotions that cry out for expression. What happens to these children, who feel invisible and silent to part of the school community, much less to the larger society? If immigrant children live in insecurity for over 6 years, what happens to their psychological and social development?

If not allowed expression, immigrant children can turn inward into morbid introspection (Grossenbacher, personal communication, May 21, 1988), fearing that they'll never make it in school, feeling helpless and hopeless. In the epilogue of my doctoral thesis (Igoa, 1988) at the University of San Francisco in California, five children from Vietnam, the Philippines, China, and Hong Kong spoke in unison:

> This is a totally different environment than I have been used to. The change is different because it upsets the kind of life I had. It was different back home. School was different, teachers were different. I feel depressed because I miss my friends in my country.

> I want to stay close to my family, I am afraid to leave them, but I must go to school. It is hard to go into a classroom. It is new and I feel as if everyone is looking at me and staring at me.

> I am having a difficult time adjusting. I don't like going to school. I am not sure I will make it. I can't speak English. I don't understand what they are saying. I am scared, afraid to express the emotions.

> I am afraid people will laugh and make fun of me because I am feeling different from others. I have no friends. I am lonely and alone and sad.

> I need someone to care for me, to hold my hand, and say, "It's all right, I'll help you. Don't be afraid." I need someone to set me on the right track. I need her caring so that I can be stronger. I just need enough confidence so that I can begin to do things on my own.

LOSS OF SELF-IDENTITY

The feeling of being different is a recurrent theme with immigrant children, who once belonged to a cultural collective in their countries of origin. There they expressed themselves in a common language or languages, lived in the dominant culture, and shared cultural symbols. They had a nest.

To find themselves out of that milieu is for them to feel like outsiders; they wonder how they can find friends when others have "nothing" in common. To a child, these feelings take on a negative connotation. Many children conclude that to feel a sense of belonging, it is necessary to be the same; that in order to act like others, one must put on a mask so no one can see the true ("different") self.

In the classroom, an immigrant child's loss of cultural self can manifest itself in any number of behaviors that inhibit learning. Many immigrant children are observed to be "living in another world," and the teacher may be apt to label such children as inattentive or "spacy." Other children engage in disruptive behavior. The classroom "clown" who makes others laugh may be trying to find a way to feel good inside, crying for relief from the uncomfortable feeling of academic as well as cultural invisibility and loneliness.

If an immigrant child is to successfully acculturate to a new social environment, the child's deeper self must be liberated to "breathe." This can be accomplished through warmth, understanding, and a reverence for listening and observing closely what the child is saying both verbally and nonverbally.

THE LOSS OF CULTURAL IDENTITY

This year, I worked with a boy who was the only child from El Salvador. Juan Carlos had been in a Spanish bilingual classroom and had been feeling alone because the majority of Spanish-speaking children were from Mexico. For some time he wondered when his culture would be respected and made visible to the others. This I realized when he wrote in his journal:

> Some people make fun of me because when I get into a fight they make fun (of) how I talk in Spanish in my country. Some people make me mad because they say I'm a Mexican just because I speak Spanish. That makes me very mad. They think Mexicans are the only ones who know how to speak Spanish. I'm from El Salvador. We speak Spanish in our country.
>
> —Juan Carlos

This boy seemed more "at home" when he got the chance to draw his Salvadoran artifacts and symbols which made him unique, and when he could experience how his artwork was seen and appreciated by his teacher and classmates. As Juan Carlos' artwork hung in the room the entire year, I often observed how he looked at his work admiringly.

Artwork by Juan Carlos, a student from El Salvador.

A LOSS OF CONFIDENCE

To listen to the children speak about their experience of school when they first arrived from their homeland is to make one wonder why schooling is such a painful experience for many, and to ask what can be done to direct the children's energies to a more productive life for themselves and for others. A few of the children's difficult experiences at school might give us further insight as to how much they cry out to be well received, accepted, liked, and seen as intelligent.

> *When I first went to school I was sent down to a classroom and all the students were all staring at me. The teacher told me to sit at the back because I don't have a desk and a chair yet, and they stared at me all the way to the back. I wanted to say, "stop staring at me", but I couldn't because they might not like me.*

—Child from the Philippines

I hated fifth grade because I never had friends. They didn't like me because they thought I was dumb. Many of the girls picked on me and I was scared of them. I hate this.

—Child from Fiji

In the second grade I felt horrible, sad and lonely. There was no one to play with when they don't know about you. They just walk away and don't even say a word. No one would even help me.

—Child from Afghanistan

WHEN IMMIGRANT CHILDREN LOOK BACK

Just as immigrant children have a lot to say about what they feel and need, they also give us solutions. When I met up years later with many of the children from an early class of mine, they gave me these recommendations and messages to teachers:

Be patient [with an immigrant child] because it is very difficult for a person to be in a new country and learn a new language. Be hopeful because if the teacher who is the closest friend gives up, then the child might as well give up.

—Dennis

[Immigrant children feel] left out. Until today there is still discrimination against people from other countries.

—Alice

Try to understand the background of the individual students. Many children don't express what they feel verbally and so they would be upset or real quiet. Try to get it out of them because they have doubts ... When can I communicate back? Will I be able to reach that point?

—Cindy

The kid is in school most of the time. You learn a lot from school, not just study, but about life ... Putting an immigrant child who doesn't speak English into a regular classroom with American students scares the hell out of her or him because it is so different. [Teachers] should start slowly and have special classes where the child could adapt and learn a little bit about American society and customs.

—Dung

I have kept their messages in mind as guidelines as I continue to work with immigrant children, as the children allow me into their inner world through our conversations and dialogues, and as I readjust the curriculum to fit their needs.

There is no formula for teaching immigrant children, but there are several clear truths to keep in mind:

1. Even before they master the complexities of the English language, immigrant children need a language to express themselves and to make themselves visible to society at large.
2. They need to feel that their true selves and their cultural identities are valued.
3. They need to become more confident about being in school.

A SECOND LANGUAGE KNOWN TO ALL

Art is a vibrant second language that is universally available to all human beings. Through art, immigrant children can communicate in more expressive and expansive ways than their oral and written language skills permit. The artwork lets the teacher become a keen observer of the children's aural silence and an active "listener" for what the child has to say through his or her drawings and paintings. Through art, the children stay in touch with their feelings.

In my nearly 17 years of teaching immigrant children, I have used art as a way of listening to the children and engaging them in a dialogue. Even with limited English-language skills, they have so much to tell. Using their drawings as a framework, immigrant children have found the words to write and to tell me of wolves and tigers chasing after them, yellow eyes staring at them, a weary and lonely bear walking in the woods, and a squirrel injured by a fall. The children illustrated stories of a mixed-up world where everything was upside down—clocks, cups, and even their names.

Then there was the tale of a little egg in a nest in America that "just sat there winter, summer, spring, and fall." For 2 consecutive years, this egg sat in the nest and hatched into a "beautiful bird" that flew out into the world and back to Vietnam only after she had been nurtured and cared for by a teacher who understood her. The Vietnamese bird grown strong by kindness found a mate and together they built their nest. Both birds stayed connected with the understanding teacher by visiting her each year—all this in the imagination of a child who sought expression through art.

These children spoke of the cultural and psychological aspects of themselves that, if respected, are necessary for their academic achievement in school. Their stories, art symbols, images and sources of academic success and difficulties are explained in much more detail in the book, *The Inner World of the Immigrant Child* (Igoa, 1995). Since I wrote the book, the children have taken me to a deeper understanding not only of the importance of art in their lives, but of why art is a second language for them.

Through art, the child's inner world is made visible. The child can channel his or her energies and come out of silent introspection. Although it is often forgotten in the budget cutting of the 1990s, art is a natural language for all children, because art has no barriers. In particular, art allows immigrant children, especially those from nonindustrialized parts of the world, to communicate in a state of pure creativity, channeling the anger and other human emotions that are a result of their uprooting anxiety, "loss of language," insecurity, and conflicts about integrating their native culture with the new.

ETHNOGRAPHY OF A CLASSROOM

In my sixth-grade class this year, I inherited a classroom full of immigrant children from eight different cultures and languages—Iran, Pakistan, Afghanistan, Vietnam, the Philippines, Nicaragua, El Salvador, and Mexico. Although each day I had a Farsi-speaking teacher assistant for two periods, Spanish- and Vietnamese-speaking assistants for one period, and an ESL teacher for one period, 31 children from eight countries all day long was nevertheless a challenge. The children came with varying levels of English-language development—from recent arrivals to those who had been in the American school system since first grade. Because many immigrant children are often in a state of mobility due to the parents' economic needs, by the end of the year, my class had 28 children, a somewhat easier student–teacher ratio.

Having been in dialogue with immigrant children for years, it was not difficult for me to intuit what the children were thinking and feeling. I could sense the depressing quality of life in the room—the feelings of helplessness and despair. I read the previous teachers' comments about the children so I could know where to begin with them:

- *She needs a lot of support in doing assignments.*
- *Fights, angry.*
- *Does not do assignments.*
- *In responsibility room* (time-out room for troubled children).
- *Attitude problem*
- *"Red dot"* (warning that the child is trouble for the teacher).
- *"Spacy"– off into his own world.*
- *The class clown.*

The thought of living with these children for an entire year was over-whelming, and I felt somewhat put upon. Inadvertently, I had missed an after-school meeting when the children were assigned and my colleagues stood firm by some unwritten school law, "You snooze, you lose." I therefore ended up with all the most difficult cases.

And there were complications beyond that! More than half the children were neither strong in their own language nor in English because of mobility factors, and they lacked motivation to succeed or basic academic skills. Three were classified as borderline "special education," one had been unschooled altogether in her early school years, and two had the very blank look of having just arrived. Another two children from war-torn Afghani-stan were still coping with their war within.

Three children were articulate and playful. That left only three serious about their school work. As I reviewed the quality of the work some had turned in, it was obvious that most of the children had given up ever making it in school. I had to find a new second language that would be common to all and that would give them the confidence they needed to succeed in school. I was determined to find a way for the children. This I found through art.

ART AS A SKILL TO BE MASTERED

Understand what it feels like to be an immigrant child. Listen and don't rush them. Help them be successful by giving them things that they can do and not things that they cannot do.

—Rosario, student from the Philippines

The wisdom of this child gave me direction. I also had past experience with art and a real sense of its importance to the immigrant child. Art helps build powers of observation and concentration. While they draw, children can forget for a time all their negative feelings about being "dumb" and invisible. As a medium of communication, art allows children to become fully expressive. Through art, they can begin to gain inner confidence because their first "masterpieces" can be hung around the room, making them instantly visible.

This group of children in particular needed a new avenue to challenge their blocked energies and to help them see that they could be successful, even if only in one area at first. Then they could build on that success to other areas of the curriculum. Nevertheless, the children at first showed tremendous resistance to beginning their "academic life" through art. This was not surprising; when I asked how many were good in art, only 2 of the 31 children raised their hands. The others saw art as a waste of time and something they did in kindergarten. Also, it was clear that these children were not in the habit of completing assignments, and those assignments that actually got turned in were done carelessly and in haste. This indifferent attitude was transferred to art assignments, no matter how easy that task.

As I walked around the room in the early days of class, their facial expressions showed me the feelings they were experiencing—"no good, bad, ugly, horrible." The only thing they seemed to enjoy was chattering with their friends who spoke the same language. Their incessant talking gave them a lot of comfort and freed them from their feelings of inadequacy. They could have chatted all day long had I let them. But I was intent on finding something they could build on—something they could do, not something they could not do.

I met with their parents, speaking through translators about the importance of art, how I was to lead them to building one skill at a time, and how I would transfer each skill to subject after subject. I showed the parents the beautiful artwork of the previous class. That did the trick! The parents supported me and spoke to their children. I only hoped that I could deliver to the parents what I promised. I had a sense that I could once the children committed themselves.

I started my plan by counting the required number of hours for the teaching of art each year. Rather than teaching art once a week for an hour, I decided to teach art for a couple of hours daily for several weeks so that the whole class could be immersed in it. The solid block of time in the classroom for art gave it a credible and significant standing in academia, and the children began to respect it. Homework often included assignments to draw things from their living rooms, kitchens, and gardens, and from the classroom. As the children progressed artistically, I reduced the amount of time for direct instruction. I used several books as references. These I include at the end of the chapter.

I would not accept work done haphazardly. Even the most simple cylinders—the first step in learning to draw—had to be done with thought and care. Many children had to do simple assignments up to three times before I would accept them. Often a child would come up to me and say, "Teacher, would you accept this work?" only to receive a response, "Not yet." When the children got the idea that only careful and thoughtful work would be accepted, the children began to rise to that high expectation level. Their attitudes became more mature and their drawings also began to mature.

This is artwork drawn by the same student before and after art intervention.
(taken from Fall and Spring semesters)

Art as a Way Toward Visibility

Once the children were committed to the task of beautiful artwork, they became more visible. We worked diligently at developing their skills through peer tutoring, teamwork and individual attention. The focus on art engaged them in such a way that a child from Mexico stopped watching TV as he got more involved in artwork. Every night after dinner he would clear the table and practice his drawings while his uncle looked on. Several other children also spoke of no longer watching television at night and became more engaged in drawing.

In September, when I asked the children how many of them were artists, two of them had raised their hands. By the end of the year, the 28 students with acquired as well as natural talent could declare that they were good in art. The room was filled with energetic artists proud of their work and applauding each other. We filled the room with color, designs, and drawings, and when the children were ready, the artwork spilled outside the classroom and onto the walls of the corridors, doors, and bulletin boards.

The children enhanced their science reports and history reports with art. They created toys and painted school murals. A few teachers hired some of the children at 5¢ a word for their calligraphy on charts and posters. A group of special education children presented themselves at the door one day and asked if the immigrant children could tutor them in art. Another group of "mainstream" children also requested tutelage and again the immigrant children responded. The mainstream children entered the immigrant children's "territory" and the two groups worked together. Often, mainstream children are mixed into classrooms to be English-language role models, but in this situation, the immigrant children were the role models for art as a second language. The immigrant children felt their strength, and through their artistic talents, they became quite visible and respected in the school.

I should point out that the children were producing beautiful and profound artwork long before they "went public," and their creations were seen outside their families and our classroom. If immigrant children experienced people looking at them with suspicion, if they were ridiculed for wearing their native clothing (referred to as "costumes"), if they were laughed at for the foods they brought to school or the language they spoke, all of this happened away from the nests of family and the "safe" classroom. The corridor from the classroom door, therefore, may represent this unsafe "real world," that harsh actuality from which they often yearn to hide their insecurities.

If artwork is placed in the corridor too early in the children's development of self-acceptance and pride, their fear of the unknown may be awakened, prompting them to shrink back into hiding themselves from others who may "stare or laugh at them." It is important for the teacher to obtain the children's collaboration before bringing them "outside" the classroom through their artwork. When the children become eager to show their work to the world, then I know that they are pleased with their work and with themselves. We work all year to achieve this goal of self-confidence, to allow oneself to be visible through art.

As people passed through the corridors and saw the beauty of the immigrant children's inner worlds, their vibrant colors and symbols, appreciation evolved into admiration and respect. Vandals marred the walls with graffiti and tore down decorations, but the immigrant children's art was left untouched, perhaps recognized as too beautiful and sacred to destroy.

A view of the school corridor containing the children's artwork.

Art as a Stepping Stone to Other Skills

Just as the children's earlier lackadaisical attitude toward school was reflected in their initial performance of art and other assignments, the reverse
became true; as the children became strong in art, they became strong in
other subjects. Their artistic skills and diligence transformed their lackadaisical attitude and gave them the foundation to build proficiency in language
literacy and writing. In the development of artistic competence, the children
learned how to focus and concentrate, how to observe and compare. They
discovered the importance of attention to detail and patience; they internalized the concept of completing steps in order to complete a task. These
skills were transferred to other academic subjects. It became easier for them
to achieve the hand–eye coordination necessary to "draw" alphabet char-
acters. Art also gave the children a framework to sharpen their imaginations
and to identify their thoughts and feelings, making it easier to articulate
themselves in speech and writing.

In September, 75% of the children could not read a fifth- or sixth-grade
novel in English that I had selected for the class. By the end of the year, 85%
of the children could read and comprehend the novel and answer in-depth
questions in writing. The remaining 15% had made significant progress in
expanding and strengthening their literacy skills. They read simple books at
first, slowly building their way up to more complex assignments and increasing their literacy skills daily and in the evenings, just as they had done in
learning art. For many, the progress they made in English also strengthened
their primary language. Their attention to detail gave them the ability to
compare and to learn about the differences in the languages. Thus, one
language was building on the other. Another aspect of the children's art
experience and success in other subjects was reflected in their increased
initiative. During recess and lunch, and even in the last week of the school
year, children voluntarily stayed to peer tutor each other, to read, to question
and to test.

Art as a Way Toward Appreciating Being "Different"

At the beginning of this article, we heard immigrant children speaking about
how badly they felt about being different. I used art as a medium to demystify
the feeling of being different by encouraging the children to emphasize and
celebrate their differences. The children were then able to see in their own
artwork the beauty and variety and color of their souls.

In one assignment, I asked the children to do a first draft of sketching designs and patterns that belonged to their individual cultures. They found them on rugs at home, in clothing, and in books. Their task in the second and final drafts was to place those designs and patterns on art paper so that it filled the space. We then placed their individual cultural drawings in a circle and as we walked around in silence, we applauded their differences; the children did not compare, they just accepted what each had done as unique as it was beautiful. We then hung the work inside or outside the classroom as the children wished.

Starting from the top panel and moving from left to right, row by row, the children's artwork represents the cultures of Mexico, Fiji, Vietnam, Afghanistan, Nicaragua, the Phillipines, and Vietnam.

Art as Cultural Expression

Immigrant children sometimes fear that they will be swallowed up by another culture and often need to express their cultural identities in their artwork. This is a healthy sign because it shows that they are in touch with their true inner selves. I often worry about the child who thinks that giving up his or her roots is the answer to finding friendships and a sense of belonging in the new society. These children overidentify with the new culture and thus lose what gives them meaning and connection to their families at home and to their countries of origin. It indicates the risk that later on, they will be caught in a culture clash, being accepted neither by their own culture nor by the new. Angry and confused, they may opt to live out of a persona—their true selves could be lost. However, if the environment in the classroom fosters the expression of the whole child, then the children feel free to say a lot about who they are and what is on their minds. This gives them a sense of security and a feeling of well-being. They will not have to regain their cultural identities later.

For example, as I prepared a lesson on how to draw cylinders, pots, and steins one day, the children were impatient and restless. They tried to rush through the process at first. Then I mentioned that they were free to add designs and patterns to enhance them. The room quieted down. Their cultures permeated their artwork, reminding me of their presence. They said a lot in these colorful pots and steins, more than words could say.

Display of children's artwork in the outside corridor.

Symbolic Art as an Expression of the Soul

Once immigrant children have gained mechanical skills, a whole spectrum of cultural experience comes through their art. Having a framework for communication, for the expression of imagination, they reveal themselves totally—culturally, intellectually, and psychologically.

Religion, so deeply embedded in culture, is often integrated in the art of the children who want the whole of who they are to be visible to the world. Having once lived in cultures where spirituality is freely expressed, these children want to express this spirituality and make it visible. The children from Mexico often draw pictures of the Virgin of Guadalupe as representative of their culture. The children from Afghanistan draw the mullah, or priest, in front of a mosque. The children from the Philippines often draw a church, steeples, and the cross—symbols of Christianity.

Deeper yet than the religious imagery is their abstract art, which carries their cultural, their spiritual symbols as well as profound personal messages to the world. A beautiful 12-year-old from Mexico wrestled with both

Spanish and English and used art as an outlet for her imagination, feelings, and beliefs. She came into the classroom one morning enthusiastically. In her hand was her abstract art—a gift. Colors filled the page, but upon closer examination I sensed that behind the colors were words, messages. Her art spoke of a vibrant interior life. I embraced it and placed it on the chalkboard—she was visible and so was her message. When I could free up a moment in my teaching day, we sat down together and I asked her to tell me what the drawing said. In a breathless story, she told of her historical connection to the Aztecs, the importance of her home where she finds a connection with herself, and the spiritual beliefs that give meaning and strength to her life. I saw that it was all there in her art in color. It took color for her to express all sides of herself.

At the center is the spirit of Mexico. It is where God lives and on either sides are the cascades of our wishes and dreams. Underneath is our home surrounded by feathers of the Aztecs.

If you enter the center of the home it is because you have done something good with your life and you can connect with God. You can enter the center of the spirit where God lives and you can go out to see the people, but the people cannot see you.

Above , the sun shines behind the clouds. It shines on the bridge where people cross.

Behind the sun is the rainbow. The rainbow signifies that there will be no more rain nor thunder and life will be more tranquil.

(a translation from the Spanish)

En el centro está el espíritu de Mexico. Es donde vive Diós y en los lados están las cascadas del deseo y de los sueños de nosotros. Debajo está nuestro hogar y alrededor están las plumas de los aztecas.

Si entras en el centro del hogar es porque has hecho algo bueno en la vida y puedes conectar con
Dios—puedes entrar en el centro del espíritu donde vive Diós y salir a ver a la gente. Pero la gente no te puede ver,

Encima el sol brilla detras de las nuves. Brilla hacia el puente donde cruza de la gente.

Detras del sol es el arco iris. El arco iris significa que ya no habrá lluvia ni tormenta y la vida será más tranquila

—Vicki Ibal, student from Mexico, age 12 (taken from her actual words, February 25, 1996)

CLOSING REFLECTIONS

How quiet the room becomes when the children draw. It becomes even more quiet when they are drawing something that gives them meaning. I use these quiet times to meet the children in the back of the room and to work with them individually or in small groups to increase their math and literacy skills and to lessen the teacher–pupil ratio. Measuring their growth in languages, art, and English, and comparing their ability with their mainstream peers, I found that in just a few months they had mastered art and reached beyond their grade level. As their artistic confidence increased, so did their confidence in all other subjects. One skill built onto another.

Art, their second language, developed naturally. Through art, the vitality level in the room was transformed, the blocked energies unblocked. Visitors stopped by to admire the children's work and artwork. We were honored by a visit from Marylou Shockley, vice president of Pacific Bell Company, who heard about the children's beautiful art. A colleague, Dr. Constance Beutel, donated an honorarium of $250 and our Room 9 Foundation was estab-

lished. From this small Foundation, six children applied and received
scholarships to go to Chabot's Summer College for kids and 10 children on
their own accord signed up for the school district's summer school. I had
taken a risk in my teaching approach to the children and they came through
beautifully. Through art, they could communicate their entire selves to the
world around them. They had a channel for their thoughts, feelings, and
imagination. They worked hard until they were both seen and heard.

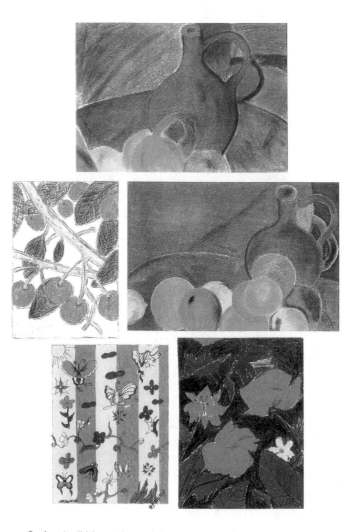

Students' still life art of jug and fruit are taken from a painting by Paul Cezanne.

SUGGESTED READINGS

Albert, K. (1993). *Spanish girl and boy paper dolls*. Mineola, NY: Dover.

Blake, W., & Petrie, F. (1981). *Starting to draw*. NY: Watson-Guptill Publications.

Brookes, M. (1986). *Drawing with children*. NY: Putnam.

Brookes, M. (1991). *Drawing for older children and teens*. Los Angeles, CA: Jeremy P. Tarcher, Inc.

Bruhns, K. O. & Weller, T. (1973). *A coloring album of ancient Mexico and Peru*. Berkeley, CA: St. Heironymous Press, Inc.

Carter, P. (1994). *Illuminated calligraphy*. Kent, Great Britain: Search Press Limited.

Du Bosque, D. (1991). *Draw! Cars step by step*. Molalla, OR: Peel Productions.

Du Bosque, D. (1991). *Learn to draw now!* Molalla, OR: Peel Productions.

Du Bosque, D. (1994). *Draw! Ocean Animals Step by Step*. Molalla, OR: Peel Productions.

Gaadt, G. (1994). *I can draw* series (Designed and produced by Morris Publishing, Inc.) Tustin, CA: Walter Foser Publishing, Inc.

Green, J. (1992). *Little exotic birds stained glass*. NY: Dover.

Linse, B. (1991). *Art of the Mexican folk*. Larkspur, CA: Arts Publications.

Miller, H. (1973). *Paint as you like and die happy*. San Francisco, CA: Chronicle Books.

Paramón Ediciones Editorial Team. (1992). *The basics of artistic drawing*. Barcelona, Spain: Paramón Ediciones, S.A.

Pereieda, R. & Rossin, L. (1982). *Beginning drawing for young people.* Cranbury, NJ: M. Grumbacher, Inc.

Shepherd, M. (1986). *Calligraphy alphabets made easy.* NY: Putnam.

Shepherd, M. (1988). *Modern calligraphy made easy.* NY: Putnam.

Simakoff, N. (1993). *Islamic designs in color.* NY: Dover.

REFERENCES

Ada, A. F. (1993). *Mother-tongue, literacy as a bridge between home and school cultures: The power of two languages.* New York: McGraw-Hill.

Cummins, J. (1986). Empowering minority students: A framework for intervention. *Harvard Education Review, 56,* 18–36.

Igoa, C. (1988). *Toward a psychology and education of the uproted: A study of the inner world of immigrant children.* Unpublished doctoral dissertation, University of San Francisco.

Igoa, C. (1995). *The inner world of the immigrant child.* Mahwah, NJ: Lawrence Erlbaum Associates, Inc.

5

Urban Appalachian Children: An "Invisible Minority"[*] in City Schools

❧ • ❧

Kathleen Bennett deMarrais
Northern Arizona University

The Appalachian mountains form a distinctive highland region in the eastern United States between the eastern seaboard and the Midwest. The region's landscape is one of quiet beauty with old, forested mountains, deep valleys, and swift-flowing rivers and streams. Geologists consider this range one of the oldest in North America, with the ancient Appalachian chain laying an unbroken line from Newfoundland to Alabama. The main backbone of the chain now extends from Maine to Georgia with a small extension into northern Alabama (People's Appalachian Research Collective, 1991). Since the 19th century, geographers have attempted to define the region with different variations for the exact boundaries of the region (cf. Raitz & Ulack, 1991). As romantic and colorful descriptions of Appalachian people appeared in popular magazines and novels in the latter part of the 19th century, Appalachia began to be known as a distinct sociocultural region in addition to its

---

[*]The title of this chapter is borrowed from *The Invisible Minority: Urban Appalachians*, by Philliber and McCoy (1981).

identity as a unique geographical region. Authors of these accounts de-scribed Appalachians as self-reliant, independent, isolated, quaint, poor, simple, and strong (Raitz & Ulack, 1991). Since that time, social scientists, writers, and educators have explored Appalachia and its people. John C. Campbell's *The Southern Highland and His Homeland* (1921) is one of the early classics describing the land and people of this region.

Although the Appalachian region has been defined differently through the years by social scientists, writers, and politicians, the most recent political definition of Appalachia grew out of efforts to establish the Appa-lachian Regional Commission (ARC) to address social, educational, and economic concerns of the area. In 1965, the federal government, at the urging of the region's state governors, created the ARC with representatives from 13 states. This commission divided the region into three distinct subregions; northern, central, and southern Appalachia. Portions of 13 eastern states, some that had not been considered Appalachia before (parts of Ohio, Pennsylvania, New York, and Mississippi) were considered in this new definition of the Appalachian region. Currently, the total Appalachian region includes 397 counties in the states of Mississippi, Alabama, Georgia, Tennessee, South Carolina, North Carolina, Kentucky, Ohio, New York, Virginia, Maryland, and western Pennsylvania, as well as the entire state of West Virginia (Obermiller & Maloney, 1994).

The people of Appalachia share a rich cultural heritage that includes a strong sense of kinship, a love of the land, a rich oral tradition, and a commitment to personal freedom and self-reliance. They also share a long history of poverty, economic exploitation, and inadequate schooling. In stark contrast to the lovely landscape of the region, poverty in parts of Appalachia is clearly evident in the substandard housing that dots the hillsides. Many rural and urban Appalachians today continue to struggle to provide basic necessities for their families; the poverty rate in central Appalachia is twice the national average. High rates of unemployment, illiteracy, and school dropouts continue to plague the region (Tickamyer & Tickamyer, 1987). Given this geographic and sociocultural introduction to Appalachia, I now turn to a discussion of my own involvement with the region followed by a brief description of Appalachian culture and values. I then examine the migration of Appalachians to northern cities, with a focus on the schooling experiences of urban Appalachian children. In this portion of the chapter, I discuss barriers facing Appalachian students in schools including negative stereotypes, the relationship between poverty and edu-cational attainment, cultural differences between home and school, and rigid bureaucratic school structures that inhibit students' fit with the institution. I conclude the chapter with a discussion of ways we can transform school structures to better meet the needs of Appalachian youth.

My first experiences with Appalachian families were in the early 1970s when I began teaching in a small, rural community in the mountains of upstate New York. My classroom was full of Appalachian children whose families had migrated from West Virginia to work in the ash forests cutting timber for use in the manufacture of baseball bats. I later moved to the greater Cincinnati area where I worked for 10 years with urban Appalachian children in northern Kentucky's public schools. Although I grew up in a small town on the outskirts of Camden, New Jersey, my own working-class background in a traditional, authoritarian, and patriarchal family was similar in values to those of my students and their families. Much of my professional life has been spent either in rural mountain communities or in working with families who migrated from the hills to urban neighborhoods.

My work in public schools, particularly with Appalachians in northern cities during the 1970s and 1980s, raised serious questions for me about the ways we, as educators, worked with Appalachian children and their families. I found teachers and principals frequently did not see Appalachians as a distinct minority group in the schools, but tended to view them simply as poor children who spoke "nonstandard" English and came to school without the parental support and other advantages afforded to middle-class children. These children were the "invisible minority" described by Philliber and McCoy (1981) in that they physically looked like mainstream White children but their unique cultural backgrounds were neither recognized nor accepted by school personnel. When the students were not successful in school they were often diagnosed with special education labels and segregated from regular classroom instruction or became early dropouts or pushouts from schools. Our school structures were inappropriate to meet the needs of urban Appalachian children as indicated by the low achievement and high dropout rates of many of our students. My discomfort with the interactions between the schools and Appalachian families led me to explore Appalachian culture more fully, in particular urban Appalachian culture, in a doctoral program at the University of Cincinnati. Since that time, I have continued to explore Appalachian culture as well as the relationship between Appalachian families and schools. I currently own a farm in a rural East Tennessee community where I appreciate the Appalachians' love of the green rolling hillsides and enjoy the warmth and kindness of my neighbors there.

A NOTE ABOUT LABELS

The Urban Appalachian Council of Cincinnati (1985) defined an *Appalachian* as one who was born, or whose parents or grandparents were born, in one of the counties making up the Appalachian region. *Appalachian migrant* is used for those first generations of people who moved from rural mountainous regions to urban manufacturing centers in northern cities. According to Obermiller and Maloney (1994), the term *urban Appalachian* was coined in the early 1970s and became the "favored term to describe those people and their descendants who had come from the Appalachian region to live and work in cities outside Appalachia" (p. 3).

APPALACHIAN VALUES

In his classic essay on Appalachian values, Loyal Jones (1975) explained that a strong sense of family, a love of the land, independence, self-reliance, and pride are of utmost importance to Appalachian people. These values are crucial to the maintenance of a sense of freedom. Early settlers to this region, primarily Scots–Irish, moved to isolated mountain regions where they could be free to enjoy the solitude and beauty of the land, to support their families, and to live without the constraints of a more populated, and therefore regulated, society. Jones (1975) explained that Appalachians value being able to take care of their own without having to depend on others:

> Our forebears were individualistic from the beginning, else they would not have gone to such trouble and danger to get away from encroachments on their freedom. Individualism and self-reliance were traits to be admired on the frontier. The person who could not look after himself and his family was to be pitied. The pride of the mountaineer is mostly a feeling of not wanting to be beholden to other people. We are inclined to try to do everything ourselves, find our own way when we are lost on the road, or suffer through when we are in great need. We don't like to ask others for help. The value of self-reliance is often stronger than the desire to get help. (pp. 509-510)

Appalachians identify with place, with their rugged hills, lush valleys, and mountain streams. Their bond to the land is the glue that binds these people to each other and to past generations of Appalachians. It was this mountainous land that initially provided for the Appalachians a subsistence living in the form of crops, game, and wood for heat and shelter. It was a land in which small upland farms could be created in the valleys and hollows of the mountains. The temperate climate nurtured an abundance of herbs, grasses, vegetables, nuts, and flowers that grew wild and were readily gathered. Much of this land was not desirable for those interested in larger scale farming or access to markets. It was a place where people could surround themselves with natural beauty while they worked hard to provide their families with a simple living. However, overcrowding of the small farms, exhaustion of the soil, extinction of game, and the discovery of coal in the region were primary reasons for the Appalachian people's history of economic struggle and exploitation in the 20th century.

MIGRATION FROM APPALACHIA TO NORTHERN CITIES

Economic survival led to one of the largest migrations of people in the United States in the 1940s and 1950s as Appalachians moved northward looking for work. This migration began during World War II and although it peaked during the 1950s, it has not stopped since that time as people continue to look for economic opportunities (Obermiller & Borman, 1994).

First generation Appalachian migrants to northern cities used family networks to obtain employment at busy automobile factories and steel mills when blue-collar manufacturing jobs were plentiful during World War II and postwar years. Cincinnati, Dayton, Akron, Cleveland, Detroit, and Pittsburgh became primary centers for this first generation of Appalachians who established urban enclaves where they settled with other migrants from rural areas. This kinship migration stream from the south continued over the next decades. Obermiller and Maloney (1994) described the Appalachians who migrated to northern cities as "predominately White (Scots–Irish or Anglo-Saxon cultural backgrounds), mostly Baptist or Pentecostal, and heavily blue collar" (p. 15). As was the case with other immigrant groups, the poverty and distinct accents of the first migrants to northern cities made them easy targets for stereotyping and discrimination. A poignant quote from Gertie, the main character in Harriette Arnow's *The Dollmaker* (1954), illustrates the bitter economic struggle of Appalachian families who sacrificed their mountain homeplaces to move to the cities where husbands, brothers, and even children could find work:

"What crops do they raise in this country?" the [police] officer asked, as if he didn't much care but wanted to make some sound above the child's breathing.

"A little uv everthing."

"But what is their main crop?" he insisted

"Youngens," she said, holding the child's hands that were continually wandering toward the hole in his neck. "Youngens fer th wars an them factories" (pp. 24–25).

In subsequent decades, the decline of the automobile and steel industries in these northern cities drastically reduced the availability of blue-collar jobs. Urban Appalachians were forced to move to new growth centers in the south and west, to seek work in service industries, or to rely on social service agencies. Those with more education and better economic opportunities assimilated into mainstream White suburbia and often no longer self-identified as Appalachian. Others continued to live in urban enclaves with other Appalachian families and friends. Today third and fourth generations of urban Appalachians are permanent residents in these northern cities with varying degrees of ties to kin in rural Appalachia.

URBAN APPALACHIAN CHILDREN IN SCHOOLS

Historically, educational opportunities have been limited for Appalachian youth primarily because of parents' needs for children to work to help support the family. Young boys left school to work in the rural coal mines, whereas young girls left to help out at home with chores and younger children. With the migration to northern cities, these economic struggles persisted so that children continued to contribute to the economic well-being of the family by early entry into the workforce.

In addition to economic barriers, the first migrants to northern cities faced particularly difficult experiences in crowded inner-city schools where their dialect and differences were obvious. We can see the difficult relationship between teachers and Appalachian migrant families portrayed by Arnow (1954) in a scene where Gertie attended an open house at school to discuss her son's progress with his teacher:

It was getting late, the children marching homeward through the halls, before she reached the one room she dreaded—Mrs. Whittle's. It was empty save for one other mother just coming out, and a woman who Gertie knew was Mrs. Whittle, for she was taking her purse from an open desk drawer. She hesitated in the doorway ... She waited a moment longer, then cleared her throat and said, "Miz Whittle."

... Gertie moved a step nearer and stood by the desk ... "I come to talk to you about my younGen—boy."

Mrs. Whittle, with a crinkling hiss of paper, was removing the hat from a green paper sack. "Yu'll have to hurry," she said, her voice somehow matching the paper. "It's late and I've been teaching and talking to mothers all afternoon."

"Th slip my youngens brung home said th teachers ud talk to us atter school," Gertie said, speaking with difficulty, choked up at being forced to speak to the woman's back. ... "The child's name?" she asked, bringing out her lipstick, turning again to the mirror.

"Reuben—Reuben Nevels."

Mrs. Whittle gave no sign that she had heard ... Mrs. Whittle turned, looked briefly at Gertie, then spoke as she opened the desk drawer, and took out gloves, "Well, what is the matter? Did your child fail to pass? A percentage do, you know."

"No, he passed," Gertie said, fighting to keep her voice smooth. "But—but you're his ... " She had forgotten the name, the kind of teacher. "You've got him more'n th other teachers, an you'll keep on a haven him an ..."

"Are you trying to say that I'm his home-room teacher?" Mrs. Whittle asked, drawing on a glove.

Gertie nodded.

"Well, what is the matter?" She was smoothing the drawn-on gloves finger by finger now.

"He—he don't seem to be a doen so good—not in his homeroom. He ain't happy; he don't like school, an I thought mebbe ..."

Her words, though halting and stumbling as they were, caused Mrs. Whittle to glance up from the second glove, and for the first time the two women looked at each other. Mrs. Whittle smiled, the red mouth widening below the old woman's angry glaring eyes. "And of course it's his teacher's fault your child is unhappy. Now just what do you expect me to do to make him happy?"

"That's what I come to ask you," Gertie said. "He kinda likes his other classes, an back home he was ..."

"Back home," Mrs. Whittle said, as if she hated the words, her voice low, hissing, like a thin whip coming hard through the air, but not making much noise. "You hill—southerners who come here, don't you realize before you come that it will be a great change for your children? For the better, of course, but still a change. You bring them up here in time of war to an overcrowded part of the city and it makes for an overcrowded school. Don't you realize," she went on, looking again at Gertie, looking at her as if she alone were responsible for it all, "that until they built this wartime housing—I presume you live there—I never had more than 32 children in my section—and only one section. ... Now I have two sections—two home rooms, one in the morning with forty-three children, one in the afternoon with forty-two—many badly adjusted like your own—yet you expect me to make your child happy in spite of ..." Words seemed inadequate, and she was silent while she reached into her purse.

"But I've got three more in school, an they git along an—"

"What did you say your name was?"

"Nevels. My boy's name is Reuben. Maybe you don't recollect him but—"

"I don't what?" And she frowned as she might have at a child giving the wrong answer.

"'Recollect, I said," Gertie answered.

"Does that mean 'remember'?"

When Gertie continued to stand in choked silence staring down at her, she went on, after taking a bunch of keys from her purse and closing it. "I do remember now—too well. Your children came up for discussion in faculty meeting the other day. ... The others have, I understand adjusted quite well, especially the younger boy and the older girl, but Reuben—I remember him ...He has not adjusted. His writing is terrible—he's messy; quite good in math but his spelling is terrible. I'm giving him a U in conduct because he just won't get along with other children." (pp. 299–302)

BARRIERS FACING APPALACHIAN CHILDREN
IN URBAN SCHOOLS

Like Reuben and Gertie in the Detroit of the 1940s, urban Appalachians today continue to face barriers in their struggle for an education. Obermiller and Maloney (1994) argued that urban Appalachians in Ohio drop out of school at higher rates than other racial and cultural groups. They reviewed educational attainment figures reported on the Greater Cincinnati Surveys in 1980 and 1989 for urban Appalachians living in the Cincinnati metro-politan area. Although dropout rates decreased from 27% in 1980 to 17% in 1989 and college graduation rates increased from 36% to 45%, urban Appalachians were less likely than non-Appalachian Whites surveyed to complete high school and college. Urban Appalachians in the survey fared better than Blacks in educational attainment measures on these surveys, except when the sample was confined to those living in inner-city neighborhoods. According to Obermiller and Oldendick (1989), educational out-comes for Blacks were better than for Appalachians living in Cincinnati's inner-city. In another study, Borman (1991) reported that urban Appala-chian adolescents had the highest dropout rates, proportionate to their numbers, in Cincinnati public schools.

Obermiller and Maloney (1994) described the situation for inner-city Appalachians as "grim." They reported that "half of the adults in these neighborhoods have no more than a high school education, school dropout rates are as high as 75%, and youth unemployment is a serious problem" (p. 11). At the same time, they argued that the urban Appalachians in their study maintain strong family bonds, support and use their own cultural institutions and organizations, and devise new ways to deal with old problems.

Although there are many urban Appalachians who succeed in school and go on to find economic opportunities for themselves and their families, we know there are far too many youth who are not successful in our school systems. In the next section, I discuss some of the barriers urban Appalachi-ans face in their continuing struggle to succeed in schools, including persistent negative stereotypes, the relationship between poverty and schooling, and cultural differences and school structures.

STEREOTYPES OF APPALACHIANS

Stereotypes of Appalachians are overwhelmingly negative and often carry derogatory labels such as "hillbillies," "ridgerunners," "hilljacks," "briars," "briarhoppers," and so on. These stereotypes become permanently fixed through films such as *Deliverance*, comic strips such as "Snuffy Smith" or "L'il Abner," and television shows like "The Beverly Hillbillies." Appalachians are generally portrayed as lazy, poor, ignorant, dirty, incestuous, clannish, bare-foot and pregnant, and immoral. As a group, Appalachians, particularly in the northern cities where they migrated, are the brunt of ethnic jokes that affirm and escalate this negative stereotyping. In an article by Sullivan and Miller (1990), Evelyn Hurt Bolton described her experiences of ethnic discrimination as a 13-year-old Appalachian migrant in Cincinnati:

> [When we first moved in] the kids were mean, like cruel, you know. They would call us names like "hillbilly" or "briarhopper." Lookin' at us [we] did not look a bit different. Maybe. ... No, we didn't look any different. We were shy The kids up here were so wild and loud ... And full of confidence, seemed like. I think it's bullyness's what they was full of, you know. But I remember wishin' I had some of that ...

It was weeks and weeks I'd go home almost every day cryin' because one of 'em would call me a hillbilly. I don't know why that hurt my feelings so bad but I knew it was an insult. One of them would pull my hair or they'd run up and hit me and run you know—those kinds of things. (p. 113)

Stereotypes die hard. Despite years of living in northern cities, urban Appalachian children continue to face discrimination based on stereotypic notions of who they are. Klein (1995) reported that when she asked educators and human service professional in several northern cities who Appalachians were, their responses typically were based in derogatory stereotypes such as the following: "poor Whites from the south," "hillbillies," "briars," "I think they beat their kids" (p. 12). In a study that explored teachers' attitudes toward urban Appalachian families, Starnes (1990) found teachers' stereotypic attitudes toward Appalachian culture negatively influenced their teaching strategies and communication with these families. When educators hold negative perceptions about a particular group of people, their expectations for school success are clearly communicated to the children through their daily classroom interactions and practices.

CHILDREN OF POVERTY

Both rural and urban Appalachians have struggled to provide for their families throughout their long history in the United States. Many urban Appalachians who have become permanent residents of inner-city neighborhoods continue to live in poverty. McCoy, Trevino, and McCoy (1994) reported that research shows that urban Appalachians' occupational status is lower than that of other groups, either other migrants or natives, and that they are concentrated in unskilled or semiskilled jobs with few holding professional or managerial positions. In their own study of urban Appalachians, these researchers found occupational patterns similar to those in previous literature. They reported that:

The pattern of stratification as shown by income and occupation data reveals a lower level than in the general population of cities such as Cincinnati. A great number of Appalachians hold blue-collar jobs; a greater number maintain traditional jobs, working at home; fewer Appalachians hold white-collar jobs. Between 1962 and 1982, migrants became even more entrenched in the blue-collar work force. (p. 45)

For years, sociologists have examined the relationship between social-class background and educational attainment and found that the most powerful predictor of educational level is the social class background of parents as measured by income level, occupation, and education (deMarrais & LeCompte, 1995). Whereas quantitative studies found students' standardized achievement test scores were stratified by social class, qualitative studies explored the relationship between teachers' perceptions and their placement of children into ability groups or academic tracks. deMarrais and LeCompte (1995) summarized this research:

> In the 1970s a strong interest in microlevel observation of classroom interaction developed. This work began to demonstrate how profoundly social class affects the placement of children in ability groups, because it showed the extent to which teachers grouped students on the basis of their perceptions of how able students are, rather than entirely on the basis of assessed competence. These perceptions are based on daily interactions with others and negotiations with teachers and are complicated by children's gender and cultural identities. Because lower-class children often lack the cultural capital congruent with school life, they are judged to be less able. Teachers classified children who were clean, were quiet, and acted respectfully as brighter. Teachers also tended to favor children who shared their own values, regardless of the student's measured ability. Sometimes teachers were notably poor judges of actual ability. They also had difficulty giving failing grades to students they liked. Unfortunately, since most teachers either were born into or have acquired the cultural capital, habits, or aspirations of the middle class, they now find many students in their classrooms who do not share their values. (p. 186)

In the following account (deMarrais & LeCompte, 1995), Jean, a rural Appalachian woman, explained how poverty and her Appalachian cultural capital conflicted with school values and practices:

> People of rural Appalachia have been discriminated against for decades. I am one of these people. There is a distance between the poor Whites and upper class Whites that exists even today. As a child I knew these differences existed, but it was not until I started to school that I learned I was different. I lived in a rural area with no other children to identify with. Going to school in town, the only school in town, was a big step for me. There I learned about culture. Culture, I gathered, was something only the rich could attain or had a right to. I had a culture all my own but did not know this. My culture was not respected by my teachers or peers. Maybe they did not know that I lived in abject poverty not more than ten miles from the school. Maybe they did, but instead of bringing my family's lifestyle to light, I believe now that I was deculturalized. Soon, I began to fit the mold, or tried to, although I never did. I had very few friends throughout school who understood my way of life. I could not have friends home from school to sleep over. I could not ask them to sleep in a cold house or to eat what food we had—food they were not used to like fried potatoes, gravy, and biscuits, when we were out of other staples such as beans and meat. I cannot deny that living in poverty has left its scars on me. (p. 245)

As we can see from this discussion, social-class background and cultural capital are inextricably linked and can result in unfortunate school experiences and lack of educational attainment for Appalachian children. I turn next to an examination of specific aspects of Appalachian culture and ways they conflict with school values and practices.

CULTURAL DIFFERENCES AND SCHOOL STRUCTURES

In my own ethnographic study in a public school in an inner-city Appalachian neighborhood, the district supervisor described the area as one of "poverty, high crime, child abuse, and despair" (Bennett, 1991). Educators see urban Appalachian children in inner-city neighborhoods as poor, but not necessarily as a distinct cultural group. They are often unaware of the language, values, and traditions that are distinctly Appalachian, and so cannot use this knowledge to develop school programs and practices that better meet the needs of urban Appalachian students.

Although Appalachians value self-reliance and independence, a key Appalachian value is a strong sense of kinship with both the family and the community. Jack Weller in *Yesterday's People* (1965) describes this strong sense of community relationships:

> He wants to be liked, accepted, and noticed, and he will respond in kind to such attention. He is reluctant to separate himself from any group in which he finds this acceptance. His life goals are always achieved in relation to other persons and are a product of participation in the group. Without such a group, the goals cannot be achieved. (p. 50)

Appalachian cultural identity is grounded in a sense of belonging in both the family and the community. Relationships with others and a sense of responsibility to the group are of primary importance in this culture. These values and daily practices are in direct conflict with urban school bureaucracies where children are sorted into large, formal classrooms by age, and often by ability level. With large class sizes and limited resources, teachers in inner-city schools have little time to develop the informal relationships essential to the success of urban Appalachian children. Personal relationships with children and families are not part of the structure of schools for urban Appalachians. Consequently, Appalachian parents and children are not comfortable in schools and feel they are not able to communicate with school personnel. Obermiller and Maloney (1994) reported that school administrators blame absenteeism and parental lack of interest in education for high dropout rates. They argued that Appalachian families view schools as "large, impersonal bureaucracies with little cultural sensitivity" (p. 8).

This absenteeism issue is an interesting one in relation to the way educators view Appalachian families. Family relationships come before anything else, so when the children are needed or wanted at home, family activities take precedence over school attendance. In first- and second-generation urban Appalachian families and in many of these families still today, ties to family at "home" in rural Appalachia play a significant role in family life. Trips back to see the family take precedence over school attendance and can result in what teachers and administrators view as "excessive" absences. School personnel may interpret this as a lack of interest in education on the part of urban Appalachian families. From the perspective of these families, they are certainly interested in their children's education, but tend to judge family to be more important.

Language differences are another place where conflicts between school and home cultures become highlighted. Language is a central aspect of the cultural capital described previously. Urban Appalachian children often come to school with distinct dialects that are not valued by educators and are perceived to be inferior to the "standard" or formal English expected by schools. Children with dialectical differences are often viewed by teachers as having less ability or intellect than those whose speech more closely resembles middle-class or school English. These children are more likely to be placed in lower ability groups and tracks in schools.

Not only can dialectical differences between school and home language lead to misperceptions, they can be detrimental for young children in learning to read and write. In my study of ability-grouped reading instruction in an inner-city Appalachian first grade (Bennett, 1991), I found the formal philosophy of the district espoused a concern for the needs of culturally different and economically disadvantaged children. The district's curriculum guides expected teachers to use "the pupil's particular language pattern as a powerful motivator for learning." These written guidelines emphasized the necessity to use the natural language patterns and life experiences of culturally different children. However, at the same time, the district mandated teachers to use a particular set of basal reading materials that utilized ability-grouped reading instruction and formal scripted lessons where there was no place for the natural language of children. The reading materials used controlled vocabulary in rather boring short stories that had little relationship to the lived experiences of these students. Children, particularly those at beginning reading levels, participated very little in real reading. Instead, they used isolated sounds and skills in a heavy focus on phonetic instruction.

This type of formal instruction placed children with Appalachian dialects at a distinct disadvantage. Children, unable to use their language strengths in reading and writing instruction, were actually forced to learn a new dialect in order to break the reading code. For example, in Appalachian dialect, the vowel sounds short *i* and short *e* as in the words pin and pen are quite similar to one another. A heavy phonics emphasis focused on vowel sound discrimination at the first and second grades puts these children at a severe disadvantage. At the end of the year, only 10 of the 31 children I studied were considered to be "on grade level." Four of the children were retained in first grade, one was assigned to a special education classroom, and of the other 26 students who were promoted to second grade, half were placed in groups that would continue to use first-grade reading books for instruction. I have no doubt that Jenny, who offered the following account, went through school in a similar system. Jenny, an urban Appalachian woman, poignantly described her experiences in finally learning to read as an adult to Victoria Purcell-Gates (1993):

> It's hard not knowin' how to read. A lot of these women, you know, they think it ain't that hard to read. Just sit down and read .... It's not easy. ... That's why it was a little hard for me startin' to like ... sound my words out ... 'cause I talk different ... 'cause I'm, you know ... countrified. And my words don't come out the way they're supposed to. (p. 211)

Clearly, there is a need to take seriously the educational achievement of urban Appalachian students. I provide one last story as a way to introduce some strategies we might explore to transform educational experiences for urban Appalachian students. This story illustrates the struggles of one young man, Les, who went through 12 years of school and actually graduated without accomplishing the basic academic skills we would expect of a second grader. It portrays the misunderstandings and miscommunications that led to educational failure for Les. I include this account as an example of the disjunctures between the needs of Appalachian students and the structures and practices of schooling. However, within Les' story, we can see places where his experiences might have been interrupted with more positive, successful ones.

The following account is taken from an oral history interview as part of a study (Center for Literacy Studies, 1992) that explored the lives of Appalachian adults with limited literacy skills. In this part of the interview,

Les described his educational history beginning with his experiences in a rural elementary school and then when his family moved to Knoxville, an urban center in Appalachia.

Les remembered doing well throughout the elementary grades: "I was making A's and B's all the way up to the sixth grade." Then, a pivotal incident occurred in sixth grade when one of his teachers would not help Les with his math assignments. He recalls:

> I couldn't do the math and she grabbed the math book and started hittin' me in the head with it and I said, "Well, I'm not doin' this math" and she said, "Fine!" From then on I quit tryin'. That's the only thing I remember (Center for Literacy Studies, 1992, pp. 59–61).

The rest of Les' educational history is best told in his own words:

> I quit school down in Riceville [in sixth grade] and moved back to Knoxville. My mother and my older brother made me go back to school and they took me up Carter High School and I enrolled in the seventh grade there. About a week and the following Monday they come to me and said I was too old to be in the seventh grade .... I was 16. I come back to Knoxville when I was 16 years old. They said I was too old to be in the seventh grade, so they moved me up to the ninth grade and that's the only reason. They didn't give me no other reason why. ... I went a half a year and again they come to me and told me I was too old. ... One of my teachers come to me and told me I was too old for the ninth grade and I was in vocational rehab and they moved me up to the 10th grade ... So I finished that half of the year out in 10th grade. The next year I graduated to the 11th and I done half of that year and again they come to me [and moved him to the 12th grade].

> It was goin' kinda fast seemed like to me. I didn't see why they were movin' me up like that 'cause there was a lot of 'em in there 17 and 18-year-old and they wasn't movin' them up. ... I don't understand why they did it. You go to 'em to try to get 'em [teachers] to give you some help and they say, "Go back there and try to figure it out."

> And when they moved me up to the 12th grade and I finished it out and they told me, says, We'll mail you your diploma. I said, "Can't I go through the line-up?" And she said, "No. We'll just have to mail you your diploma."

> They [his teachers] wouldn't try to help you. ... Mostly you sit at your desk and do nothin'. You wouldn't do no work. It wasn't learnin'. It was a story.

Despite this rather grim picture of school, Les remembered one teacher who he described as a "good teacher":

There was one teacher that did [try to help]. Shop teacher. He got in there with you and showed you how to do things but the teacher in the class, I only had one class, all she done was sit up and read a book.

Les seemed to learn best when someone demonstrated for him rather than explained it without a demonstration. Traditional models of schooling in which teachers lecture and give assignments to students obviously did not work with Les. "You show me one time and you won't have to show me nothin' else. ... Anything I start, even though I don't know how to do it or can't read it ... it will be done!" (Center for Literacy Studies, 1992, pp. 59–61).

HOW CAN WE TRANSFORM SCHOOLS TO FIT THE URBAN APPALACHIAN COMMUNITY?

It seems we can learn much about schooling for Appalachian families from the stories of Gertie, Evelyn, Jean, and Les shared in these pages. We know that for schooling to be most beneficial to students such as these, the school must find its place within the community—it must become a part of the community rather than an uninviting bureaucracy.

When I bought my farm in East Tennessee in the early 1990s, Dewey, the owner of the property, was very concerned that whoever he sold it to would be a family who would "fit into the community." After several full days of talking with him and his family over the course of a month or so, my husband and I were able to establish a personal relationship with him. He was able to assess our "fit" and agreed to sell us the farm. He explained that he wanted to be sure we would become part of the community. In thinking about this process in relation to the fit between urban Appalachian communities and the public schools housed in those neighborhoods, we might consider what schools would be like if they had to prove their fit in a similar manner. For years, urban Appalachians have been force fit into rigid school structures and practices. As we have seen, the result has not been overwhelmingly beneficial to these families. If we were to turn the process around and fit the school into the inner-city Appalachian community, what would schools and classrooms be like?

From the stories recounted earlier, we know that, first and foremost, positive and personal relationships between teachers, administrators, and families are essential. Many urban Appalachians have had neither successful nor positive experiences in northern schools. Due to past poor relationships between urban Appalachians and school personnel, families tend to distrust teachers and administrators. For a better community fit, school personnel need to reach out in personal ways to the community to break down these barriers between schools and families. In contrast to current city schools, neighborhood schools and small classrooms that are more inviting to children and families would be a start. Research indicates that the bigger the school, the higher the dropout rates, especially for minority students (Turner, 1989). Teachers in small community schools working with children over longer periods of time can get to know their students and respond to their needs more quickly. It is more difficult to lose students when the bureaucracy is small. Deborah Meier, codirector of Central Park East Secondary School, explained: "Most human beings need to be known, and it is more critical when other things are also fragile. Kids are dying in these large schools" (National Center for Restructuring Education, 1994, p. 4).

In addition to small size, schools and classrooms need to be built on the principles that support individual growth and development. Rather than batch-processing children by age levels and perceived ability levels, why not use multi-age classrooms that reflect the family structures within the community? Appalachian children are responsible for household chores and for the care of their siblings at very young ages. A multi-age classroom where children are actively engaged in a variety of active learning experiences would enable children to help one another and work collaboratively with one another as the teacher facilitates their growth. A multi-age structure where teachers or teams of teachers could work with the same children for several years could help develop long-lasting, personal relationships with the children and their families. Teachers would then have opportunities to get to know individual children and their siblings, and to engage parents in ways that supported educational growth.

Another requirement for the school to fit into the community would be an examination of school schedules and calendars. Most districts, particularly in urban areas, have rigid schedules within the school day that have little relationship to students' academic needs. Even at elementary school levels, these schedules are based on the delivery of discreet subject matter in short periods where teachers attempt to pour content into students rather than have them explore it in more meaningful ways. Fifty-minute periods are inappropriate for students whose academic success requires building personal relationships with teachers and active involvement with learning materials. They are also inadequate for any meaningful, in-depth academic learning to occur.

In addition to daily schedules, the school calendar is based on early labor market needs when students were needed to help with farm work during long summer months. How might the school calendar be organized to better fit into current needs of urban Appalachian families? In order to know this, school personnel need to involve families in authentic decision making that is based in community needs and practices. Real reform efforts where teachers and families participate with administrators in making school policy is necessary for better relationships in these urban communities. When students and their families sense that their voices are heard, they are more likely to be participants in their own schooling.

Obermiller, Borman, and Kroger (1988) provided a model of community-based schooling for adult education that may help us to visualize what could work for K–12 schooling. Lower Price Hill, an inner-city Appalachian neighborhood in Cincinnati, is the site of Lower Price Hill Community School, founded in 1972 by neighborhood residents. It is a one-room school that offers basic literacy and high school equivalency programs, and has a two-year satellite college program offered as a project of a local university. A board consisting primarily of neighborhood residents and graduates of its programs is responsible for overseeing the work of the school and for ensuring enough funds are raised to support it. Learning is accomplished in an informal, comfortable environment that resembles a family. Student attendance is voluntary. Personalized recruitment of students, understanding and respect for students' cultural backgrounds, and individualized instruction all combine to meet the needs of the students in this community school. In addition to academic offerings, the school serves as a community center where meals, nutrition classes, and child-care services are regular activities. The authors described the school as a community center:

> The school's role as a social hub reflects the students' view of their lives as a web of interconnected concerns and responsibilities. Neighborhood life is not easily divided into separate categories of public and personal issue. The school makes learning more accessible by integrating it with meals, child care, and opportunities to relax, socialize, and discuss mutual concerns. This is a logical extension of the homelike physical environment the school cultivates. (p. 130)

The Lower Price Hill School, now into its third decade of work within this inner-city Appalachian neighborhood, provides clear, simple guidelines for ways K–12 public schooling might be structured for Appalachian students.

TEACHING, TEACHER EDUCATION, AND CLASSROOM PEDAGOGY

Given these structural changes, what would teachers and teaching be like if they were to fit the needs of inner-city Appalachian youth? It seems as though the teachers in many of the stories recounted in this chapter were insensitive or unkind to culturally different children. We prefer to think most teachers are well-meaning professionals who do the best they can, given both their education and the circumstances in which they find themselves. We need to remember that many of these teachers work in difficult school environments with little power within urban bureaucracies to provide more appropriate schooling for children. As we are so powerfully reminded in the work of Jonathan Kozol (1991), social-class backgrounds of students are often replicated in the schools they attend. Consequently, teachers in inner-city Appalachian neighborhoods work in overcrowded classroom with inadequate resources with little control over their own work lives. They may have minimal support from administrators or central office personnel and often do not have a sociocultural knowledge base from their teacher education programs that would support their work with children who are culturally different.

For teachers to better meet the needs of urban Appalachian youth, they might first become knowledgeable about the history and culture of Appalachian people. In addition to the academic literature available, there are wonderful Appalachian novels available for adults and children that provide rich and moving portraits of the strengths of Appalachian culture. Becoming engaged in this literature will undoubtedly enrich educators' knowledge base and destroy some of the stereotypes and misperceptions they may hold of Appalachian families and communities. It is not necessary to specifically teach about Appalachian culture in schools, although it may be appropriate at times. However, it is important for teachers to have an understanding of the children and communities in which they work as well as the changes in the culture within the communities over time. Obermiller, Borman, and Kroger (1988) described the position taken by teachers in the Lower Price Hill Community School:

> [T]he school does not objectify Appalachian culture; no effort is made to teach about Appalachia as such. Rather, a subtle understanding of what it means to be Appalachian infuses everything done at the school. It is a subject freely spoken about but not artificially inserted in the learning process. Appalachian consciousness grows among the students along with their understanding of grammar and their ability in math. (p. 129)

In considering appropriate pedagogical practices for urban Appalachian youth, we find Les' story of his shop teacher illustrates a core principle—that of being shown; learning by doing and becoming actively engaged in hands-on activities. Les' teacher "got in there with you and showed you how to do things." He was able to be successful when he felt the teacher was right there with him engaging him actively in the learning process. What Les is describing is what educators should know from current research. Whole-language processes that utilize children's own language strengths in emergent literacy programs, curricula that begin with students' prior knowledge and is integrated across content areas, and project-centered learning are all appropriate educational practices for inner-city Appalachian children. Like Les, children need to feel that teachers are "right in there with them."

Urban Appalachian children, like most children across cultural groups, begin school eager to learn. Five- and 6-year-old children have no reason to believe they will not learn or be treated any differently by teachers than they are by their parents. They are fully participating members of their families where they share language, behaviors, and norms. From a 5-year-old's perspective, it would seem that these expectations would extend into the kindergarten classroom. However, because of school structures and practices, as well as the beliefs of some teachers, these young children find themselves in places that are not comfortable and conducive to learning. They recognize, maybe for the first time in their lives, that their language is not understood by others or that they are considered different—an uncomfortable kind of different. Teachers correct their language and behaviors for more appropriate school behaviors and begin to construct identities of these children as less able than their mainstream peers. Children learn early and clearly where they stand in the hierarchy of schooling.

Are urban Appalachian children really invisible to teachers and administrators in city schools? Yes, in that educators do not recognize them as a unique cultural group and are unaware of the history and culture these children bring to school. Yes, in that urban Appalachians continue to suffer discrimination based on hurtful stereotypes. Yes, in that this particular group of inner-city children continues to lag far behind mainstream European American students on all measures of educational attainment. Yes, in that these children attend city schools that are often crowded, underfunded, and ill equipped. Urban Appalachians are not invisible to one another. Do they need to be invisible to educators? Recognition of urban

Appalachian ethnicity is a beginning step for educators as they work to develop schools that truly fit into the community to meet the educational needs of urban Appalachian children.

REFERENCES

Arnow, H. (1954). *The dollmaker.* New York: Macmillan.

Bennett, K. P. (1991). Doing school in an urban Appalachian first grade. In C. Sleeter (Ed.), *Empowerment through multicultural education* (pp. 27–47). Albany, NY: SUNY.

Borman, K. (1991). *Urban Appalachian children and youth at risk.* Cincinnati: University of Cincinnati.

Campbell, J. C. (1969). *The Southern highlander and his homeland.* Lexington, KY: University Press of Kentucky. (Original work published in 1921)

Center for Literacy Studies, University of Tennessee, Knoxville. (1992). *Life at the margins: Profiles of adults with low literacy skills.* U.S. Congress Office of Technology Assessment, Contract #3.5365.0. Washington, DC: National Technical Information Service.

deMarrais, K. & LeCompte, M. D. (1995). *The way schools work: A sociological analysis of education.* NY: Longman.

Ergood, B. & Kuhre, B. E. (Eds.). (1991). *Appalachia: Social context past and present* (3rd edition). Dubuque, IA: Kendall/Hunt.

Jones, L. (1987). Appalachian values. In R. J. Higgs & A. N. Manning (Eds.), *Voices from the hills: Selected readings of Southern Appalachia* (pp. 507–517). NY: Frederick Unger. (Original work published in 1975)

Klein, H. A. (1995). Urban Appalachian children in northern schools: A study in diversity. *Young Children,* 10–16.

Kozol, J. (1991). *Savage Inequalities: Children in America's Schools.* New York: Crown.

McCoy, H. V., Trevino, D. G., & McCoy, C. B. (1994). Appalachian women: Between two cultures. In K. M. Borman & P. J. Obermiller (Eds.), *From Mountain to metropolis: Appalachian migrants in American cities* (pp. 33–48). Westport, CN: Bergin & Garvey.

National Center for Restructuring Education. (1994). *Schools and teaching newsletter.*

Obermiller, P. J., Borman, K. M., & Kroger, J. A. (1988). The Lower Price Hill Community School: Strategies for social change from an Appalachian street academy. *Urban Education, 23*(2), 123–132.

Obermiller, P. J., & Maloney, M. E. (1994). Living city, feeling country. In K. M. Borman & P. J. Obermiller (Eds.), *From mountain to metropolis: Appalachian migrants in American cities* (pp. 3–12). Westport, CN: Bergin & Garvey.

Obermiller, P. J. & Oldendick, R. W. (1989). Urban Appalachian health concerns. In *Health in Appalachia: Proceedings of the 1988 University of Kentucky Conference on Appalachia.* Lexington, KY: Appalachian Center.

People's Appalachian Research Collective. (1991). Why study Appalachia. In B. Ergood & B. E. Kuhre (Eds.), *Appalachia: Social context past and present.* (3rd ed., pp. 3–7). Dubuque, IA: Kendall Hunt.

Philliber, W. W., & McCoy, C. B. (1981). *The invisible minority: Urban Appalachians.* Lexington: University Press of Kentucky.

Purcell-Gates, V. (November, 1993). "I ain't never read my own words before." *Journal of Reading, 37*(3), 210–219.

Raitz, K. B., & Ulack, R. (1991). Regional definitions. In B. Ergood and B. E. Kuhre (Eds.), *Appalachia: Social context past and present.* (3rd ed., pp. 10–26). Dubuque, IA: Kendall Hunt.

Starnes, B. (1990). Appalachian students, parents and culture as viewed by their teachers. *Urban Appalachian Advocate, 1,* 1–4.

Sullivan, M., & Miller, D. (1990). Cincinnati's urban Appalachian council and Appalachian identity. *Harvard Educational Review, 60,* 1, 106–24.

Tickamyer, A. R., & Tickamyer, C. (March, 1987). *Poverty in Appalachia* (Appalachian Data Bank Report #5). Lexington, KY: Appalachian Center, University of Kentucky.

Turner, R. L. (1989). *Organizational size effects at different levels of schooling.* Paper presented at the meeting of the American Educational Research Association, New Orleans.

Urban Appalachian Council. (1985). *Urban Appalachian fact sheet.* Cincinnati, HO: Urban Appalachian Council.

Weller, J. (1965). *Yesterday's people: Life in contemporary Appalachia.* Lexington: University of Kentucky Press.

Young, A. J. (Ed.). (1991). *Rural education: Issues and practice.* New York: Garland.

6

Traditional Stories of Female Students in an Alternative School

❧ ◆ ❧

Linda Steet
The University of Michigan–Flint

For a little over a year I worked as a volunteer at an alternative public high school for adjudicated teens. My association with the school included teaching a weekly class on popular culture to 12 girls, organizing educational outings with the girls, consulting with the school's director on gender issues, and developing a school/university student mentoring project. This association, with its range of activities, was also an opportunity to carry out qualitative research in the area of gender, female juvenile delinquency, and education. This chapter is about layers of invisibility in some girls' lives. Here, the aspects I am most concerned with are those related to sex, which play an all too dominant and oppressive role in the girls' lives.

Among the layers of invisibility is one I as a researcher am implicated in producing. I am speaking for them, representing them. I am speaking about them, analyzing them, interpreting them, and choosing which parts of their lives should be examined by us. Both me and my representations of them are visible; they, as actual beings, remain invisible. They are not here speaking for themselves; I am the "authenticating presence" (Alcoff, 1995).

Feminist philosopher Linda Alcoff (1995) argued in her essay "The Problem of Speaking for Others" that

> Persons from dominant groups who speak for others are often treated as authenticating presences that confer legitimacy and credibility on the demands of subjugated speakers; such speaking for others does nothing to disrupt the discursive hierarchies that operate in public spaces. (p. 99)

I agree with Alcoff and recognize that the current crisis of representation is long overdue. But here I am, speaking for others. And the structural features of my carrying out qualitative research and publishing it seem uncomfortably like Trinh's (1989) characterization of anthropology as "mainly a conversation of 'us' with 'us' about 'them'" (p. 65).

So, I have to acknowledge contributing to the invisibility of the girls by representing them here. And while I once found false comfort in thinking, "Well, if I don't tell their stories they won't be heard at all," I no longer do. Nor do I feel any longer that I've taken care of my responsibilities as a critical researcher by pointing out the crucial difference between being and representing or the asymmetric power relationship between me and given research subjects. Qualifiers, caveats, and apologies about research cannot change the fact that I haven't created ways of structuring and presenting this research that actually disrupt existing discursive hierarchies. So, until a concrete move in that direction happens, my representing subjugated others remains problematic.[1]

Another layer of invisibility in the girls' lives is the one that hides the boys and men who oppress and abuse these girls. In educational literature we essentially ignore these males; we have not researched their gendered practices and beliefs. This invisibility is variously tied to sexism, blaming the victim, and, in spite of all the talk, still not having a politics sophisticated enough to account for gender, race, and class.

Many of us educators haven't figured out how to process and respond to what boys and men do to girls, despite the fact that this subject finds space even in mass print media. A *Newsweek* article (Klein, 1996) reported that several studies revealed some disturbing facts:

---

[1]I considered referring to the girls by numbers rather than giving them fictitious names in order to keep their invisibility in sight through the awkwardness of reading about Girl #3 or Girl #6. I decided against ruffling the reader this way because I did not want to suggest that qualitative researchers who create names for their research subjects don't recognize the crisis in representation. There are many examples of critical qualitative research (e.g., Biklen, 1995; Britzman 1991; Fine, 1992; Thompson, 1995; Weis, 1990) directed toward developing better practices.

- Sixty-six percent of all teen mothers surveyed had children by men who were 20 years old or older.
- A 1990 California survey seemed to indicate that the younger the girl, the older the guy. (Among mothers aged 11 to 12, the father was an average 10 years older.)
- A 1992 Washington state study found that 62% of 535 teen mothers had been raped or molested before they became pregnant; the offender's mean age was 27.4 years.

And a *Chicago Tribune* article (Schodolksi, 1996) reported on a controversy in Orange County, California over the growing practice of allowing young girls to marry or live with the men who made them pregnant, instead of prosecuting the adult men for statutory rape or child molestation. The age difference in some of these cases finds 13- to 16-year-old minors marrying men in their 30s.

The older teenage boys and men in these reports and in the stories of the girls at the alternative school remain largely invisible in educational discussions about female juvenile delinquency. Sexual abuse, general sexual mistreatment of girls, and girls' miseducation about their bodies and sexual matters, are intimately connected to many of the problems the girls get into. But these issues are often not given the attention needed to help girls get control of their lives. Instead, we focus on the consequences of this situation and rail about wild girls, children having children, girls in gangs, and so on. We rail, we don't actually deal with girls' lives because they are made invisible. And girls participate in producing this invisibility because they suffer so quietly, and their troubles stay hidden.

Clearly, it is theoretically complex to drive gender through territory sometimes occupied by lower socioeconomic classes or ethnic and racial groups who themselves suffer serious forms of discrimination—but we must. The girls I have worked with are routinely mistreated, psychologically and physically, by boys and men who are victims of systemic oppression themselves, but are also dominant players within gender arrangements that crush girls. And it is this role and its negative consequences to girls that must be made visible. We need to develop a theory and practice that recognizes that gender is a power relation, no matter what the socioeconomic class or cultural group.

Another layer of invisibility in the lives of some girls is tied to their own performances. The girls are invisible because they perform someone else.

Psychologist Mary Pipher (1994) reported that during early clinical work in the 1970s, she taught a sex education class to delinquent teenage girls and was struck by

> how unsophisticated and utterly ignorant they were about sex. They swore like longshoreman, but they knew little about their own bodies, contraception or pregnancy .... The lack of physical information was bad enough. Worse was that these girls didn't have any guidelines for making decisions about sex. They were barely aware of what they were doing and afterward often "forgot" that they had had sex. They didn't know they had the right to make conscious decisions about sex. They didn't know how to say no .... Their experiences had been confused, hurried and impersonal. Intercourse happened to them. Most of them had been coerced into sexual encounters. None had had sex as the result of a conscious choice to share love in a relationship. (pp. 208–209)

Pipher's description of those 13- to 16-year-olds absolutely mirrors the current situation I found teaching a class on popular culture to a group of similarly aged girls at a school for adjudicated teens.

The girls flirt aggressively with males, making comments about physical looks sprinkled with sexually explicit suggestions. They *act* completely confident about initiating advances and at times seem to actually scare some of their male targets. (It is important to note, however, that the girls practice this style of flirtation when they are with at least one other girlfriend; it isn't a game played solo.) The girls share dirty jokes regularly, swear colorfully, and have a full repertoire of meaningful hand gestures. They *appear* to be in control of their sexual lives and aware of their sexual desires and how to satisfy them. They *appear* so, but they are the very same girls Pipher described.

The girls I taught had all been sexually active since between 12 and 13 years of age and had had numerous sex partners. However, none of the girls had ever had an orgasm. They all preferred not to undress completely while having sex (to conceal perceived body flaws), and they explained that men have sexual needs that, if left unattended, cause a painful condition called blue balls. Recounting their first sexual experience, the girls, without exception, described the event as unromantic, painful, regrettable, and a result of pressure (psychological or physical) from older teens or adult men. This information contrasts with the way the girls appear at first glance, the way they perform.

This discrepancy between the girls' performances and what their stories revealed was always there. One way it surfaced made a particular impact on me because of its visual power. I found the girls, in preparation for Valentine's

Day, addressing Valentine cards. I was shocked to see that the cards were the very same kind used by elementary school children—those familiar one-sided, 2 x 3 inch cards that carry pictures and messages such as a child with a bow and arrow who's "Aiming for you, Valentine" or an elephant with the message "I like you a ton, Valentine." Other Valentine cards were from recent Disney films such as "The Little Mermaid" and "Beauty and the Beast." It was when I saw the girls with these cards that I realized what young children they were. Girls who were in legal trouble, sexually active, and, in some cases, mothers were sending the same Valentine cards as elementary school children. The girls are young children, but we see them perform as tough, older girls.

And it was as young children that these girls had their first sexual experiences. One story I heard exemplifies vividly the way the girls generally characterized the "first time." Tina's first sexual experience took place on a bathroom floor at age 12. Her strongest memory of that event is the pain she felt from the jagged floor tile cutting into her back every time the 18-year-old guy pushed against her body as he tried to penetrate her. She remembers thinking: "When will he finally get it in? How many more times will he have to ram me before it's over? ... God, my back was all cut up and bleeding. I don't think I ever noticed what was going on down there." I asked her why she didn't tell the guy about her back and she answered, "I don't know. I think I felt embarrassed or something. I just wanted him to finish."

Such stories are in stark contrast to the girls' surface language and behavior when they're performing. An example of the girls *acting* like savvy, sexually liberated teens occurred during class when we were discussing the predictable gender formula found in fairy tales such as *Snow White, Cinderella*, and *Sleeping Beauty*. I talked about creating alternative fairy tales and suggested we try to rewrite these familiar tales. Amy volunteered to tell an alternative tale, but warned me it might not be exactly what I wanted. This is her alternative *Cinderella* story:

> Cinderella is talking to her fairy godmother and telling her that she can't go to the ball because she just got her period and doesn't have any tampons. The fairy godmother says, "Don't worry, I'll turn this pumpkin into a tampon for you." Then the fairy godmother tells her to be sure to be back by midnight because then everything will turn back to what it was and Cinderella goes to the ball. But at midnight Cinderella isn't back. She doesn't return until like 3:00 in the morning. When she finally gets in the fairy godmother says, "Why are you so late? I told you to be sure to get home by midnight." And Cinderella says, "Oh, you'll never guess who I ran into, Peter Peter Pumpkin Eater." (Personal Communication, April 16, 1996)

Amy may sound like someone who is in charge of her sex life and can hold her own in a relationship with a guy, but she isn't. She has been used and abused more times than she can remember. She has had sex with more than 20 guys and says that if she had it to do over, she'd only sleep with one of them again. She admits the rest were all bad choices and were just using her for sex. She keeps making the same mistakes in her search for love and romance. Amy desperately wants a boyfriend because, "There's nothing worse than being alone on New Year's Eve or not having anyone to think of you on Christmas."

Sex is so much a part of these girls' lives because they don't control it. Others make decisions concerning sex for them. Others have always made these decisions: when and where they will have sex, what sex acts they will do, and if it will be protected sex. None of the girls know sex as something that gives them direct physical pleasure. Any satisfaction comes indirectly from giving men pleasure and being able to provide guys with "what they need." To the agreement of the other girls, Amy said, "I feel really good when a guy is getting off and going all crazy because of me. That's the part about sex I like."

Although the girls have all had several years of sexual experience and many partners, not one expected to be in a relationship where her needs were identified and met. Their knowledge, views, and behaviors concerning sex are very traditional. These are not sexually informed or empowered girls. If they seem (or are) out of control sexually, it is a situation similar to that described by Pipher (1994) of young girls with serious eating disorders who are "oversocialized to the feminine role. They are the ultimate people pleasers" (p. 170). Also, like girls who suffer from bulimia or anorexia, these girls are paying a high price as people pleasers. Among the 12 girls at the alternative school while I worked there, Sherry and Tina were mothers. Tina, then 14, became pregnant with her second child. Crystal and Maria also became pregnant during the school year. Liz, following continued pressure from her boyfriend, reluctantly moved into his apartment. Julie was being medically treated for a sexually transmitted illness, and Gloria was gang raped.

Gloria's rape is a story most of us have heard. She and a girlfriend were drunk when they accepted the invitation of five guys to attend a party at a motel room. Once there, the five pulled Gloria into the bathroom and locked the door. They raped and beat her while her girlfriend pounded helplessly on the bathroom door trying to convince them to let Gloria out. When the guys were done with Gloria, they left. Gloria was afraid to go to the police because she had been drinking and, like the other students at the alternative school, was already in legal trouble. For these same reasons, she also decided not to tell her parents what had happened. (Gloria's bruises were not immediately apparent because of her dark skin color, use of make-up, and clothing choices.) The next day, Gloria, bruised and in pain, attended school. She was obviously in a great deal of discomfort and the school's director knew something was wrong. Gloria broke down crying and told the whole story. The director promised Gloria she'd stand by her and then called her parents and the police. This part of the story is also familiar to us: Gloria knew only the first names of two of the five guys involved in the rape. She and her girlfriend were drunk and willingly went with strangers to a motel room, and she didn't report the rape soon enough for proof to be collected. The police took descriptions of the guys, but were not optimistic about it going anywhere. A "blame the victim" attitude was shared, to varying degrees, by all the authorities involved—school, parental, and police. Gloria's bad judgment was as apparent as the guys were invisible. The more foolish and careless she looked, the more distant the role of the five guys became.

A couple of days after this incident we discussed in class the cultural construction of romance and dating, and how it's used to sell everything from toothpaste to cars. In an attempt to demystify the culture industry's version of "the couple," I asked the girls to identify what important things they got out of their relationships with guys that couldn't be had outside of such relationships. Gloria immediately yelled out, "Sex. We need guys to give us sex. That's why they're important. How else do you expect us to have sex?" Gloria was performing and rendering invisible the girl who was so recently gang raped.

This performance and self-silencing should not be considered a survival strategy because it (unintentionally) secures those gender arrangements that oppress girls and ensures continued invisibility. Linda Brodkey and Michelle Fine (1992) examined how university women produce a mind/body split in their narratives of personal experiences with sexual harassment. They see the women as

> trying to reproduce a version of scientific discourse by positioning themselves as narrators who, having transcended their bodies, are then entitled to use their dispassionate observations as the bases of their clinical explanations of men's motives and cynical speculations on institutional reprisals. (p. 82)

With this mind/body split, the women are offering to pay an impossible price by not problematizing what happened to their bodies and, instead, by attempting a "presence of mind in the absence of body" strategy. Gloria's gang rape, her reluctance to report it, and her self-silencing performances leave her with something even beyond the university women's mind/body split. Gloria produces an absence of mind and absence of body.

Sharon Thompson (1995) said the 1970s saw a gradual increase in the number of girls willing to have sex. Given the new balance in supply and demand, boys no longer had to endure "a certain amount of merging [combining love and sex] in return for sex" (p. 42). "The new script was good for traditional boys but not for girls," Thompson says, as boys raced ahead with sexual triumphs proving their masculinity like nothing else can. And girls, hoping for love and caring, were left behind, setting themselves up for one disappointment after another while waiting for their real prince to arrive.

I would add to this that the quantitative change in the number of sexually active girls has not, for the girls I worked with, produced a qualitative change in their traditional, gendered role. As we have seen, although the girls at the alternative school appear learned in a discourse of desire, they are merely reciting someone else's script. Even speaking about them as sexually active girls doesn't really capture their situation because very different and unequal gender roles are being played. Sexually active boys and sexually active girls are not playing the same game. What these girls experience might better be characterized as sexual *misactivity*. As Thompson (1995) put it, "Gender still loads the dice of difference … sex is too often a danger, too seldom a pleasure" (p. 245).

Michelle Fine (1992) maintained that girls need a sex education curriculum that combines two important aspects, desire and victimization. She pointed out that "the female victim and subject coexist in every woman's body" and critiqued a sex education discourse centered around woman-as-victim, which "may actually disable young women in their negotiations as sexual subjects" and continue to reproduce positions of passivity (pp. 48–49).

This passivity is tied to what philosopher Hilde Lindemann Nelson (1996) contends about girls: They grow up learning "the lesson of cognitive deference" and are "taught to distrust their own judgments in the service of boys and men" (p. 92). Cognitive deference helps explain how girls repeatedly allow others to assume authority over them. The girls at the alternative school have had years of training in underestimating themselves as "moral deliberators" and in depending on dominant men. The girls desperately need a different education. Nelson suggests that this include learning to create a counterstory—a narrative whose aim is to resist and undermine a story of domination. Its teller uses her standpoint as Other to feature certain details and moral ideas the dominant story ignores or underplays, retelling the story in such a way as to invite interpretations and conclusions that are at odds with the ones the dominant story invites. (p. 98)

Creating a counterstory is a process where girls, writing in diaries or in a circle of friends, first learn to read the dominant story, which is a difficult and long process of interpretation (Nelson, 1996). As they develop an understanding, they also begin working on the counterstory and resisting dominant versions. Our public schools must develop intellectual and political space where girls can begin this work and become visible.

I want to conclude this chapter by putting the unmet needs of girls—needs that have long been identified and long been shared by an ever increasing number of girls and by ever younger girls—alongside the needs of another group of students recently highlighted in my local paper. This small example demonstrates how gender determines different educational practices and policies. An article in *The Ann Arbor News* (Mathis, 1997) reported on a proposed program to handle "disruptive students" in Ann Arbor public schools. The recommendation was for a $700,000-a-year plan to respond to the disruptive behavior of elementary students who are "usually boys—who are smart, who are very savvy, and who come to school very needy." This problem, according to the article, has escalated in the last 10 years and is one that ranks "high on the stress scale of district teachers." The suggested plan "incorporates a 'wrap around' concept in which the student and family would be served by an interagency intervention team including representatives from education, mental health, health, social services, family, and community."[2] Disruptive boys are very visible and, therefore, demand attention.

Where is the wrap around concept in our public schools for girls who quietly get pregnant and have babies; for girls who are too ashamed, embarrassed, or afraid to tell their stories; for girls who can't find anyone to listen to their stories; and for girls who don't even think they have stories to tell?

---

[2] I find this proposed plan for "disruptive students" very problematic. However, this isn't the place for my critique of it. I am referring to the plan for the limited purpose of demonstrating gender differences in the identification and treatment of problems in schools.

REFERENCES

Alcoff, L. (1995). The problem of speaking for others. In J. Roof & R. Wiegman (Eds.), *Who can speak? Authority and critical identity* (pp. 97–119). Chicago: University of Illinois Press.

Biklen, S. K. (1995). *School work: Gender and the cultural construction of teaching.* New York: Teachers College Press.

Britzman, D. P. (1991). *Practice makes practice: A critical study of learning to teach.* Albany: State University of New York Press.

Brodkey, L., & Fine, M. (1992). Presence of mind in the absence of body. In M. Fine (Ed.), *Disruptive voices: The possibilities of feminist research* (pp. 77–95). Ann Arbor: University of Michigan Press.

Fine, M. (1992). Sexuality, schooling, and adolescent females: The missing discourse of desire. In M. Fine (Ed.), *Disruptive voices* (pp. 31–59). Ann Arbor: University of Michigan Press.

Klein, J. (1996, April 29). The predator problem. *Newsweek, 32.*

Mathis, J. C. (1997, February 27). Schools consider program for disruptive students. *The Ann Arbor News,* pp. A1, A9.

Nelson, H. L. (1996, Winter). Sophie doesn't: Families and counterstories of self-trust. *Hypatia, A Journal of Feminist Philosophy, 11*(1), 91–104.

Pipher, M. (1994). *Reviving Ophelia: Saving the selves of adolescent girls.* New York: Ballantine Books.

Schodolski, V. (1996, September 12). Marriages of pregnant teenagers being criticized as child abuse. *Chicago Tribune,* 1.

Thompson, S. (1995). *Going all the way: Teenage girls' tales of sex, romance, and pregnancy.* New York: Hill & Wang.

Trinh, T. Minh-ha. (1989). *Woman, native, other: Writing postcoloniality and feminism.* Bloomington: Indiana University Press.

Weis, L. (1990). *Working class without work: High school students in a de-industrializing economy.* New York: Routledge.

7

"Before Their Time:" Social Age, Sexuality, and School-Aged Mothers

❧ • ❧

Nancy Lesko
Indiana University–Bloomington

Representations of teenage mothers abound, and they are generally dense webs of significations. For example, the New Right portrays young mothers as immoral social problems who cause family deterioration, a portrait that draws heavily on familial and reproductive ideologies (Coontz, 1992; Luker, 1996; Murcott, 1980). From a deconstructive angle, feminist analyses emphasize the gender, race, and social class dimensions of sexual activeness, birth control, abortion, and keeping a baby (Eisenstein, 1994; Kunzel, 1993; Lesko, 1995; Solinger, 1992). The problem of teenage pregnancy has been described as a moral panic (Murcott, 1980) and a keyword of the United States welfare state (Fraser & Gordon, 1994). Indeed; teenage pregnancy approaches an "epidemic of signification" (Treichler, 1987).

In general, educators have not focused on this population of students (see Lesko, 1995). Although highly visible in the last decade in United States society and politics, school-aged mothers have remained marginal to educational discourses of curriculum, school reform, and pedagogy. The empirical research on school-aged mothers has primarily sprung up in fields such as medicine, social work, psychology, and history. Thus, I characterize school-aged mothers as a largely invisible group for educators.

In this essay, I examine the marginalized presence of teenage mothers in educational discussions by scrutinizing normative age chronologies in both theories and institutionalized practices. I examine normative coming-of-age scripts utilizing Homi Bhabha's (1995) concept of the disjunctive present—a time that emphasizes contingency and the possibilities of the indeterminate. The concept of a disjunctive present prompts us to examine the staging and timing of social order, and here that means investigating the life scripts of youth. The concepts of the disjunctive present and normative age chronologies allow us to reflect on how our theories and school practices promote and maintain socially young adolescents. When we maintain "socially young" teenagers, their sexuality is thereby staged as a "shock" and pregnancy as a terrible, inconceivable blow to our views of them. From the vantage point of the disjunctive present and feminist political theory, I argue that our marginalization of school-aged mothers is emblematic of our denial of sexuality among youth and our marginalization of sex education in schools. In order to see teenage mothers in different ways, we need to add a sense of contingency to coming-of-age narratives via a concept of social age. The concepts of social age and reproductive rights to sex education make school-aged mothers visible to us as figures of both necessary change and hope.

MODERNITY, FUTURE-DRIVE, AND THE DISJUNCTIVE PRESENT

Homi Bhabha (1995) interrogates the temporal ordering of modernity, and his work situates the future-directed order of schools within a larger critique of modernity. When the view of modernity as progress (with its negative ontologies of "lack" or "excess") is halted, as it is in the problem of teenage pregnancy—a problem that "rends the social fabric" ("Children," 1985)—the production of modernity as forward movement is visible. Bhabha theorizes that in such situations, binarisms of past/present are decoupled. "The linear, progressive time of modernity" reveals its construction, its necessary terms, and structures (p. 58). When the past/present dialectic of modernity (that is, the dynamic that we in the present are advancing and are more advanced than those in the past) is brought to a standstill, the "temporal action of modernity, its progressive future drive" is temporarily halted (Bhabha, 1995, p. 58). Bhabha identifies this temporal lag—the unmasking of the constant drive toward the future and the interpretations of past and present tied to that future drive—as a "disjunctive present" when the past, rather than being speedily surpassed, is "sutured to the present." Thus, the disjunctive present is produced through an accidental bumping up and overlapping of past and present, terms usually set as binary opposites, kept separate and hierarchically ranked. "This lagged temporality ... is a mode of breaking the complicity of past and present to open up a space of revision and initiation" (Bhabha, 1995, p. 59). To view life as uncertain, as contingent — rather than through the veil of progress in which the future is deemed to be brighter as we work our way "forward" — opens possibilities. Bhabha (1995) marks this contingency as positive: "Indeterminism is the mark of the conflictual yet productive space in which the arbitrariness of the sign of cultural signification emerges within the regulated boundaries of social discourse" (p. 48).

I am utilizing Bhabha's theorizing as a way to emphasize the problem of school-aged mothers as a disjunctive moment, a moment when conceptions of adolescence and youth are revealed as "staged" or produced. Adolescence is a thoroughly modern concept, imbued with the dynamics of past/present, as youth point unflaggingly to the future. Youth are invariably talked about as *our* future.

Adolescence is an Emblem of Modernity, and Time is its Defining Mode

In my view, adolescence enacts modernity in its central characterization as *developing* or becoming[1]; youth cannot live in the present, they live in the future, that is, they exist only in the discourse of "growing up" (Graff, 1996). Adolescence reenacts the evolutionary supremacy of the West over primitive others in its psychologized internal progress from (primitive) concrete operational stages to (advanced) abstract ones. Adolescence continuously enacts Western progress carried in the oppositional positions of past and present, and ever points toward even greater futures.

Central to successive psychological prescriptions for adolescence to lead to proper human development and the progress of the race was the postponement of sex, for unrestrained sexuality was the hallmark of "savages"

---

[1]I have argued elsewhere (Lesko, 1996) that G. Stanley Hall's invention of adolescence in the early 1900s took colonialist dichotomies of civilized/savage, White/Black, progress/stagnation, and the obsession with threats to progress (decadence and unmanly men and middle-class White women who prioritized careers over motherhood) to produce an object that both exemplified the problems of development and held out hope for the proper socialization of the next generation.

(Ross, 1972, 1984). Teenage pregnancy and motherhood call into question the future drive and the present-is-better ideology. When New Right critics label school-aged mothers as the source of family and social deterioration, these mothers are positioned as backward, both individually and as signs of the social fate. The future of sleek technological progress on the information superhighway and in the global economy is disrupted by images of young pregnant women. The individual citizenry progress from education to work to stable family life is disturbed. This disturbance allows us to examine the staging of the progress and upon what bodies the progress works. Thus, teenage mothers are a disjunctive moment that focuses us on the present and offers us the possibility to think differently about the relationships of past, present, and future. Instead of linked in a unilinear future-centered drive, in which adolescent bodies are produced for the good of the future, we may be able to contemplate youth and time in alternative arrangements.

THE TIME OF ADOLESCENCE

Age and normative life chronology are central in the linguistic and visual representations of school-aged mothers: Teenage mothers are "children having children"[2] and mothers "before their time."[3] Thus, integral to depictions of teenage mothers as social problems is their violation of normative chronology. Annette Lawson (1993) explains:

> The overwhelming hegemonic ideal orders events much as follows: childhood and education, work and sexual experimentation …marriage and children ….The very young mother is deviant by virtue of her obvious rebellion against the proper chronology of events as she flaunts her out-of-time acts. (pp. 111-112)

The moral panic over teenage mothers is aroused, in part, by the

---

[2]This phrase is synonymous with the 1980s depiction of the problem of teenage pregnancy, and varies from earlier language of unwed mothers. The headline for the December 9, 1985, cover story in *Time* magazine was "Children Having Children." The Children's Defense Fund (1985) used this phrase as the title of one of their early booklets, *Preventing Children Having Children*. Leon Dash, a journalist, published *When Children Want Children* in 1989.

[3]The phrase "before their time" is not as frequently invoked, but does appear often as a shorthand phrase for teenage mothers. For example, see J. Sander (1991).

disorderly, out-of-time acts.[4] Lawson's analysis supports the importance of temporal (dis)ordering in the problem of teenage pregnancy and motherhood, which is in keeping with Bhabha's concept of disjunctive time.

Another aspect of the disjuncture of teenage pregnancy is the sexuality of girls and young women. Children have been defined as pure and nonsexual (Foucault, 1976; Kincaid, 1992), and part of the political force of the term "children having children" is the juxtaposition of children with sexuality and child-bearing. The time of childhood and young adults is meant to be asexual. The pregnancy of a 15- or 16-year-old flies in the face of such deeply entrenched beliefs, and news magazines have regularly featured photos of young faced girls with swollen bellies to emphasize the out-of-time acts.

Bakhtin's study (as cited in Holquist, 1990) of the relation between chronology and plot in different narrative genres is useful to point out how time/event are related. Holquist (1990) explains that "there is no purely chronological sequence inside or outside the text" (p. 116). Holquist links Bakhtin's work with Einsteinian ideas about the inseparability of time and event:

> An event ... is always a dialogic unit in so far as it is a *co*-relation: something happens only when something else with which it can be compared reveals a change in time and space ....[E]*verything will depend on how the relations between what happens and its situation in time/space is mediated* [emphasis added]. (p. 116)

From this perspective, the meaning of an event resides in the process of comparison with another event and its time/space location. Thus, teenage pregnancy or children having children is implicitly compared with orderly childbearing, once schooling is finished, employment secured, and a marriage consummated.

---

[4]The voluminous research on teenage pregnancy and motherhood, much of which begins with an assumption that school-aged mothers are problems, enacts a critique based on out-of-time perspectives. First, teenage mothers are likely to be bad mothers (thus contributing to the New Right discourse on family deterioration), they are irresponsible (which connects to a failure to have hope for a bright future), and they are likely to become and remain dependent on the state (Lesko, 1995). The "out-of-time" dimension plays in each of these domains: They're too young to be good mothers (still children themselves); they are emotionally disordered in failing to believe ideologies of progress and ability to succeed if they try hard enough; and by not completing their education and entering the workforce before having children (or, failing that, by not marrying), they are plunging themselves into poverty. Sara Ruddick (1993) argues that judgments about untimeliness of teenage motherhood vary with individual and social circumstances.

Some more recent analyses have begun to emphasize the problem of young mothers as poverty rather than age (e.g., Weatherley & Cartoof, 1988). Austin (1989) characterized teenage pregnancy as a failure of the schools, the economy, and the health system to provide education and opportunities for youth.

Historian Harvey Graff (1996) finds that children and youth only exist within the "discourse and experience of growing up" (p. 10), although numerous paths to adulthood exist in different historical periods and among children of different social, racial, and gender groups. Sociologists Allison James and Alan Prout (1990) similarly identify time as central to the construction of childhood and youth, and urge the systematic study of the "temporal underpinnings of different representations of childhood" (p. 217). James and Prout write: "It is during childhood (and old age) that time and perceptions of time have the greatest social significance" (p. 217).

Drawing on the work of Graff and James and Prout to examine childhood and youth critically, we need to extricate them from the discourses of growing up, to re-present children and youth, that is, to consider empirically and theoretically the temporal dimension of childhood. We need to be able to consider children and youth separate from the narratives of growing up and biologically based developmental schemas. Thus, in the terms of this anthology on visible and invisible young people, to make youth differently visible, we need to disrupt the normative narrative of youth with its dominant time/event relation. To begin this task, James and Prout recommend scholarly focus on age-prohibited activities of youth—for example, sex—and transition times. School-aged mothers provide a focus on both the prohibited sexual activity of youth and upon the transition time of teenage motherhood, and, thereby, respond to James and Prout's proposed sociological agenda.

In the next sections, I examine the changes in contemporary life scripts, life chronologies of some teenage mothers, and how they exemplify the concept of "social age."

CONTEMPORARY LIFE SCRIPTS OF YOUTH

In his recent historical work on youths' narratives of growing up, Graff claims there is a compacting of the growing up narrative in the contemporary era, at least for some youth. That is, whereas a series of transition events were once ordained to occur over a number of years, to allow a slow ("developmental") process of maturation, Graff finds that for some contemporary youth, growing up occurs in one event and that fact produces tremors among adults and youth. Concluding from his own work and that of other historians, Graff (1996) finds "an absence of uniformity across a cohort or age grade, and a lack of a lengthy period of postponement or moratorium in youth or adolescence, regardless of theories and expectations to the contrary, which nonetheless retain their force" (p. 333).

The work of sociologist Marlis Buchmann (1989) confirms Graff's view of the variety across life scripts. Her research compares the life events of 1960 and 1980 U.S. high school graduates. According to Buchmann, three transitions have historically marked the move into adulthood; the end of formal schooling (and entrance into the workforce), marriage, and having children,[5] and these occurred in that order. However, in the contemporary United States, adults and youth may be in extended formal schooling together (due to economic uncertainty and job instability), marriage is being replaced with cohabitation and a substantial increase in single adult households, and having children has been decoupled from marriage. Buchmann concludes that her research "suggest[s] a greater complexity and diversity in transition patterns to adulthood" (p. 181). Although socioeconomic position still exerts a strong impact on life chances, Buchmann writes that "the 1980 cohort's orientations and actions show more individually stratified patterns" (p. 184). Traditions and customs constrain her 1980 cohort less, whereas increased standardization (through rationalization and bureaucratic credentialing processes) of public identities works against the individualization:

> More flexible and discontinuous, and increasingly diversified and individualized, life course patterns have been discussed as effects of the mutually reinforcing processes of rationalization at the level of social organization and the elaboration of the ideology of individualism. (Buchmann, 1989, p. 186)

The transition to adulthood, in Buchmann's (1989) macrosociological and actor-centered perspective, is transformed into a "more extended, diversified, and increasingly individualized period" (p. 187). The differentiation between adult status and youth status is increasingly blurred. Buchmann (1989) writes that "structural and cultural changes over the last two decades have made youth as a life stage increasingly obsolete, while they have simultaneously extended it indefinitely" (p. 188). Here is another illustration of the disjunctive present—the disordering of a well-established

---

[5]The compulsory heterosexuality of this account of growing up can only be noted here. Space does not permit a critique of this heteronormativity, but see Sedgwick (1993) for a relevant analysis.

time/event relation. If the contemporary coming-of-age patterns vary more, other social institutions, such as the media, may work harder to re-infantilize youth.[6]

TEENAGE MOTHERHOOD AS ALL-AT-ONCE GROWING UP

Teenage motherhood appears to be a narrative of swift and all-at-once growing up. Thus, teenage motherhood violates proper age chronology and what is believed about biological age; it is also a compacted or condensed narrative of growing up that violates the leisurely, extended adolescence thought proper and necessary by psychologists from Hall to Erikson, and institutionalized in compulsory school attendance laws and child labor prohibitions. Teenage motherhood perplexes secondary school educators and challenges their assumptions of schooling's role in "preparation" for adulthood. If school-aged mothers are already adults, at least in one domain, what can school do for them? And how should it treat them?

In the next section, I use interviews with school-aged mothers to explore the all-at-once growing up scripts and some of their time/event relations.

Students at Bright Prospects Alternative School[7]

The perspective of the teachers, counselors and nurses at Bright Prospects School was that young teenagers can be good mothers. The alternative school was founded in 1980 in a city in the southwestern United States, a city reputed to have above national averages of pregnancy, drug abuse, and suicide among youth. The city's ethnic diversity was reflected in the school population of 54% Hispanic, 30% Anglo, 8% Native American, and 7.5%

---

[6]Patricia Holland's (1992) study of contemporary print media's portrayal of youth depicts recurrent representations that make the adult/youth border unambiguous and demonstrate clear adult superiority. Similarly, expert knowledge such as developmental psychology retains its rigid age-based stage demarcations. Thus, despite Buchmann's findings of greater blurring of adult and youth status from the perspective of life scripts, other social arenas continue to promote the view of inferior, undeveloped, and immature youth.

[7]All proper nouns are pseudonyms.

Black. The economic base of the city rests largely upon a military base, tourism, and the main branch of the state university. Salaries remain low.

Debbie, a 16-year-old mother attending Bright Prospects alternative high school for school-aged mothers, noted, "*It seems when you get pregnant, you mature just like that* [emphasis added]. We're not old," she added quickly to uniform laughter from her peers, "You just mature." Debbie portrayed an all-at-once growing up experience, in which responsibilities appear to demand that youth become serious about their actions and consequences. The group of six young mothers whom I interviewed agreed with Debbie's perspective, and supported it with other examples. Suzanne claimed she had decided to give up drinking and smoking pot in order to set an example for her son. Esther recounted her maturity in her relationship with school: "Before [I got pregnant] I didn't go to school; I partied all the time ....Now I respect myself more. I don't do things to embarrass myself."

For some of the young mothers, the all-at-once growing up occurred in contexts of strict (often religious) family backgrounds that utilized ignorance as an approach to morality.[8] Theresa, a 16-year-old junior at the time of the research,[9] explained the role of Catholicism in her young "social age":

> It's not that I didn't know about birth control, it's just something we [Theresa and her steady boyfriend] never really thought about—til I got pregnant ....I was brought up in a strict Catholic family, so even the thought of having sex before you were married was not allowed. That kind of shied me away from talking to my mom about it [birth control].

When they found out she was pregnant, Theresa and her boyfriend made some hard decisions. First, they decided not to get married, and then they decided to release the baby for adoption. Together they went through the open adoption procedures, and they reviewed applicants' files, interviewed them, and chose the adoptive parents:

---

[8]Research indicates that higher teenage pregnancy rates occur in countries with the least open attitudes toward sex. In addition to different attitudes toward sex, contraceptive information is advertised differently and made available in different ways. See the two volumes of comparative research by Jones et al. (1986) and by Jones, Forrest, Henshaw, Silverman, and Torres (1989).

[9]The research at Bright Prospects School was conducted from 1986–1988. More extensive data on Bright Prospects are presented in both Fernandez et al. (1987) and Wehlage, Rutter, Smith, Lesko, and Fernandez (1990). Elsewhere I have analyzed the students' perspectives differently (see Lesko, 1990, 1991).

[Open adoption] makes me feel better about what I did, knowing that he [her son, Nicholas] is in a good home. I got to choose the parents, so he didn't just get placed in a home. And I get pictures and a letter three times a year, so you don't feel so isolated.

Theresa found being at Bright Prospects during her pregnancy was important in that she was among girls in the same situation, one in which understanding and nonjudgmentalism were promoted. Her comments on learning about the labor-intensive work of caring for a child shed further light on social age and pregnancy, for both boys and girls. She believed few of the teenage fathers, like the mothers, knew anything about caring for a child. Even one day in the Bright Prospects nursery would temper certain attitudes:

A friend of mine—the father of her baby—won't let her give it up for adoption. He wants to keep the baby. Well, he's 16 years old and I don't think he has any idea of what it's like to take care of a baby. And if he came over here and worked for one day [in a nursery], he'd lay off and leave her alone.

Two alumni of Bright Prospects also presented their pregnancies as all-at-once adulthood scripts. Betty, 24 at the time of the interview, described the state she was in when she got pregnant at 16: "I was headed for dropping out; I was headed down. I hadn't been doing well in classes. Getting pregnant really made me grow up ....It sort of saved me."

I am not suggesting that Debbie, Suzanne, or Betty speak for all teenage mothers, rather I use them to highlight a perspective on school-aged mothers that has been omitted—the relationship among sexuality, pregnancy, and all-at-once growing up. The concept of social age helps us think about the socially constructed age dimension of sexuality and pregnancy.

Social Age

In various contexts and dynamics, many of these young women were kept "young," both in their own behaviors and in what was expected of them by others, especially parents. For example, Gina was 21 when I interviewed her, having graduated from Bright Prospects 2 years earlier. Before her pregnancy and enrollment at Bright Prospects, she had been suspended from several schools in two states. Gina reminisced: "In a way I wanted to get pregnant. She [my mom] was so strict: no phone calls, no dates, no make-up. At 16 I could only wear mascara."

Part of the precipitating events in young pregnancies, in these narratives and elsewhere (e.g., Rains, 1971), is the failure to take one's life, and especially one's sexuality, seriously. Prudence Rains maintains that the failure of young women to use contraception is interwoven with their inability to see themselves as rightfully sexual and as sexually active people. To have sexual feelings is difficult to accept, and the girls she interviewed "resolved" this difficulty by denying the need for contraception and by seeing themselves as being swept away by particular situations. Thus, they could continue to view themselves as virginal and childlike. Their negotiated "young social age" maintained their innocence concerning contraception, and helped create unplanned pregnancies.

The concept of social age denaturalizes biological age and allows us to see the negotiated, thus *produced* character of age. Anne Solberg (1990) researched 12-year-olds in Norwegian families, and her study revealed a range of practices around the household obligations and rights of children that either made them "grow" (i.e., have an older social age) or stay small (i.e., maintain a younger social age). In this intriguing work, Solberg shows the constructedness of age through obligations and rights of children in households and develops the concept of a mutually negotiated social age that was variable whereas biological age was constant.

Although I have no comparable empirical studies of negotiated social age in U. S. schools and families upon which to draw, the concept of social age can be employed to read the above-quoted statements by school-age mothers. Strict attitudes toward sex and contraception or dating, or few expectations for school achievement seemed to be part of a negotiated young social age. Schooling, with its emphasis on preparation and slow development, may help construct the problems of teenage mothers by maintaining the young social age.

The maintenance of a young social age in the area of sexuality is common across the United States. Comparative studies of the United States and other industrialized countries demonstrate that the United States has less of an open attitude toward sexuality, and that reproductive information and services are harder to find and to travel to (Jones et al., 1986, 1989).

An anecdote from Indiana illustrates one way schools perpetuate young social ages around sexuality. On a fall, 1996 visit to a high school in Indianapolis with my undergraduate multicultural education class, a counselor referred to the "epidemic proportions of teenage pregnancy" in the school. Of course, the counselor added, the Indianapolis school board policy prohibits discussion of birth control and only permits abstinence to be taught. My students and I had numerous encounters with teenage mothers that day. The student I shadowed had a 9-month-old son; she was an honor student in a highly visible program for college-bound youth (in a strongly working-class school). There were many other honor students and average students who attended school while they were pregnant and as young mothers.

This school system refuses to acknowledge the sexuality and sexual activeness of teenagers. In its prohibition of useful and meaningful sex education, the school defines these students as sexually immature. By virtue of the lack of knowledge and ability to discuss themselves as sexual beings, the students are kept at young social ages, at least in relation to sexuality. This young sexual age is part of the production of the problem of school-age pregnancies. School programs and policies, supported by theoretical perspectives on adolescence and human growth and development, perpetuate a young social age, one particularly significant dimension of which is the childlike approach to sexuality. These immaturity-maintaining practices help produce unplanned pregnancies, which disproportionately impact young women. These immaturity-maintaining practices are both within the domain of sex education and contraception and more generally in secondary schools that assume slow development toward adulthood. Finally, when all-at-once maturity occurs, with pregnancy its most potent symbol, schools generally cannot adapt or connect with these "too quickly mature" youth. Once again, schools fail them in the lack of child-care facilities, the lack of sex education, and the minimal coursework regarding childrearing and parenting (Lesko, 1995). The assumption of schools of a normative and proper, slow development of youth is effective in keeping many youth "socially young," a fact that clearly contributes to being "sexually young." Being sexually young, in turn, contributes to an inability to consider responsible sexual practices, including use of contraception (but not limited to that).[10]

Young mothers at Bright Prospects School spoke about their maturity regarding contraception. Numerous students emphasized their regular use of birth control. Dolores spoke for many others: "I have my son on my lap. There is *no way* I will forget to take my birth control pill ... with him there as a constant reminder." Most of the girls with whom I spoke wanted more children, but not until they were ready. "Maybe when I'm out of college and I don't have to depend on anyone, when I can take care of myself," Esther summarized. "I know not to do it again until I'm ready."

---

[10]See Michelle Fine's (1988) important critique of sex education from a feminist perspective.

FEMINIST POLITICS, REPRODUCTIVE RIGHTS, AND SOCIAL AGE

Feminist politics can aid us in reconsidering school-age mothers and sexuality from the perspective of age domination (hooks, 1981), the accepted practices of seeing children as deficient and as adult property (Lenzer, 1993).[11] Zillah Eisenstein's (1994) feminist politics around reproductive rights, including health care, sex education, AIDS prevention, and so forth, is necessary to end the domination of teenage mothers from the perspective of their age. Eisenstein argues that focusing on reproductive rights as a central facet of a feminist, antiracist, and progressive politics ought not to be confused with abortion politics:

> Reproductive rights enlarges the issue of abortion to related concerns [italics added]: affordable and good health care; a decrease in infant mortality and teenage pregnancy; reproductive health; health services for infertility; and access to appropriate contraceptives. (p. 220)

Eisenstein writes that "contraceptive services, sex education, and AIDS prevention outreach are as important to any woman needing them as abortion is for others" (p. 220). Reproductive choice is an essential part of this right. The Supreme Court upheld restrictions on teenage access to abortion, via a required parental consent or a court approval; these restrictions mean that teenagers do not have reproductive choice. Eisenstein argues that we must reinvent democracy from the starting point of the pregnant bodies of women of color, building connections across women of color and White women around reproductive health, broadly conceptualized. These ideas regarding feminist support of reproductive rights, the centrality of pregnant women's bodies in a reinvention of democracy, and the roles of schools in those processes focus our attention on the necessity of reproductive rights education in schools.

CONCLUSION: VISIBILITY, REPRODUCTIVE RIGHTS, AND SOCIAL AGE

The analysis presented here argues that the dominant life script of adolescence is a slow, over-a-long-time development from youth to adult. This

---

[11]Interestingly, the youth rights movement wrote a Youth Bill of Rights, which lists nine rights, including the rights to liberty, safety, survival, education, and so forth, but omits any mention of reproductive rights (Lenzer, 1995).

coming-of-age narrative is assumed to be universal. However, by looking at school-aged mothers, we see that this chronotype ignores various life situations and, most specifically, reproductive bodies (Eisenstein, 1994). It assumes and maintains a seemingly generic youth in a male body, who can grow up slowly, planning and reflecting on his future adulthood. In these ways the dominant theory of adolescence, with its narrative of a slow developmental progression, makes sexually active and reproductive young women impossible to consider. They can remain only marginal and deviant. Furthermore, this normative view makes sex education marginal to education, rather than a reproductive necessity.

A second major emphasis in this chapter is the rethinking of teenage mothers, from social problem to an emblem of the disjunctive present—a time in which the staged emphasis on the present surpassing the past is stalled by school-age mothers, who are said to deteriorate the social fabric of family life. Views of slowly developing youth and views of children as nonsexual are belied by scores of school-aged mothers.[12] Sociologist Buchmann articulates the disjunctive present through her vision of the obsolescence of youth, yet its perpetuation for more and more years. This disjunctive present allows us to see how we produce youth as socially young and keep them that way. It allows us as educators to consider the social age of youth and schools' roles in treating them as young. Thus, the concept of the disjunctive present points both to how schools help produce forever young teenagers—as part of their structural relations to other social institutions (families and workplaces)—and to how this structural relation is supported by theoretical narratives that make it seem natural and proper to maintain young teenagers as youngsters, especially in the arena of sexuality. From this perspective, we see how the social age roots of teenage mothers must remain invisible and how seemingly universal theories of adolescence privilege males.[13]

In these ways, school-aged mothers bring our narratives of adolescence and imbedded scripts of growing up into relief. Shall we continue to make school-aged mothers only visible as disordered chronologies and sexual

---

[12]Recent figures report that the rate of births to teenagers is down from 62.1 births per 1,000 in 1991 to 56.9 births per 1,000 in 1995 ("Teen birthrates," 1996).

[13]There are racial and social class dimensions to the adolescence discourse, too. I do not develop them here, but see Lesko (1996) for more of an historical analysis of the discourse on adolescence. For the contemporary period, see Giroux (1996).

deviants? To do otherwise involves educators' active renegotiation of social age and political support for the feminist agenda of reproductive rights.

REFERENCES

Austin, R. (1989). Sapphire bound! *Wisconsin Law Review, 539*–578.

Bhabha, H. K. (1995). Freedom's basis in the indeterminate. In J. Rajchman (Ed.), *The identity in question* (pp. 47–62). New York: Routledge.

Buchmann, M. (1989). *The script of life in modern society.* Chicago: University of Chicago Press.

Children having children. (1995, December 9). *Time.*

Children's Defense Fund (1985). *Preventing children having children.* Washington, DC: Author.

Coontz, S. (1992). *The way we never were: American families and the nostalgia trap.* New York: Basic Books.

Dash, L. (1989). *When children want children: An inside look at the crisis of teenage parenthood.* New York: Penguin.

Eisenstein, Z. R. (1994). *The color of gender: Reimaging democracy.* Berkeley: University of California Press.

Fernandez, R., Geary, P. A., Lesko, N., Rutter, R. A., Smith, G. A., & Wehlage, G. G. (1987). *Dropout prevention and recovery: Fourteen case studies.* Madison, WI: National Center on Effective Secondary Schools.

Fine, M. (1988). Sexuality, schooling, and adolescent females: The missing discourse of desire. *Harvard Educational Review, 58*(1), 29–53.

Foucault, M. (1976). *The history of sexuality: Vol. 1. An introduction.* (R. Hurley, Trans.). New York: Random House.

Fraser, N., & Gordon, L. (1994). A genealogy of dependency: A keyword of the U. S. welfare state. *Signs: A Journal of Women in Culture and Society, 19*(2), 309–336.

Giroux, H. A. (1996). *Fugitive cultures: Race, violence & youth.* New York: Routledge.

Graff, H. J. (1996). *Conflicting paths: Growing up in America.* Cambridge, MA: Harvard University Press.

Hall, G. S. (1905). *Adolescence* (Vol. 1). New York: Appleton.

Holland, P. (1992). *What is a child? Popular images of childhood.* London: Virago Press.

Holquist, M. (1990). *Dialogism: Bakhtin and his world.* New York: Routledge.

hooks, b. (1981). *Ain't I a woman: Black women and feminism.* Boston: South End Press.

James, A., & Prout, A. (Eds.), (1990). *Constructing and reconstructing childhood: Contemporary issues in the sociological study of childhood.* London: Falmer Press.

James, A., & Prout, A. (1990b). Re-presenting childhood: Time and transition in the study of childhood. In A. James & A. Prout (Eds.), *Constructing and reconstructing childhood: Contemporary issues in the sociological study of childhood* (pp. 216–237). London: Falmer Press.

Jones, E. F., Forrest, J. D., Goldman, N., Henshaw, S., Lincoln, R., Rosoff, J. E., Westoff, C. F., & Wulf, D. (1986). *Teenage pregnancy in industrialized countries.* New Haven, CT: Yale University Press.

Jones, E. F., Forrest, J. D., Henshaw, S., Silverman, J., & Torres, A. (1989). *Pregnancy, contraception, and family planning services in industrialized countries.* New Haven, CT: Yale University Press.

Kincaid, J. R. (1992). *Child-loving: The erotic child and Victorian culture.* New York: Routledge.

Kunzel, R. G. (1993). *Fallen women, problem girls: Unmarried mothers and the professionalization of social work, 1890–1945*. New Haven, CT: Yale University Press.

Lawson, A. (1993). Multiple fractures: The cultural construction of teenage sexuality and pregnancy. In A. Lawson & D. Rhode (Eds.), *The politics of pregnancy: Adolescent sexuality and public policy* (pp. 101–125). New Haven, CT: Yale University Press.

Lenzer, J. (1993). Politics of youth: Youth liberation. *Z Magazine, 6*(2), 49–52.

Lenzer, J. (1995). Youth summit '95. *Z Magazine, 8*(9), 22–25.

Lesko, N. (1996). Past, present, and future conceptions of adolescence. *Educational Theory, 46*(4), 453–472.

Lesko, N. (1995). The "leaky needs" of school-aged mothers: An examination of U. S. programs and policies. *Curriculum Inquiry, 25*(2), 25–40.

Lesko, N. (1991). Implausible endings: Teenage mothers and fictions of school success. In N. Wyner (Ed.), *Current perspectives on the cultures of schools* (pp. 45–63). Cambridge, MA: Brookline Books.

Lesko, N. (1990). Curriculum differentiation as social redemption: The case of school-aged mothers. In R. Page & L. Valli (Eds.), *Curriculum differentiation: Interpretive studies in U.S. secondary schools* (pp. 113–136). Albany, NY: State University of New York Press.

Luker, K. (1996). *Dubious conceptions: The politics of teenage pregnancy*. Cambridge, MA: Harvard University Press.

Murcott, A. (1980). The social construction of teenage pregnancy: A problem in the ideologies of childhood and reproduction. *Sociology of Health and Illness, 2*(1), 1–23.

Rains, P. M. (1971). *Becoming an unwed mother*. Chicago: Aldine.

Ross, D. (1972). *G. Stanley Hall: The psychologist as prophet*. Chicago: University of Chicago Press.

Ross, D. (1984). American social science and the idea of progress. In T. L. Haskell (Ed.), *The authority of experts: Studies in history and theory* (pp. 157–179). Bloomington, IN: Indiana University Press.

Ruddick, S. (1993). Procreative choice for adolescent women. In A. Lawson & D. Rhode (Eds.), *The politics of pregnancy: Adolescent sexuality and public policy* (pp. 126–143). New Haven, CT: Yale University Press.

Sander, J. (1991). *Before their time: Four generations of teenage mothers*. New York: Harcourt Brace.

Sedgwick, E. K. (1993). How to bring your kids up gay. In M. Warner (Ed.), *Fear of a queer planet: Queer politics and social theory* (pp. 69–81). Minneapolis: University of Minnesota Press.

Solberg, A. (1990). Age in Norwegian families. In A. James & A. Prout (Eds.), *Constructing and reconstructing childhood: Contemporary issues in the sociological study of childhood* (pp. 60–77). London: Falmer Press.

Solinger, R. (1992). *Wake up little Susie: Single pregnancy and race before Roe v. Wade*. New York: Routledge.

Teen birthrates down in nearly every state, survey shows (1996, November 6). *Education Week*, p. 8.

Treichler, P. (1987, October). AIDS, homophobia, and biomedical discourse: An epidemic of signification. *October, 43*, 31–70.

Weatherley, R. A., & Cartoof, V. G. (1988). Helping single adolescent parents. In C. S. Chilman, E. W. Nunnally, & F. M. Cox (Eds.), *Variant family forms* (pp. 39–55). Newbury Park, CA: Sage.

Wehlage, G. G., Rutter, R., Smith, G. A., Lesko, N., & Fernandez, R. (1990). *Reducing the risk: Schools as communities of support*. London: Falmer Press.

8

Heterosexism, Homophobia, and the Culture of Schooling

Richard A. Friend
University of Pennsylvania

As a microcosm, school culture in the United States reflects the conflicts and tensions of the broader society. While neither powerless nor without responsibility, schools reflect and re-create a society whose perceptions render some of its members invisible. As Books suggests in the introduction, "invisibility" is evidenced by socially devaluing others' experiences so that alleviating the often difficult conditions of their lives is not a social priority. Rendering others invisible also subjects them to hurtful, narrow stereotypes that construct them as something other than they are. Those who are not seen are often educationally neglected in the sense that the quality of the schooling they receive, if any at all, is poor. Finally, their voices and experiences are inadequately represented in classrooms, in the curriculum, or in the attention paid by scholars in the field of education. Often called "the invisible minority," the lives of lesbian, gay, bisexual, and transgendered people are marked by all these forms of invisibility and silencing.

Who are these invisible members of school culture? Do not refuse to see. Those rendered invisible are always around:

These children are your students and the adults are their parents and your colleagues. They are the class clown, the high school star athlete, the class valedictorian, the ordinary kid next door, your neighbor, your sibling, your child, your principal, your teaching partner. Unfortunately, because of the invisibility, it is often virtually impossible to identify the lesbian and gay community in your school. Tragically, this invisibility has led to our collective ability to ignore the problem and failure to design a curriculum that will address these issues. ... Each child that dies by their own hand is a child with loved ones who are left behind to pick up the pieces of their shattered lives. Each child that dies by their own hand could have become that adult who found the cure for cancer. Each child that dies by their own hand could have been that adult that made world peace possible. Each child that dies by their own hand may have been that invisible child in your school. (Sivertsen & Thames, 1995, p. 6)

Antigay and antilesbian violence and harassment as well as epidemic rates of sexual minority youth who attempt or complete suicide, drop out of school, or run away are part of the price paid for the sanctioned silences and institutionalized invisibility of the lives of lesbian, gay, bisexual, transgendered (l/g/b/t), and questioning youths in the fabric of public schooling.

As McLaren (1995) argued with regard to sexuality and sexual politics:

The current historical juncture is precisely that perilous mixture of historical amnesia and cultural intensity in which society is attempting to reinvent itself without the benefit of knowing who or what it already is .... We rely as a society on perceptions that have been filtered through constellations of historical commentaries rooted in xenophobia, homophobia, racism, sexism, the commodification of everyday life, and the reproduction of race, class, and gender relations. Schools both mirror and motivate such perceptions, reproducing a culture of fear that contributes to a wider justification for vigilance surrounding sexual practices through polar definitions of youth as morally upright/sexually deviant, and approvingly decent/unrepentantly corrupt. (pp. 105–106)

Framing the lives of l/g/b/t people as "the other" contributes to constructing the lives of heterosexual people as moral, normal, natural, and blessed (Rubin, 1984). Marginalizing a group as the other serves two key human functions: It provides a sense of belonging and contributes to the need for power and status. According to Babad, Birnbaum, and Benne (1983):

The conflict in heterogenous society is the struggle between distinct groups ... each vying to attain more power and status, better opportunities for its members, and more control over society's various resources. For a group identity to be viable and meaningful, the group boundaries must be well defined, and there must be a recognizable "out-group," that is, those who do *not* belong in the group. (p. 100)

It is important to recognize not only how other people benefit from the marginalization of l/g/b/t youth, but also how the layers of silencing and invisibility can contribute to educators, researchers, advocates, and parents focusing on the tragedies rather than on the successes. The fact that many students emerge with strength and power must not be overlooked or minimized. More and more, l/g/b/t students experience school in a paradoxical mix of empowerment and conflict. The challenge for educators, and anyone else concerned about youth, is to work to understand the socioemotional context in which students exist and to provide resources for overcoming and dismantling the systems that lead to silencing and victimization. The good news is that public schools in the United States contain seeds of the same forces working outside schools to interrupt heterosexism and homophobia. Given the many common elements of oppression, schools that manage to undo heterosexism and homophobia are likely to be places of incredible possibility for all youth.

What follows is an analysis of how heterosexism and homophobia are institutionalized into the culture of schooling, followed by a discussion of the impact of these forces on students. Finally, recommendations for interrupting and undoing heterosexism at an institutional/systemic level are presented. For more than 15 years I have worked with teachers, administrators, counselors, school secretaries, bus drivers, cafeteria workers, nonteaching assistants, custodians, parents, and youth around these issues. The lessons, stories, and research I have collected as a result of this work both in and out of schools inform this chapter.

HETEROSEXISM, HOMOPHOBIA AND SEXISM

Heterosexism

Heterosexism, homophobia, and sexism function in schools to sustain and reproduce specific power relations. Heterosexism is the systematic process of privileging heterosexuality relative to homosexuality. Heterosexism is the assumption that everyone is heterosexual, or if not, should be (Friend, 1987a, 1987b, 1989, 1990, 1992, 1993, 1994; Neisen, 1990). As such, it is both an assumption and a value. The assumption of heterosexuality renders invisible all who are not, and the value implied in "should be" elevates heterosexuality relative to homosexuality. Lorde (1988) described this process as "a belief in the inherent superiority of one pattern of loving over all others and thereby the right to dominance" (p. 26). Rich (1980) referred to this universal assumption of heterosexuality as "compulsory heterosexuality."

I am reminded of the pervasive assumption of heterosexuality operating in schooling when I ask educators, "What is life like for the lesbian, gay, and bisexual students in your classrooms or schools?" The most common answers are, "I don't know," or "I never thought about it," or "Well, I had one once, but ..." My response always is, "If you don't know what life is like, or are surprised by the question, that tells you something about what life is like for lesbian, gay, and bisexual youth." Living invisibly, or in a closet, is an experience unto itself.

The assumption of heterosexuality encourages individuals to assume or prejudge that those around them are all heterosexual (hence excluding or rendering invisible the existence of lesbian, gay, and bisexual identities). When an individual, an institution, or a culture has the power to impose this prejudice, an "ism" results (Friend, 1992; Neisen, 1990). Heterosex*ism*, therefore, reflects the beliefs and systems, sustained by power arrangements, which render invisible the lived experiences and contributions of l/g/b/t members of society. The loud silence that results resonates throughout history as well as in the halls, playgrounds, and classrooms of contemporary schools. It also means that to interrupt the silence is both dangerous and possibly subversive.

Coming Out

Heterosexism is the arrangement that necessitates "coming out." If heterosexuality is assumed, those who are lesbian, gay, or bisexual must constantly face and deal with that incorrect assumption. Coming out is a cognitive, affective, and behavioral process. In part, it is a process toward self-acceptance whereby individuals either internalize heterosexist information (which results in low self-esteem and marginal self-acceptance) or deconstruct the heterosexist hegemony and reconstruct their identity in positive and affirming ways (Friend, 1987a, 1987b, 1990, 1991). The behavioral component has to do with if, and how, the individual informs others of their identity. Given the pervasiveness of heterosexism, coming out is generally an ongoing and lifelong process. As long as people continue to make the wrong assumption, lesbian, gay, and bisexual individuals must navigate the risk of challenging this assumption and make a decision on whether the many benefits to coming out are worth the potential costs. Herdt and Boxer (1993) described the process of coming out:

> The challenge to the individual comes in the way that expressing same-sex desires undermines the received theory of "human nature" in American society which is learned in growing up. ... First, he or she must unlearn the principal of "natural" heterosexuality, especially the "essentialist" assumption that to marry and parent with the opposite sex is the only right and normal mode of development. Second, they must unlearn the stereotypes of "homosexuality" as they apply to their own development .... Third, they must learn how to be gay and lesbian, which requires them to reconstruct their social relationships in American society, based on new and emerging social status and cultural being in the gay and lesbian culture. This latter process is the end product of coming out, except that, in fact, the process is lifelong and never really ends. (p. 15)

Developing a positive gay identity entails facing the regular personal and political challenges of using oneself as a catalyst for social change through education and awareness. In the words of José, a 19-year-old Puerto Rican male living in North Philadelphia:

> I knew I was gay, I never sat there and denied it. It was a learning process. I knew that [the messages] wasn't me and I knew that wasn't some of my friends. I knew there were myths about Puerto Ricans, and I knew they weren't right. But I didn't know how to make that connection that these were myths or misinformation. It was just "something's wrong here." It took me years to learn what it was: "Oh, they're myths, hello!" Now I'm constantly educating people. I need to be paid 24 hours a day. That's what I hate about being gay, it's like a job. It comes with a political part about it, and an educational part. (personal communication, November 9, 1996)

Homophobia

The invisibility and devaluing of homosexuality, which are products of heterosexism, also result in the fear and discomfort labeled as "homophobia" (Friend, 1987a, 1987b, 1989, 1990, 1992, 1993, 1994; Herek, 1984; Weinberg, 1972). This can be the fear and discomfort of one's own potential same sex attraction (internalized homophobia), or negative feelings that occur in response to the real or perceived homosexuality of others.

Whenever I teach or conduct training on these issues I ask, "How can you tell if someone is lesbian or gay?" Often people say, "You can't unless they tell you," but others will frequently say, "Sometimes you can tell by the way they look." I am quick to quote a lesbian colleague of mine who says,

"It's not the way we look. It's the way we look back!" Then I introduce a concept called "gaydar," defined as the sixth sense lesbian, gay, and bisexual people are said to develop in order to find one another (like radar). Then I say, "Let me demonstrate 'gaydar' for you. I am going to point to the lesbian, gay, and bisexual people here. When I point to you, I want you to stand." Generally there is nervous laughter, people avoid eye contact with me, and shift in their seats. After what seems like a very long pause, my response is, "I can't do that. But if you felt uncomfortable and/or afraid, if you worried, 'Oh my God. What if he points to me?' chances are what you were feeling was homophobia." This is a quick and effective way to help people experience the powerful nature of fear and discomfort associated with the perception of homosexuality. Homophobia ensures that violating the rule of heterosexuality has consequences.

Sexism

The root of heterosexism is sexism, and one of the fundamental enforcers of sexism is homophobia (Pharr, 1988). If "heterosexism" assumes that people are or should be heterosexual, "sexism" is the set of assumptions and arrangements about how women and men "are or should be." It is not by accident that many of the stereotypes of lesbian and gay people have to do with gender-role nonconformity. Homophobic expressions and sentiments (such as "faggot," "dyke," "queer," or "punk") are often used against those who violate our expectations of appropriate gender-role behavior.

The boy who is "too sensitive" or "too emotional" is often first labeled a "sissy." If he continues to demonstrate these so-called "feminine traits," he is later called "fag" or "punk." Given that sexism values "masculinity" more than "femininity," feminine boys, who are seen as abandoning a position of power, are generally more of a source of concern (and ridicule) than are masculine girls (Friend, 1993).

A girl who is too rough and tumble is called a "tomboy." If her assertiveness and independence continue, there may be concern that, "God forbid, she might grow up and some day be able to live without men." This is generally of less concern than for her feminine male counterpart. Although she may then be labeled a "dyke" or "the big 'B'," sexist reasoning concludes that at least assertiveness and independence are socially valued traits. All females and males, no matter what their age or sexual orientation, are then subject to social control that is informed by sexism and homophobia.

José's memories of his third-grade English teacher illustrate this relation-ship between heterosexism and sexism. The teacher, Ms. Douglas, divided up the class into two teams for an activity. According to José,

> She said, "The girls on one side and the boys on the other." And when she said that, I knew what was going to happen. I knew it. Everybody said, "Where is José gonna go?" I knew it was going to happen and I didn't want to play the game. (personal communication, November 9, 1996)

José's capacity to predict what was going to happen reflects the pressure for gender-role conformity and the use of homophobia as a weapon against those who are perceived to violate these gender role expectations. Although it was clearly not the intent of the teacher to set José up, her assumption that this dividing technique was benign not only reinforced competition between the genders, but was indicative of her lack of awareness of the consequences of heterosexism for l/g/b/t youth. The unrelenting teasing of his peers and the lack of support in his school environment were the primary reasons José dropped out of school during the eighth grade.

Maintaining Heterosexism: Systematic Exclusion and Systematic Inclusion

Heterosexism is demonstrated and maintained by two interrelated power processes, systematic exclusion and systematic inclusion. Systematic exclu-sion is the process whereby positive role models, messages, and images of, by, and about l/g/b/t people are publicly silenced. One way this happens is through the absence of an inclusive pedagogy (Friend, 1993; Prince, 1996), for example, when there is no mention of sexual orientation in the official curriculum, even in the most obvious places. When studying the lives of James Baldwin, Virginia Wolf, Walt Whitman, Gertrude Stein, Willa Cather, Bessie Smith, or Bayard Rustin, for example, without referencing how living as gay or lesbian people may have influenced their work, systematic exclu-sion has occurred.

Advocates of an inclusive pedagogy face an increasingly organized and vitriolic opposition. The stealth approach of the far right has lead to government hearings, restrictive legislation, and the threat to cut public funds for schools that are inclusive around a range of social issues. In December of 1995, the U.S. House Subcommittee on Oversight and Inves-tigations of the Committee on Economic and Educational Opportunities held hearings entitled "Parents, Schools, and Values." These hearings, initially described as an investigation into the "promotion of homosexuality in public schools," were held at the request of the far right Traditional Values Coalition's Rev. Lou Sheldon. Although the hearings resulted in no legislative action, they lent "legitimacy" to similar hearings and actions at state and local levels.

Salt Lake City's Board of Education, for example, voted in February of 1996 to ban student clubs rather than allow equal access to Gay Straight Alliances in their high schools. Many other state and local governments are drafting legislation that would withdraw aid to public schools and community colleges that promote homosexual practices, equate homosexual behavior to heterosexual behavior, or equate sexual orientation to race or national origin.

On September 17, 1996, the Elizabethtown, Pennsylvania school board passed a policy entitled "the Pro-Family Resolution" that stated:

> Whereas the traditional family is under relentless attack by those who want to redefine family to include homosexual and lesbian couples, and by those who want to indoctrinate children in pro-homosexual propaganda against their parents' wishes; therefore be it resolved that ... pro-homosexual concepts on sex and family ... will never be tolerated or accepted at this school.

After the resolution passed, 200 Elizabethtown high school and 50 middle school students walked out of class in protest.

These are a few examples of codification of systematic exclusion through governmental hearings and legislation. The role of educators in addressing these issues of exclusion by legislated mandate is discussed in the last section of this chapter.

Heterosexism is further maintained by the systematic exclusion of visible l/g/b/t role models. As mentioned earlier, potential role models are lost when the lives of important l/g/b/t people are studied without mention of their sexual orientation or gender identity. The extent to which l/g/b/t teachers, administrators, counselors, and other adults in schooling feel pressure to remain invisible sends a compelling message. For both l/g/b/t youth and the children of l/g/b/t parents, the message is, "Don't talk about your lives here." Role models provide accurate information for all youth as well as a powerful sense of possibility for l/g/b/t teens.

Griffin's (1992) research documented the role empowerment plays in the professional lives of lesbian and gay educators. According to Griffin, empowerment is associated with both positive feelings about self- and group identity as gay and lesbian educators, and a better understanding of themselves as educators in a heterosexist society. Empowerment is also related to taking action to change oppressive situations and to gain more control over their work lives. Empowering educators helps them to be better teachers and positively affects the lives of their students and colleagues. Their effectiveness and productivity as educators improved when they did not have to expend energy hiding and protecting themselves. Griffin (1992) reported:

> The entire educational community has something to gain from the empowerment of gay and lesbian educators .... Visible lesbian and gay educators provide colleagues, students and parents with the opportunity to learn that their fears of and stereotypes about gay and lesbian teachers are not rooted in reality. Perhaps most importantly, young people struggling with their sexual orientation would have more realistic and hopeful expectations about what it means to be gay or lesbian. They would learn that there are gay and lesbian adults, some of whom are respected teachers in their schools, who live happy and productive lives. (pp. 194–195)

Nineteen-year-old Keesha knew some of her teachers were lesbian and gay, but also knew they did not feel comfortable or safe being "out." Ironically, Keesha was the catalyst in her school who opened the closet door for many of her peers and teachers.

> One of my teachers, for example, wasn't out. I knew and she knew I knew. I would smile at her and it made her nervous. After about a year she finally came out and told me. After that it was cool and a couple of other teachers would come up and talk with me. It made me feel good. I'm 15 or 16 and I came out, and these are teachers in their 30s who aren't out yet. The administration was weird, like they would pity me. The principal who never talked to me ever before, would come up to me and say, "Hi, Keesha. How are you doing?" Like they thought my life is horrible and I have all these problems now. I would say, "No, this is great. I'm out now, so it's cool." At the time it was really easy for me to come out. My being out made it easier for the teachers and others. I started a group too. The Gay Straight Alliance, and that was really cool because a lot of kids started coming out. It was great for me too because all these girls would come up to me on the side. That was the best thing about being the token dyke. They had nothing else to compare me with so I was just the coolest thing. I even took a girl to my prom. (personal communication, November 8, 1996)

Finally, systematic exclusion may occur when students attempt to access information in the school library. Lesbian, gay, bisexual, and transgendered youth report that the library is generally one of the first places they go for information about sexual orientation and identity in school. When students go to the library, however, they often face structured silence. If there are materials, they are often held behind the reference desk. Librarians explain that this is because the books are frequently stolen (often by desperate kids too afraid or embarrassed to check them out). Having to ask for the materials creates a catch-22, however. The students may need the books in order to begin to feel comfortable enough to ask for the books.

In spite of the sanctioned silences in school libraries, many more youth are gaining access to information today through the INTERNET. Although this may diminish the effects of systematic exclusion for the individual student who has access to a computer and the world wide web, it does little to transform the culture of schooling. The artifacts of school culture—books on the shelves, posters on the walls, pamphlets in the racks, positive role models, and inclusive policies and curriculum—all send messages about the culture. Not having these artifacts also sends a powerful message of exclusion and invisibility.

When sanctioned discussions about homosexuality do occur in schools, they are generally placed in a negative context. The process of systematic inclusion, which consistently links homosexuality with pathology, sexual behavior and/or danger, reifies heterosexism. This occurs in both subtle and obvious ways.

If information about homosexuality is part of a school library's holdings, how the material is catalogued may send subtle messages. Libraries using the Dewey Decimal system, for example, locate information on homosexuality in the HQ section. Browsing the stacks of this section, students will find books on prostitution, pornography, sexual abuse, and pedophilia. Including books on homosexuality in this group sends a message.

When the only "official" conversations regarding homosexuality occur in the context of AIDS/HIV education, another unfortunate linkage develops. Not only does this reinforce the notion of homosexuality as pathology, but undermines effective HIV-prevention education. If homosexuality is included elsewhere in the health education curriculum, it is frequently "velcro-ed" as an add on (Whitlock & DiLapi, 1983). There may be units on families, relationships, development, love, and then a separate unit on homosexuality, which implies that homosexuality is separate from families, relationships, development, and love. Heterosexuality by definition is woven into lessons on family, love, and relationships. Linking heterosexuality with these concepts while excluding homosexuality from this sphere is the source of great social and political tension today.

In spite of the fact that an estimated 6 million to 14 million children have a lesbian or gay parent (Patterson, 1992), the contention over New York City's Children of the Rainbow Curriculum, which included discussion of these families, not only became heated and controversial, but contributed to the departure of the Chancellor of Schools. The curriculum controversy, according to Lipkin (1996),

> was a rallying point for public discourse about the nature of sexuality and families. The battle over the inclusion of gay-positive instruction in a broad multicultural curriculum evinced a homophobic barrage from a multiethnic chorus, informed with religious zealotry and other biases of the Right. Some reporters observed a diversion of troops from family-planning clinics to school yards. (p. 47)

One of the most pervasive, persistent, and pernicious associations is that of equating homosexuality with sexual behavior. In the words of one 18-year-old lesbian, "They think we spend 24 hours a day in bed. Why?" (Trenchard, 1984, p.12). Controlling images and ideas about a group's sexuality is a powerful form of social control. Framing "others" as sexually dangerous, out of control, or as asexual is a common tool of oppression. History provides many examples. Images of African American men as rapists and African American women as either temptresses or asexual "mammies" have been common social constructions. People with disabilities are frequently seen as sexual predators or asexual victims to be pitied. Nazi propaganda in World War II Germany showed pictures of Jews with exaggerated genitalia. Gay people today are often assumed to be sexual predators who are threats to children and society.

Equating homosexuality with sex works in the service of heterosexism and homophobia. Current ideology sees sex as personal and private. In education, this ideology is critical because if homosexuality is equated with sex, then any discussion of it is more easily framed as private, inappropriate for children, and requiring of parental permission. Discussions of l/g/b/t issues are then automatically seen as "sex lectures."

This begs several important educational questions. If we don't require parental permission for an elementary school curriculum on families, should it be required if same-sex families (or single-parent families) are included? If we don't require parental permission for lessons on the histories of the women's movement, should it be required for a lesson on the history of the lesbian and gay civil rights movement? If we don't require parental permission for lessons on African American literature or poetry, should it be required for lessons on gay and lesbian literature and poetry? What gets framed as "controversial" as well as policies for dealing with controversial issues in schools are critical windows into the current climate of education.

Focusing on sex because of the hegemony of heterosexism ignores the broad contexts of lesbian and gay life, community, culture, and history. Lesbian and gay culture contains music, poetry, film, art, politics, and history, all of which can be taught in age-appropriate and subject-appropriate ways. Examining James Baldwin's decision to move to Europe, for example, because he felt so uncomfortable living as a gay man in the United States may enrich students' appreciation for his writing. Lessons such as this need not be discussions of sex.

Although there is a place for pleasure and sexual behavior as part of an engaged pedagogy, to have the lives of lesbian, gay, and bisexual people only located in the sphere of sex obfuscates the complexity of our lives. Gay and lesbian studies are a growing area in which educators can be informed and should be trained.

Maintaining Heterosexism: Accepting Harassment and Violence

Harassment and violence against individuals who are l/g/b/t, or who are perceived to be, is an integral part of school culture. Homophobic name calling is a strong fixture in the "hostile hallways" of schools. Homophobic epithets such as "fag" or "dyke" are some of the most common verbal weapons used to hurt, humiliate, and terrorize. In fact, the word "gay" is now frequently used as a generic put down (as in "those sneakers are gay").

When educators interrupt racist and sexist name calling in their schools, but do not intervene when homophobic comments are made (which is frequently the case), their silence communicates a message of permission (Gordon, 1983). One reason educators fail to intervene is their fear of being the target of suspicion (guilt by association). Because sexual orientation is generally more invisible than other dimensions of identity, interrupting homophobic comments and behavior may feel more risky. When a White male intervenes in response to sexist and racist comments, he is generally not worried that others will think he is a closeted woman of color.

For educators to intervene effectively, they need the confidence not to care if others "wonder" about their sexual orientation, as well as the skills to use a name calling incident as a "teachable moment." Not only should clear sanctions be given indicating that homophobic name-calling will not be tolerated, but a meaningful conversation should occur (Lipkin, 1996). The educator should explain why this type of name calling is wrong and explore with the harassing student what motivated them to use these verbal weapons in the first place.

Failing to interrupt homophobic name calling passively contributes to supporting heterosexism and homophobia. Teachers can support this oppressive ideology in more direct ways as well. The following testimony describes this process:

> As part of the [eighth grade] Physical Education program there was a one-period "Hygiene" class each week which was conducted by one of our P.E. instructors. At some point in the year we reached the chapter in our text books where it became necessary for the instructor to talk with us about sex. The only thing I remember from that course is one of the boys making a joke about how homosexuals have sex and kidding with the instructor about how he knows the instructor would like to "get boned." Our sex educator became annoyed and said, "Yeah, you let some faggot try to stick his thing up my butt, I'd break his nose and then cut his joint off." The class broke out in hysterics and I joined them to hide my embarrassment and disgust with myself. (Written testimony to the Philadelphia Board of Education, September 15, 1986; October 4, 1986; November 10, 1986)

Unfortunately, homophobic name calling is all too common in U.S. schools. According to the AAUW Report on Sexual Harassment in America's Schools (1992), students reported that they would be very upset if they were called gay or lesbian. In fact, the risk of being called gay was so great that this would be more upsetting to boys than actual physical abuse. Eighty-six percent of all students said they would be very upset if they were called gay or lesbian (85% of boys and 87% of girls responded this way). For boys, this was both the most disturbing as well as common form of unwanted behavior. According to the U.S. Department of Health and Human Services (1989), the violence and harassment is so unrelenting that it contributes to the fact that an estimated 28% of gay and lesbian youth drop out of high school because of discomfort in the school environment, and that 25% of all youths living on the streets are gay or lesbian.

Being perceived as gay or lesbian, or simply being called gay or lesbian, is a powerful weapon, as the recent Jenny Jones Talk Show murder reflects. Twenty-six-year-old Jonathan Schmitz said he was driven to kill Scott Amedure after it was revealed to Schmitz on the show that Amedure had a crush on him. That Schmitz would rather be perceived as a murderer than as possibly gay is a poignant barometer of homophobia.

Not only is verbal harassment a fixture in schools, antigay and antilesbian violence is both epidemic and on the rise (Herek, 1989). According to a report released by the U.S. Department of Justice (National Institute of Justice, 1987), lesbian and gay people are probably the most frequent victims of hate crimes, but the criminal justice system, like society as a whole, has not recognized the seriousness of this problem (Comstock, 1991). Comstock (1991) reported that "lesbian and gay crime victims report greater frequency of incidents in school settings than do victims of crime in general (25% lesbian/gay; 9% general)," that "men experienced more violence in school settings than women (29% men; 17% women)," and that people of color report more antigay and antilesbian violence in schools than Whites (p. 76).

Although most cases of antigay and antilesbian harassment and violence go unreported, on November 19, 1996, a jury in a federal district court found that two school principals and an assistant principal were liable for not protecting Jamie Nabozny from abuse by other students. The school officials agreed to pay nearly $1 million to settle the lawsuit. Jamie suffered years of antigay abuse in middle school and high school. From the 7th through the 11th grade, he was repeatedly attacked by his fellow students. These attacks included being kicked and beaten, once so severely that he needed exploratory surgery; being pushed into a urinal and urinated on; and victimized in a simulated rape in a classroom. Jamie and his mother testified at the trial that their pleas for help were brushed off by school officials with comments such as, "Boys will be boys," and, "If you're going to be gay, you have to learn to expect such abuse." Although exceptional, Jamie Nabozny and his family are not exceptions. What is so unusual about this case is not the violence and "victim blaming," but the perseverance of Jamie and his family. That they reported the incident in the first place, and then spent 8 years successfully fighting for their rights, is what makes their experience unusual.

Jamie Nabozny also had the benefit of family support in dealing with an oppressive school culture. Unlike members of other marginalized groups, l/g/b/t youth often do not have the support of their families (Gover, 1996). According to Krysial (1987), "Gay people are the only minorities that do not have a parent as a role model" (p. 304). Hunter and Schaecher (1987) reported that "violence toward lesbian and gay people comes not only from strangers but very often from family as well" (p. 180). A social worker told me a gay youth he was working with shared that "growing up gay in my family is like being Jewish in a Nazi home." As Smith (1991) said, "Lesbians and gay men are the only oppressed group that was born and raised by our oppressors." Even if families are supportive, they may not know how, or they may not have the emotional and behavioral tools for helping their children respond to this type of oppression.

Starting in the sixth grade, Sharon's mother began asking her if she was a lesbian. For a year and half Sharon lied because she was not ready for anyone in her family to know the truth. Finally, in the eighth grade, Sharon decided she could not lie any more and answered honestly the next time her mother asked. Her mother's response frightened and surprised Sharon.

> She had never been physically abusive towards me before, ever. She beat me pretty badly. Her boyfriend had to drive me home since I was bleeding. She really didn't take it well, I guess you could say. I didn't talk to her for a couple years after that. After she beat me, I hated her. I couldn't believe that she had done that. I just didn't talk to her .... I was scared shitless because I thought she was the one who would take it well. (personal communication, November 10, 1996)

Lesbian, gay, bisexual, and transgendered youth not only face violence at the hands of others, but often fall victim to violence from their own hands. Suicide is the leading cause of death among lesbian and gay youth. According to the Department of Health and Human Services (Gibson, 1989), lesbian and gay youth are two to three times more likely to attempt suicide than other young people and comprise up to 30% of completed youth suicides annually. In a 1991 study of 137 gay and bisexual male youths, 30% had attempted suicide once and 13% reported multiple attempts. The mean age of those attempting suicide was 15.5 years (Remafedi, Farrow, & Deisher, 1991).

The greatest predictor of whether a gay or bisexual male youth attempted suicide, according to Remafedi et al. (1991), was gender-role nonconformity. The extent to which perceived femininity in males is enough to make them want to kill themselves is a powerful statement about the impact of sexism and heterosexism on males.

School culture is colored by harassment, violence, and invisibility. The oppression of invisibility and silencing has costly effects, which range from confusion, depression, and alienation, to dropping out, running away, and suicide. However, within this context of oppressive silencing, there is an increasing number of l/g/b/t youths who develop strong sources of inner strength and a healthy sense of self. The good news is that some students manage to excel academically, socially, and psychologically. The evidence of resistance to oppression is only now starting to accumulate. Not only are we seeing more "survivors" today, but increasingly we are seeing "thrivers." These are resilient and empowered youth who actively resist oppression, who are organized socially and politically to combat homophobia, and who are taking a place of leadership in their communities. I discuss next various forms of response to homophobia and heterosexism and briefly discuss their effect on students of all sexual orientations.

HOMOPHOBIA AND HETEROSEXISM: IMPACT ON STUDENTS

Sanctioned silences and institutionalized invisibility about the lives of lesbian, gay, bisexual, and transgendered individuals are part of the fabric of public schooling. Although they function to maintain a traditional status quo, they do so at a price. The cost is ignorance, alienation, harassment, violence, suicide, and even homicide. Although students may act out socially, experience depression, rage, truancy, or even drop out, viewing the source of these problems as existing solely within the students rather than in the contexts in which they live their lives can contribute to a process of blaming the victim. Given the heterosexism and homophobia in schools, it is clear that the tragedies lesbian, gay, and bisexual students may experience do not center around being homosexual or transgendered, but are a result of being hated or devalued or of having their identity denied. It is within this context that youth struggle to gain an education, survive and/or thrive.

Passing/Compartmentalization

The most common coping strategy adopted by lesbian, gay, bisexual, transgendered, and questioning youth is "passing." For at least some part of their life in school kids who can, try to pass as "straight" (Herdt & Boxer, 1993). Twenty-one-year-old Ken Laparte from Northeast Philadelphia described his process of passing while in school.

> I was going around telling everyone I had a girlfriend and that I had a child and all this other stuff ... I still to this day have people come up to me and ask, "How is your daughter doing?" ... I lied because I was afraid. I didn't know how people would react. I live in a tough neighborhood and I went to a tough school where guys run up and down the hallways with guns in their hands. I was afraid I would get beat up everyday, which I always did as I was growing up. I was afraid people wouldn't accept me. (personal communication, November 8, 1996)

Some youth "compartmentalize" their lives by passing in some arenas and being open in others. Remafedi (1990) argued that healthy development for lesbian and gay teens involves cultivating a positive lesbian or gay identity and self-affirmation, along with the ability to adapt to and cope with a range of social settings and contexts. Compartmentalization of this sort is similar to developing a "bicultural" identity or "bilingual" fluency in a monocultural or "English only" environment. Youth who are "out" in some contexts but not others are similar to Asian or Latino youth who must learn to survive in a racist/ethnocentric world. Knowing where it is safe to speak openly about yourself and where one has to speak the "official language" of heterosexuality is a skill that many lesbian, gay, and bisexual youth perfect.

For the many youth who choose to hide or pass, a tremendous amount of energy and psychological cost can be spent in maintaining a facade (Friend, 1992, 1993; Gonsiorek, 1988; Gover, 1996; Herdt & Boxer, 1993; Martin, 1982; Martin & Hetrick, 1988; Rofes, 1989; Schneider & Tremble, 1986; Walling & Gonzalez, 1996). According to Minton and McDonald (1983/1984), "In choosing to hide an essential part of the self, individuals are left with a gnawing feeling that they are really valued for what others expect them to be rather than for who they really are" (p. 93). Passing and compartmentalization can lead to feeling fragmented and often contributes to lack of authenticity in interpersonal relationships.

Heterosexist Accommodation

In an effort to keep the light of suspicion off of oneself and not be the target of homophobic harassment and violence, some youth accommodate to a homophobic environment by contributing to it. These would be the youth who tell the "fag" jokes, who taunt others who are perceived to be "different," or who spread a rumor about a teacher or a peer. Given that homophobia can be both internalized and a response to the perceived homosexuality in others, Troiden (1988) reported that by harassing others, individuals distance themselves from their own homoerotic feelings. This type of behavior also deflects attention away from the individual and may bolster one's status among a heterosexist peer group. In fact, Herek (1986) argued that the social construction of heterosexual masculinity requires that to be "a real man" in the United States, one must be homophobic.

Heterosexual Overcompensation

Another strategy for fitting in is heterosexual promiscuity and teen pregnancy. In many ways, this is the perfect cover. Troiden (1988, 1989) described this "heterosexual immersion" as adolescents' hope of "curing" their homosexual interests. Heterosexual promiscuity may be a desperate attempt to affirm heterosexuality, for the gay adolescent; for straight youth it may help buffer against their own and others' concerns that they might be gay or lesbian (Schneider & Tremble, 1986; Treadway & Yoakam, 1992). Seventeen-year-old Regina described herself as one of the more popular girls in high school:

> I always dated the best looking guys. Little did they know I was playing with some of their other girls in my head while we were doing it. I got pregnant when I was fifteen because I knew my parents would have an easier time dealing with that, than my lesbianism. (personal communication, November 24, 1990)

Overachievement

Other lesbian, gay, and bisexual youth find that excelling in some area helps them to gain peer acceptance (Treadway & Yoakam, 1992). These youth may be the star athlete, perfect a musical or artistic talent, or demonstrate academic excellence. Overcompensation and proving oneself may be a way to have both peer acceptance and to participate in activities that generate feelings of accomplishment and self-esteem.

Dropping Out

For some l/g/b/t youth, dropping out of school may be a form of active resistance; a considered strategy to keep oneself safe. The Harvey Milk School, a separate public school for lesbian, gay, and transgendered youth, was founded in New York City as a result of the high number of lesbian, gay, and transgendered youth who drop out. Dennis and Harlow (1986) described this school as symbolizing both the rejection of gay teenagers by mainstream schools and the commitment of these teenagers to obtaining education free from discrimination. According to Whitlock (1988):

> In the face of such constant homophobic abuse, it is hardly surprising that gay/lesbian youth are at a high risk for truancy and dropping out. When this occurs administrators too often ignore the damage done to the young person's educational life, believing that if the student is gone, the problem is gone. Truancy and dropping out are taken as evidence that sexual minority youth are a particularly problematic population. Yet this behavior should more properly be seen as a coping strategy, born of desperation when authorities fail to provide a safe learning environment. (pp. 15–16)

Eighteen-year-old Tameeka dropped out of high school after constant antilesbian harassment and violence. When she went to GED school, she found herself the target of harassment there as well. As an "out" and visible lesbian, students and teachers in Tameeka's GED class were uncomfortable and overtly hostile. As is often the case, Tameeka found that she was held responsible, however, for the discomfort of those around her. The GED teacher made her sit in the back of the classroom, because she was "the source of so much tension." This "blaming the victim" approach culminated in Tameeka's being asked to leave the school. When Tameeka told the teacher, "I'm here for an education, not for you to like me," she believes the teacher "kind of found that smart ... and asked me to leave. That's pretty sad when you have to drop out of GED school." (personal communication, November 8, 1996)

Thrivers: Affirmation, Empowerment, and Activism

Today there is a growing cadre of youth who respond to homophobia and heterosexism with strength and fortitude (Friend, 1993; Savin-Williams, 1990; Woog; 1996). Undaunted by oppressive forces, these youth work individually and collectively to transform their worlds. They fight back politically, legally, physically, intellectually, and spiritually. These are kids working on the street to create social change, organizing self-defense classes, running for public office, and constantly educating those around them. They are the youth who are moving from surviving to thriving.

José dropped out of school during the eighth grade after the teasing and harassment he faced from students and teachers in school became intolerable. His mother and father were addicted to drugs and as a child, he lived in a shooting gallery. Today, his mother is in recovery, his father died from AIDS a month prior to our interview, and his brother deals drugs. José survived childhood by dancing and writing poetry. Today he works full time as a community educator conducting HIV prevention and antihomophobia education on the streets, in classrooms, and for social service agencies. He recently completed his GED.

Derik Cowan was thrown out of his home in Connecticut 2 years ago after his fundamentalist parents found out he was gay (Woog, 1996). The 22-year-old founded *Oasis*, the "queer youth Web'zine" that attracts more than 10,000 people a month.

Today, 20-year-old Timothy Ryan is coordinator of Youth Pride, Inc.'s HIV education program in Providence, Rhode Island (Woog, 1996). After coming out at age 15, Timothy spent 4 years working for the successful passage of a state gay rights bill. Currently he's organizing a support group for HIV-positive youth; 2 years ago he tested positive.

Adam Sofen is 17 years old and was a catalyst behind the creation of Gay and Lesbian History Month. After Adam wrote a letter to *Newsweek* complaining about the lack of gay role models, Rodney Wilson, a Missouri teacher, and the Gay, Lesbian and Straight Teachers Network (GLSTN) came up with the history month idea. Adam speaks regularly at staff training and teachers' meetings as well as runs cross-country and track. He hopes to be "the first Jewish, openly gay, somewhat socialist president of the United States" (Woog, 1996, p. 52).

Eighteen-year-olds Mike Hobbs and Adam Rosen broadcast their ideas and concerns on their own St. Louis radio show. They address a range of issues for lesbian and gay youth by reviewing books, interviewing guests, and taking calls from listeners (Woog, 1996).

Seventeen-year-old Miguel Ayala founded the first Gay Straight Alliance in a Chicago public school. Not satisfied with organizing at a local level, Miguel founded Pride USA, a national organization whose mission is to assist students who want to start organizations in their school and serve as the national alliance of all such clubs. He secured 501(c)(3) status and has established a Web site for the group. He recently became the first openly gay person to serve in Chicago's Board of Education (as a student representative; personal communication, October 24, 1996).

These thriving youth demonstrate the vision, the character, and the strength necessary to exercise leadership in their own lives and in their communities. In interviewing resilient youth, a few common themes emerge from their stories. Each of them has had the mentoring, love, and support of a caring adult or family member in their lives. José talks about how David, a local gay activist and poet, forced him to get his GED and helped fine-tune his politics. Sharon and her lover identify Janice Pinto, the high school teacher who helped them start their gay straight alliance, as their mentor. Tameeka's mother, brother, and aunt are continued sources of support and encouragement. Each found a peer group of l/g/b/t youths and engage in mutual support and socializing. They are also all involved in "giving back" in some sort of way.

The process of "service," be it through educating others, organizing support groups, volunteering, or working in social service agencies, is a common thread in the stories of the youth interviewed here. Helping others seems to help. Not only does this teach the skills of planning, decision making, and negotiation, it is grounded on a value of community responsibility. So often these youth found this type of community responsibility contradicted in their own experience. Now they model the way.

The lessons embedded in the lives of these resilient youth also contain the seeds for creating change in public schooling. What follows are recommendations for interrupting homophobia and heterosexism in schools.

IMPLICATIONS FOR PUBLIC SCHOOLING

Shared Leadership

For effective culture change to occur, there must be multiple champions throughout the system exercising leadership at the top, the middle, the bottom, and from the outside. This includes principals and administrators; teachers, counselors, and staff; parents, students, unions, and community organizations. The role of leadership is to inspire a shared vision. The vision must go beyond having a hostile-free or safe school, and must clearly describe an inclusive school culture.

Inclusive schools are not only safe schools where all children can learn, but are school cultures where hate, violence, harassment, and suicide will not be tolerated. Inclusive schools provide more information about the world, not less. Inclusive schools are grounded on the philosophy that critical thinking skills to understand complex pedagogy in an engaged manner is better than limited information and passive thinking. Inclusive schools subscribe to the belief that in order to prepare the next generation of citizens and workers, schools have an obligation to teach the skills necessary to manage differences as a value-added opportunity.

This vision is a moral imperative: Promoting harassment, violence, suicide, low self-esteem, hate, and ignorance is morally wrong. Framing the vision in this way helps transformational leaders set the agenda and appeal to the widely shared values of respect, honesty, compassion, and safety.

Jonathan Wilson served on the Des Moines, Iowa School Board for 12 years. After being verbally attacked and threatened by the antigay organization "The Report," Wilson outed himself as a gay man during a televised School Board meeting. Although he lost his reelection, Wilson's demonstration of integrity and leading by example reflect the values of inclusive schooling. According to Wilson (1996):

I would submit to you that an essential component today of a basic, quality citizenship education is an appreciation for the rich diversity that makes up the world in which we already live.... Where there is community consensus about values ... the public school should teach without apology to anyone, including parents on the fringe. When it comes to issues on which there is not yet a community consensus, such as interracial dating, abortion, and homosexuality, the public schools should acknowledge that opinions in the community may differ on the right or wrong of the issue, and then teach tolerance and respect, and answer factual questions, all factual questions, as honestly and accurately as possible, and without apology to anyone. (p. 4)

To put into practice the vision that public education can and should be a place of possibility and growth for all people—no matter what their race, class, ethnic identification, gender, ability/disability status, or sexual orientation—school culture must frame inclusiveness as a moral career for all participants. In this way combating sexism is seen as good for boys as well as for girls. Dismantling racism is understood as important for Whites as well as for people of color. Coming out against homophobia is framed as enhancing the lives of people of all sexual orientations.

Given that leadership by definition involves counter-hegemonic action, educators express a range of concern regarding interrupting heterosexism. These concerns reflect the power of the current hegemony. One concern has to do with "undue influence" or "encouragement," demonstrated in the fear that "if you talk about it, they'll do it."

This fear of encouragement is expressed in debates over comprehensive sexuality education. It is supported by the notion of "childhood innocence" and the concern that by raising these issues, the innocence of youth is lost. Like sex and sexuality, youth are already thinking about homophobia in profound and powerful ways. This is reflected in the number of gay, lesbian, and bisexual youth who are either coming out or deciding not to. It is evidenced in those youth who actively resist oppression and thrive, or internalize it by contemplating or completing suicide. Boys who attack and hurt kids who are perceived to be gay as a "right of passage" ("boys will be boys"), and kids who taunt each other in hostile schoolyards are evidence that we are not introducing a new conversation, but trying to interrupt an oppressive dialogue that limits the opportunities for *all* students.

The number of l/g/b/t youths who are failed by the system and drop out reflects this powerful social arrangement. The extent to which adolescent males disproportionately represent perpetrators of antigay and antilesbian violence (Comstock, 1991) indicates that the ideas are already in their heads. They are "doing it." The issue at hand is "how do *we* feel about the 'it' that they are doing?"

"If you talk about it, they'll do it" is also based on the belief that people are all born heterosexual and become influenced (usually by an adult homosexual) or "recruited" into homosexuality. Talking about sexual orientation in inclusive ways will only influence students' self-acceptance and their comfort with those who are similar or different from themselves. Hidden here is also the assumption that none of the students are lesbian, gay or bisexual, or that even if we could influence students' sexual orientation, that it would certainly be better to develop heterosexual orientations than homosexual ones. Both these assumptions reflect the deeply rooted ideology of heterosexism.

The concern of "undue influence" is grounded on a moral imperative to protect children. The sexualization of homosexuality and the framing of homosexuals as sexual predators often links this concern with fear of "access to children." The mythology is that teaching about lesbian and gay issues sets the stage for homosexuals to have sexual access to children. Protecting children is central to the rhetoric of those opposed to inclusion. This is as true today as it was when Anita Bryant formed her "Save the Children" campaign in the 1970s and the "Protect Our Children" slogan used in Oregon's 1994 antigay referendum; or when the Nazis accused Jews of kidnaping and killing Aryan youth. Protecting children is a universal value that needs to be reclaimed and expressed by educators as they set the agenda for a cultural change toward inclusion (Jennings, 1996). Access to schools *is* access to children. We need to protect children from harassment, violence, and ignorance, and from not being prepared to live and work effectively in an increasingly diverse world. It is to this moral cause that we should recruit children (Armstrong, personal communication, October 24, 1996).

Although leadership is a *shared* responsibility, without champions situated at the top, the process of culture change takes much longer and is much harder (Friend, 1996). Individuals whose professional role charges them with organizational power and responsibility are critical as change agents. Their behavior must match their rhetoric. They must also enforce the values of inclusiveness through the policies and practices that they set.

Inclusive Policies, Practices, and Pedagogy

For the vision of inclusiveness to become part of the foundation of school culture, formal and informal policies and practices have to be aligned with the vision. An engaged and inclusive pedagogy (Freire, 1996) connects "the will to know with the will to become" (hooks, 1994, p 19).

Inclusive curricula and pedagogy not only incorporate lesbian and gay issues throughout the curriculum, but do so with a willingness to accord the work of those considered marginal "the same respect and consideration given other work" (hooks, 1994, p. 39). Many educators worry, however, that teaching inclusively opens the flood gates to tremendous controversy and chaos. I believe, however, that a risk-free environment is a learning-free environment. Intellectual risk taking, trying out new ideas, and challenging the status quo are part of the process of critical thinking and are not mutually exclusive with safety.

The "banking system" of education where educators pass on information to passive students like currency (Freire, 1996) is central to a control-and-manage pedagogy. "Decentering" this control makes many educators feel unsafe. However, in a seemingly "safe and controlled" educational setting, there are many students who feel unsafe and unrecognized. According to hooks (1994), "Many students, especially students of color, may not feel at all 'safe' in what appears to be a neutral setting. It is the absence of a feeling of safety that often promotes prolonged silence or lack of student engagement" (p. 39).

When heterosexist language is avoided through the inclusion of story problems in math class that use gender neutral pronouns or in discussions of situations that refer to partner choice and family, for example, a decentering of heterosexism occurs. The message, while subtle and powerful, helps to build an inclusive learning community that recognizes multiple voices.

The policies and practices of schooling also need to support the values of safety and respect. Clear nondiscrimination and antiharassment policies that include sexual orientation as a protected status must be developed and actively publicized and enforced throughout the school community (Anderson, 1994; Treadway & Yoakam, 1992; Walling, 1996). In July 1991 The National Education Association passed a resolution supporting nondiscriminatory personnel policies inclusive of sexual orientation and a resolution deploring incidents of harassment and hate-motivated violence based on real or perceived sexual orientation. Policies such as these provide direction and authority for educators to act proactively and reactively in support of inclusiveness.

Nondiscrimination and domestic partnership benefits also contribute to a school culture where lesbian and gay adults are likely to feel the freedom to be open about their lives in the same ways as their heterosexual colleagues. Not only does this provide access to information and role models for all members of the school culture, but it increases the talent pool from which to recruit future school personnel.

There also need to be multiple practices and structures that support students coming together around issues of sexual orientation. There are four types of models commonly used for this purpose. These support models used collectively help to promote inclusion.

One model involves peer support groups such as Gay–Straight Alliances (GSAs or SAGAs) which are open to any student interested in understanding issues of homophobia and sexual identity. These forums provide education, awareness, and a focused space of inclusion. In December 1993, Massachusetts became the first and only state to outlaw discrimination in public schools on the basis of sexual orientation. The number of public schools with GSAs in Massachusetts rose from two in 1992 to 20 in 1993 (Dorning, 1993). This fact demonstrates the way in which policies and practices weave together to form a net of support.

Another form of support is grounded on a psychotherapeutic model. Trained counselors who can provide individual and group counseling play an important role in supporting youth in conflict. Not all youth need this type of support, however, and to have this be the only type of support group available may send a message of pathology rather than inclusion.

A third model is to infuse issues of lesbian and gay inclusion into the mission of other school-sponsored organizations (such as Amnesty International). It is important to help students understand the connection of individual social issues to a larger whole. A stand-alone GSA is probably necessary, however, if not all groups are able to act inclusively in interrupting homophobia (and most are not).

A final model that is used is the creation of safe spaces or harassment-free zones. These clearly identified locations (whether a classroom, a counseling room, or an administrator's office) are visibly marked (often with a pink triangles) as places students can go if there is a problem. The goal of inclusiveness, however, is for *all* space to be safe and free from harassment.

The practice of having visible lesbian, gay, and bisexual role models as well as "straight allies" (Washington & Evans, 1991) is important for interrupting homophobia and building inclusion. Knowing someone personally who is lesbian or gay is critical in reducing stereotypes. If there are no out role models available within the school, this says something about the current school climate. Inviting presenters and speakers in from local youth groups or organizations can be used as an intermediary step.

School-sponsored social functions such as proms, dances, film, and theater presentations should also be inclusive in theme. Invitations to these events should be worded using inclusive language that clearly welcomes all people and all couples.

Incorporating lesbian and gay issues appropriately throughout the curriculum, having clear nondiscrimination and antiharassment policies, supportive groups and safe space, and available role models and allies are some of the key policies and practices that contribute to the creation of an inclusive school environment.

Another key resource is training. Staff need to have comfort, understanding, and effective skills for promoting and maintaining an inclusive culture (Friend, 1992, 1996). Lipkin (1996) argued that staff must work out their own feelings and clarify their own values on the issues and then be trained to handle the discomfort and questions of students. Emotional content to be addressed includes feelings about the inevitable "Are you one of them?" question. Like any educational process, there is a learning curve for educators. With the right training resources and an encouraging environment, they eventually can learn to deal with this issue as they have learned to handle other controversial issues in the classroom.

To increase inclusiveness within school culture, a clear strategic approach is necessary. The plan should include anticipating opposition and building a broad base of support around the vision of inclusion. Anticipating the opposition is not the same as fearing the opposition.

Fear of opposition is strong. Teachers fear administrators, administrators fear parents, parents bring in the fear of god, and so on. Approaching the issue from a position of fear, however, means the opposition never has to do anything overt to stop the process. Without even materializing, the fear of opposition alone often preempts the conversation. Instilling fear is a potent tool of disempowering the courageous and facilitating divide-and-conquer among well-meaning individuals who are simply not clear about the vision of antihomophobia education.

Jennings (1996) recommended framing the issues in the right way using universal values such as those articulated earlier. He also recommended putting a human face on the argument. This interrupts the opposition's tool of framing gay and lesbian people as dreadful and dangerous "others." Finally, he recommended organizing across existing divisions. Building a broad base of community support is important fuel.

Have active community support from teachers, unions, parents, alumni, and religious organizations that represent a broad range of races, social classes, and ethnic backgrounds. Groups like GLSTN, Parents and Friends of Lesbians and Gays (PFLAG), associations such as the AFT, the NEA, and local PTAs as well as religious organizations that support lesbian, gay, and bisexual people are all key allies to be leveraged. This alliance building is key even in the absence of an organized opposition. It models the type of inclusive coalition building implied in the vision.

Although more easily said than done, these recommendations for building inclusiveness have been useful guides for the organizations and schools I have partnered with in addressing and interrupting homophobia. Complex systemic change requires the patience, perseverance, resources, and commitment to continuously work at achieving the vision of inclusiveness.

CONCLUSIONS

The better part of my adult life has been spent involved in facilitating individual and organizational change in order to improve the quality and outcome of schooling and work. I started this journey as an enthused and hopeful pioneer, ready to build a partnership around the vision of creating school cultures that promote equity in outcome as well as access. Although still hopeful, I am sobered by the paradoxes that reveal how challenging it is to make this vision a reality. As an optimist, I continue to hold to the vision that public schools can and should be a place of possibility and growth for children and adults alike. Today, it is the generation of resilient lesbian, gay, bisexual, and transgendered youth as well as courageous educators and change agents who fuel my optimism and inspire me to move ahead. It is my hope that anyone involved in schooling finds a role that ensures that this next generation flourishes and cuts a path toward a better future for all of us.

ACKNOWLEDGMENT

The author would like to express his thanks and appreciation to Daren R. Wade and Janice Pinto for their help and support on this project. Correspondence may be directed to the author at: 5510 N. Sheridan Rd. #16–A, Chicago, IL 60640. rafriend@msn.com, phone/fax (773) 275-1294.

REFERENCES

AAUW. (1992). Hostile hallways: The AAUW survey on sexual harassment in America's schools. American Association of University Women Educational Foundation, researched by Louis Harris and Associates.

Anderson, J. D. (1994). School climate for gay and lesbian students and staff members. Phi Delta Kappan, 76(2), 151–154.Vol. 76, No. 2.

Babad, E., Birnbaum, M., & Benne, K. (1983). The social self: Group influences on personal identity. Beverly Hills, CA: Sage.

Commission on Global Governance. (1995). Our global neighborhood: The report of the commission on global governance. New York: Oxford University Press.

Comstock, G. D. (1991). Violence against lesbians and gay men. New York: Columbia University Press.

Dennis, D. I., & Harlow, R. E. (1986). Gay youth and the right to education. Yale Law and Policy Review, 4, 446–478.

Dorning, M. (1993, November 30). Schools' support groups helping gay teens to cope. Chicago Tribune

Fine, M. (1991). Framing dropouts: Notes on the politics of an urban public high school. Albany, NY: State University of New York Press.

Freire, P. (1996). Pedagogy of the oppressed: New revised 20th anniversary edition. New York: The Continuum Publishing Company.

Friend, R. (1987a). The individual and social psychology of aging: Clinical implications for lesbians and gay men. Journal of Homosexuality, 14(1, 2), 307–331.

Friend, R. (1987b). Sexual identity and human diversity: Implications for nursing practice. Holistic Nursing Practice, 1(4), 21–41.

Friend, R. (1989). Older lesbian and gay people: Responding to homophobia. Marriage and Family Review, 14(3, 4), 241–263.

Friend, R. (1990). Older lesbian and gay people: A theory of successful aging. Journal of Homosexuality, 20 (3, 4), 91–110.

Friend, R. (1992). Listening to silenced voices: Strategies for undoing homophobia in schools. Independent School, 51(3), 33–37.

Friend, R. (1993). Choices, not closets: Heterosexism and homophobia in schools. In L. Weis & M. Fine (Eds.). Beyond silenced voices: Class, race, and gender in United States schools (pp. 209–235). New York: SUNY Press.

Friend, R. (1994). Homophobia. In V. L. Bullough & B. Bullough, (Eds.), Human sexuality: An encyclopedia (pp. 275–277). New York: Garland Publishing, Inc.

Friend, R. (1996, March 8). Being paid to induce dangerous thoughts: The paradoxes of being an anti-homophobia educator. Paper presented at the Second Annual Midwest GLSTN Conference, Chicago, IL.

Gibson, P. (1989). Gay male and lesbian youth suicide. Report of the Secretary's Task Force on Youth Suicide (pp. 36–3-142). Washington, DC: U.S. Department of Health and Human Services.

Gonsiorek, J. C. (1988). Mental health issues of gay and lesbian adolescents. Journal of Adolescent Health Care, 9, 114–122.

Gordon, L. (1983). What do say when we hear the word "faggot?" Interracial Books for Children Bulletin, 14, (3/4), 25–27.

Gover, J. (1996). Gay youth in the family. In D. R. Walling (Ed.), Open lives, safe schools: Addressing gay and lesbian issues in education (pp. 173–182). Bloomington, IN: Phi Delta Kappa Educational Foundation.

Griffin, P. (1992). From hiding out to coming out: Empowering lesbian and gay educators. In K. M. Harbeck (Ed.), *Coming out of the classroom closet: Gay and lesbian students, teachers and curricula* (pp. 167–174). New York: Harrington Park Press.

Herdt, G., & Boxer, A. (1993). *Children of horizons: How gay and lesbian teens are leading a new way out of the closet.* Boston: Beacon Press.

Herek, G. M. (1984, Fall). Beyond "homophobia": Social psychological perspective on attitudes toward lesbians and gay men. *Journal of Homosexuality, 10,* 39–51.

Herek, G. M. (1986). On heterosexual masculinity: Some physical consequences of the social construction of gender and sexuality. *American Behavioral Psychologist, 29,* 563–577.

Herek, G. M. (1989). Hate crimes against lesbians and gay men: Issues for research and policy. *American Psychologist, 44,* 948–955.

hooks, b. (1994). *Teaching to transgress: Education as the practice of freedom.* New York: Routledge.

Hunter, J., & Schaecher, R. (1987). Stresses on lesbian and gay adolescents in schools. *Social Work in Education, 9*(3), 180–190.

Jennings, K. (1996). Together for a change: Lessons from organizing the Gay, Lesbian and Straight Teachers Network (GLSTN). In D. R. Walling. (Ed.), *Open lives, safe schools: Addressing gay and lesbian issues in education* (pp. 251–260). Bloomington, IN: Phi Delta Kappa Educational Foundation.

Krysial, G. J. (1987). A very silent and gay minority. *The School Counselor, 34*(4), 304–307.

Lipkin, A. (1996). The case for a gay and lesbian curriculum. In D. R. Walling. (Ed.), *Open lives, safe schools: Addressing gay and lesbian issues in education* (pp. 47–69). Bloomington, IN: Phi Delta Kappa Educational Foundation.

Lorde, A. (1988). I am your sister: Black women organizing across sexualities. In L. Fulani (Ed.), *The psychopathology of everyday racism and sexism* (pp. 25–32). Binghamton, NY: Haworth.

Martin, D. A. (1982). Learning to hide: The socialization of the gay adolescent. *Adolescent Psychiatry, 10,* 52–65.

Martin, D. A., & Hetrick, E. S. (1988). The stigmatization of the gay and lesbian adolescent. *Journal of Homosexuality, 15,* (1/2), 163–183.

McLaren, P. (1995). Moral panic, schooling, and gay identity: Critical pedagogy and the politics of resistance. In G. Unks (Ed.), *The gay teen: Educational practice and theory for lesbian, gay, and bisexual adolescents* (pp. 105–123). New York: Routledge.

Minton, H. L., & McDonald, G. J. (1983/1984). Homosexual identity formation as a developmental process. *Journal of Homosexuality, 9,* 91–104.

National Institute of Justice. (1987). *The response of the criminal justice system to bias crime: An exploratory review.* Washington, DC: U.S. Department of Justice.

Neisen, J. (1990). Heterosexism: Redefining homophobia for the 1990's. *Journal of Gay and Lesbian Psychotherapy, 1*(3), 21–35.

Orenstein, P. (1994). *School girls: Young women, self-esteem, and the confidence gap.* New York: Double Day.

Patterson, C. (1992). Children of lesbian and gay parents. *Child Development, 63.*

Personal Responsibility and Work Opportunity Reconciliation Act of 1996, Pub. L. No. 44–103, 110 Stat. 2110 (1996).

Pharr, S. (1988). *Homophobia: A weapon of sexism.* Inverness, CA: Chardon.

Prince, T. (1996). The power of openness and inclusion in countering homophobia in schools. In D. R. Walling. (Ed.), *Open lives, safe schools: Addressing gay and lesbian issues in education* (pp. 29–34). Bloomington, IN: Phi Delta Kappa Educational Foundation.

Remafedi, G., Farrow, J. A., & Deisher, R. W. (1991). Risk factors for attempted suicides in gay and bisexual males. *Pediatrics, 87,* 869–875.

Remafedi, G. (1990, November 1). *Moving towards a healthy paradigm of teen sexual development*. Paper presented at the 33rd Annual Meeting of the Society for the Scientific Study of Sex, Minneapolis.

Rich, A. (1980). Compulsory heterosexuality and lesbian existence. *Signs: Journal of Women in Culture and Society, 5*(8), 3–32.

Rofes, E. (1989). Opening up the classroom closet: Responding to the educational needs of gay and lesbian youth. *Harvard Educational Review, 59*, 444–453.

Rubin, G. (1984). Thinking sex: Notes for a radical theory of the politics of sexuality. In C. Vance (Ed.), *Pleasure and danger: Exploring female sexuality* (pp. 267–319). Boston: Routledge & Kegan Paul.

Savin-Williams, R. C. (1990). *Gay and lesbian youth: Expressions of identity*. New York: Hemisphere.

Schneider, M., & Tremble, B. (1986). Gay or straight?: Working with the confused adolescent. *Journal of Social Work and Human Sexuality, 4*, (1/2), 71–82.

Sivertsen, W., & Thames, T. (1995). Each child that dies: Gays and lesbians in your schools. In J. M. Novak & L. G. Denti (Eds.), *Multicultures, Unity Through Diversity–A Monograph of Diversity in the Field of Education, 1*.

Smith, A. J. (1991, July 6). *From stigma to paradigm: The uses of difference*. Paper presented at the third North American Anti-Homophobia Educators Conference—Challenging Oppression: Creating Multicultural Communities, Chicago, IL.

Treadway, L., & Yoakam, J. (1992). Creating a safer school environment for lesbian and gay students. *Journal of School Health, 62*(7).

Trenchard, L. (1984). *Talking about young lesbians*. London: London Gay Teenage Group.

Troiden, R. R. (1988). Homosexual identity formation. *Journal of Adolescent Health Care, 9*, 105–113.

Troiden, R. R. (1989). The formation of homosexual identities. *Journal of Homosexuality, 17*, (½), 43–73.

Walling, D. R. (1996). Introduction. In D. R. Walling. (Ed.), *Open lives, safe schools: Addressing gay and lesbian issues in education* (pp. 1–6). Bloomington, IN: Phi Delta Kappa Educational Foundation.

Walling, D. R., & Gonzalez, C. T. (1996). How the IYG helps gay teens at risk. In D. R. Walling, (Ed.). *Open lives, safe schools: Addressing gay and lesbian issues in education* (pp. 245–250). Bloomington, IN: Phi Delta Kappa Educational Foundation.

Washington, J., & Evans, N. J. (1991). Becoming an ally. In N. J. Evans & V. A. Wall. (Eds.), *Beyond tolerance: Gay, lesbian and bisexuals on campus*. Alexandria, VA: American College Personnel Association.

Weinberg, G. H. (1972). *Society and the healthy homosexual*. New York: St. Martin's Press.

Whitlock, K. (1988). *Bridges to respect*. Philadelphia: American Friends Service Committee.

Whitlock, K., & DiLapi, E. M. (1983). "Friendly fire": Homophobia in sex education literature. *Interracial Books for Children Bulletin, 14*(3,4), 20–23.

Wilson, J. C. (1996, March 8). *Quality education: A view from an open closet door*. Paper presented at the Second Annual Midwest GLSTN Conference, Chicago, IL.

Woog, D. (1996, September). Under 21. *Genre, 41*, 50–55.

II

THE BROADER CONTEXT
OF INVISIBILITY

9

Where Have All the Children Gone? The Transformation of Children Into Dollars in Public Law 104-193

❈ ◆ ❈

Barbara Finkelstein
Reem Mourad
Elyssa Doner
University of Maryland, College Park

Children have served as symbolic repositories for generations of policymakers who, as they conduct the business of government, have invoked the condition of childhood as both reason and rationale to expand or contract the taxing power and regulatory authority of the federal government, to redistribute resources, and, in oft-times unacknowledged and invisible ways, to define the moral responsibilities of families, the norms of childrearing, and the standard of care to which children ought to be entitled (Finkelstein, 1985).

Serial generations of social reformers have invoked the needs of children to justify an array of contradictory social policies and forms of intervention into the lives of families and children. In 1819, with the passage of a so-called "Civilizing Act," Congress appropriated $10,000 to hire teachers of "good moral character" to instruct Indian children in agriculture and the 3 Rs. Part of an effort to disengage First Nation Americans from valuable land,

and to separate them from European society, the Civilizing Act was ultimately designed to detribalize Indian youth, to turn the American Indian into a New England farmer, and their children into literate Protestants. The Secretary, in 1819, gave voice to this particular sentiment by invoking a commitment to child-saving as a rationalization for federal government incursions into the tribal life of Native Americans:

> In the present state of our country, one of two things seem to be necessary. Either that those sons of the forest should be moralized or exterminated. Humanity would rejoice at the former, but shrink from the latter. Put into the hands of their children, the primer and the hoe, and they will naturally in time, take hold of the plow and as their minds enlighten and expand, the Bible will be their Book and they will grow up in habits of industry and morality. (quoted in Winer, 1972, p. 72)

Different indeed were the sentiments of Teddy Roosevelt a century later, when he urged an expansion of federal government involvement in the lives of the nation's children, by defining children as people in need of help rather than in need of moral and social reconstruction. Invoking a rhetoric of child protection rather than national defense, Roosevelt (1909) justified the establishment of a Children's Bureau that would create a children's lobby inside the federal government and justify a much expanded role for Uncle Sam in the lives of troubled youngsters:

> The state has dealt generously with her trouble-some children: but what is she doing for those who make no trouble but are simply unfortunate? Some are orphans or half-orphans, some are abandoned by heartless parents, some are victims of cruelty and neglect. They are not delinquents; they are accused of no faults; they are simply destitute and neglected. (p. 17)

Roosevelt distinguished between the deserving and undeserving poor as he justified the expansion of federal government involvement in the lives of the young, defining the role of the national government as an agency of child protection as well as moral reformation or poor relief. Defining neglected and abandoned children as a special obligation of the federal government, Roosevelt helped to redefine the relationship of Uncle Sam to the nation's children, laying a foundation for a much more elaborate expansion of the federal role in the 1930s.

A third form of federal involvement with families and children emerged in the wake of the Depression when in 1935, Congress enacted social security legislation that linked the well-being of children to the economic, social, medical, and educational condition of their families.

The aim of social security is the protection of the family life of wage earners, and the prime factor in family life is the protection and development of children. Security for families, the broad foundation upon which the welfare of American children must rest, involves economic, health, and social measures which pertain to the entire economic and social structure of our civilization. Among them are an adequate wage level; ... compensation when full employment fails; provision of adequate medical care ... provision for the old, sick, the widowed, and the orphaned; adequate opportunities for education and for vocational guidance and placement .... *All social security measures may be described, in fact, as affecting child welfare—even old age security which lifts the burden of support of the aged from those of middle age whose resources are needed for the care of children* [italics added]. (quoted in Bremner, 1974, p. 525)

The joining of child welfare to social security constituted a revolutionary transformation in the meaning of child protection—a meaning that was to become fully institutionalized after 1935, as the nation aimed to recover from the social consequences of a devastating world war and an economically shattering depression. From the end of World War II until August 22, 1996, federal legislative provisions have defined children as victims of economic and social misfortune rather than moral degeneracy, and serial congresses have elaborated two kinds of legislative strategies consistent with these views. A family tutoring legislative strategy identified the interests of children with the interests of their parents and led Congress to provide services to families in the form of parent education programs and nursery schools for their children. The establishment of child-care centers during the New Deal, Head Start, and Even Start programs in the 1960s, 1970s, and 1980s, parent education programs, and child-care service provisions in the Child Development Block Grants of the early 1990s, all deploy resources for the support of child-care centers for needy families.

Beyond arranging for the provision of social services, Congress also recognized a special obligation to the children, identified their interests with the economic well-being of their families, and channeled income directly into their homes. The welfare provisions of the original Social Security Act, Title IV of Aid for Families with Dependent Children, the Family Leave Act of 1994, and the Earned Income Tax Credit Bill all exemplify what might be called family saving legislative strategies.

For the last half-century, the federal government has deployed what some have called a "safety net," what others have called a 60-year commitment to America's poorest children, and what still others have called "the nation's social bargain with the poor" (Clinton, 1996). These approaches represent the cumulative efforts of generations of child advocates to engage the power of the federal government to right social wrongs, to protect the dependent, and to minister to the socially needy.

All of this was to end on August 22, 1996, when President William Jefferson Clinton signed the Personal Responsibility and Work Opportunity Reconciliation Act of 1996 into law and through this action reorganized the relationship of Uncle Sam to the children of the nation. This legislation, as Clinton put it on the day of the signing, "provides an historic opportunity to end welfare as we know it and transform our broken welfare system by promoting the fundamental values of work, responsibility, and family" (Clinton, 1996).

Through its rhetorical emphases and regulatory provisions, The Personal Responsibility and Work Opportunity Reconciliation Act of 1996 eliminates child protection as a legitimate rationalization for federal involvement and substitutes moral reconstruction and economic oversight instead. The goal of welfare reform, according to President Clinton (1996a), is to "make work and responsibility the law of the land." Senator Mikulski (1996) put it this way: "Welfare reform is about ending the cycle and culture of poverty ... ending the culture of poverty is about personal responsibility."

This act disjoins the interests of children from those of their families in quite the same way as traditional child-saving legislative strategies have done—by declaring families to be morally bankrupt and by deploying the disciplinary apparatus of the federal government to impose work requirements, to define who is undeserving and who is not, and to channel public expenditures into services designed to replace families with morally and politically sanctioned substitutes.

The bill does not provide support directly to families in the form of child-care services, parent education programs and/or nursery schools that parents may or may not choose to use. Nor does it provide income supports, unemployment insurance, maternity or paternity leaves, or education allowances.

Unlike its predecessors, the 1996 Personal Responsibility and Work Opportunity Act invokes no rhetoric of child protection or child rights. Through the provisions of this act, poor children come into view not as an economically bereft, educationally vulnerable, dependent class of victimized young people, but as the progeny of a morally profligate class of unmarried, undeserving, sexually promiscuous men and women in need of moral reclamation, social reconstruction, publicly administered discipline, and paid work.

The new welfare bill, as we shall see, is less about child welfare than about working parents; less about child protection than about family regulation; less about children's rights than about parent obligation. As we shall see, the new welfare law deploys the disciplinary power of the federal government to bring childrearing under the unbending control of market requirements and to divest nonworking families of the public support except for very short periods of time. It diverts direct cash payments from families, and through a labyrinthine series of highly regulated federal block grant allocations, aims to establish the two-parent family as a social norm, the working couple as a social ideal, and the state social service agency as a regulatory channel for the administration of child care services, social security insurance, and medical benefits. The Personal Responsibility and Work Opportunity Reconciliation Act (1996) also serves as an instrument of deficit reduction by streamlining services to children, cutting medical and social benefits, and by redefining the levels of care to which children are entitled. In short, this act transforms childhood policies into economic policies and state mandated prescriptions for right living.

What follows is an analysis of how this transformation works. It constitutes an exploration of how the bill deploys the sovereign power of the federal government to define the meaning of personal responsibility and to impose state-constructed norms of conduct. It suggests the ways in which the Personal Responsibility and Work Opportunity Reconciliation Act (1996) engages the federal government in definitions of welfare that construct families as interdependent economic entities rather than as sites for the rearing and protection of children. It reveals the ways in which childcare services are constructed as commodities to be purchased and businesses to be regulated rather than as safe havens for children, subject to nationally constituted quality controls, standards of accountability, levels of care, and safe provider–child ratios. Finally, it explores the welfare bill as an instrument of deficit reduction. Taken together, these four attributes reveal Uncle Sam's approach to children at century's end.

STATE-CONSTRUCTED NORMS

Strewn throughout the nine titles of the bill are an array of rhetorical assertions and regulatory principles that establish norms that should govern the relationships between mothers and fathers, parents and children, and the family and the community.

The Two-Parent Family

Title I, Section 101 of the Personal Responsibility and Work Opportunity Reconciliation Act (1996) contains the "findings" of the Congress which invoke the virtues of marriage and proclaim the evils of single parenthood as a crisis of monumental proportions.

- Marriage is the foundation of a successful society.
- Marriage is an essential institution of a successful society which promotes the interests of children.
- Promotion of responsible fatherhood and motherhood is integral to successful childrearing and the well-being of children.

Beyond attaching the well-being of children to the institution of marriage and the exercise of responsible parenthood, this Act contains a series of statistical claims that blame socioeconomic dislocations on children born out of wedlock. The bill correlates increases in the number of "illegitimate" children with rises in poverty, crime, physical and sexual abuse, disease, and school failure. Because approximately 89% of children in AFDC families live with only one parent, the bill defines children born out of wedlock as a drain on the public treasury, the offspring of parents who are often young, unmarried, unschooled. (Burke, 1996)

In an attempt to prevent increases in single motherhood, the bill (Title I, Section 103) also authorizes a state to use federal family assistance grant amounts under its Temporary Assistance Programs to provide prepregnancy family planning services (although their use for medical services is generally denied). As an inducement, the federal government also promises "out-of-wedlock bonus money"—up to $20 million for the five states that achieve the sharpest drop in out-of-wedlock births while also decreasing the abortion rate. The bill empowers states to cap family benefits when an additional child is born and requires states to deny benefits to those who fail to cooperate with child-support agencies or who incur child support arrears.

Consistent with the diagnosis of illegitimacy as a cause of social disruption, Title I of the new welfare law deploys regulatory measures designed to reconstruct the custodial arrangements of unwed mothers and fathers. Viewing the two-parent family as a social norm and, as we shall see, an economic necessity as well, the bill deploys the disciplinary power of the federal government to regulate the lives of several classes of family members. Unmarried mothers under the age of 18, in order to be eligible for benefits, must live with an adult relative or in an adult-supervised arrangement, as long as the arrangement does not subject the mother to potential harm. Similarly, the bill requires the states to provide assistance to unwed minor husbands to find suitable adult-supervised homes.

Family and Community

"Noncustodial," "nonsupporting" parents under the age of 18 are also required to adhere to the edict of personal responsibility and attain self-sufficiency through mandatory participation in community service programs, vocational education training, public housing reconstruction initiatives, and child-care service centers for the children of service program participants (Title I, Sec. 103). Beyond defining where unmarried mothers and fathers should live, the bill also requires mothers who have completed high school to attend school or an alternative training program once their children are 12 weeks old.

Beyond regulations that compel young unmarried recipients of public assistance to live in supervised homes, enter work training programs, arrange for childcare, and take prepregnancy health courses, recipients under the new welfare law must also participate in community service after they have received 2 months of benefits (unless excused by the state) and to be at work after 2 years. Furthermore, the law imposes a 5-year time limit on aid.[1]

Although the parent of a child under 12 months is exempt from this work requirement, such an exemption is available only once in the 5-year period. Through the array of prescriptions and assertions, the Personal Responsibility and Work Opportunity Reconciliation Act (1996) has defined an optimal American family as one in which parents are married, over 18, working, and purchasing day care for their children.

THE FAMILY AS ECONOMIC UNIT

The array of measures designed to redefine the structure and custodial functions of the family, to impose norms of social service and school attendance, to require education in family planning, and otherwise to

---

[1] Exceptions are made for "hardship" or "battered" persons.

reduce illegitimacy represents only one approach to the moral reconstruction of welfare recipients. The Personal Responsibility and Work Opportunity Reconciliation Act (1996) also defines family responsibility in economic terms, setting forth measures that treat the family as an interdependent economic unit in which members are defined in relationship to one another by an array of economic entitlements and obligations. In so doing, the federal government legitimizes a disposition to view the family as an economic unit with responsibilities and liabilities, rather than as a childrearing unit that should create an ideal environment to raise children. This shift in emphasis enables the federal government to justify reductions in levels of support for child care.

In an attempt to establish the primacy of work as a family necessity, the bill compels states to substitute work requirements for direct cash payments. It also requires parents to work outside the home and contribute, as necessary, to the purchase of child- and health- care services as well as to sustain the financial costs of childrearing.

Less focused on the availability of decent child care or affordable health care or housing than on the need for parents to work outside the home, the bill deploys the regulatory authority of the state to enforce work requirements. In a two-parent household, at least one parent is required to work for 35 hours per week, while single parents are subject to a work requirement of 20 hours per week until the year 2002, when they will be required to work 30 hours per week in order to receive benefits.

The bill proceeds on an assumption that children over 6 will be in school and therefore require no additional care before or after school.[2] For families with children under 6 years of age, the law requires parents to put their children into the care of other licensed providers.[3] Because of new regulations that license previously unregulated child-care centers in churches and other private spaces, the number of available centers will increase, but

---

[2]Likewise, Section 103 under the same title permits states receiving family assistance with the option of denying assistance to an adult who has received TANF or food stamp assistance if the adult fails to ensure that his or her minor dependent children attend school as required by applicable state law or is between the ages of 20 and 51 and has received such assistance if such adult does not have, or is not working toward attaining, a secondary school diploma or its recognized equivalent (unless the person is determined to lack the requisite capacity to attain such credentials). Noncomplying adults are not only "irresponsible," but are in fact liable for their misbehavior and are subsequently denied benefits.

[3]The only exceptions are for families who can show there is no decent child-care arrangement available within a reasonable distance from their homes.

control over their quality will not necessarily be assured.[4]

The new welfare law also imposes a series of disciplinary measures on welfare recipients and on state agencies that fail to establish and document paternity, enforce child-support responsibilities, establish two-parent liability, or otherwise secure paternal involvement with families.[5] Title III outlines specific provisions for child support and at the same time creates a system of personal liability. Subtitle G, Section 365 requires states to establish plans to secure child and spousal support, including specified procedures that require recalcitrant parents to work or participate in work activities that a court defines as appropriate. Furthermore, Title III permits states to disqualify custodial parents of children under the age of 18 who have an absent parent, unless the parent cooperates with the state child-support agency in establishing the child's paternity and in obtaining support for the child and the parent. The bill (Subtitle B Sections 314–315) requires state agencies to seize assets of a debtor parent by intercepting or seizing lump-sum or periodic payments, such as unemployment, workman's compensation, lottery winnings, awards, judgments, or settlements. In addition, the bill enables states to report child-support arrears to credit bureaus, to provide for liens against real and personal property, and to implement the restriction of driver's, professional, occupational, and recreational licenses of individuals owing support.

The bill also calls for the establishment of automated registries to track and locate parents quickly and efficiently, to streamline the paternity determination process, and to reduce or eliminate support for noncooperating families.[6] The law creates a complex network of regulations with which the states must abide in order to receive block grant monies. For example, the work participation rate for the caseload of single-parent families within a state begins at 25% in FY 1997 and increases by 5% each year, to a peak of 50% by 2002. Two-parent families start at 50% and increase to 90% in the same period. States that fail to enforce work requirements will have the

---

[4]Title III, Subtitle B, Sections 314–315 outlines specific provisions for child support and, at the same time, creates a system of personal liability.

[5]Subtitle B amends Part D (Child Support and Establishment of Paternity) of SEA Title IV to require state plans for child and spousal support to provide certain services related to paternity establishment or to enforcement of child-support obligations.

[6]Section 316 requires the federal government and the states to establish automated registries of child-support orders so as to quickly and efficiently track and locate parents. Subtitle III streamlines the paternity determination process. Parents who do not cooperate in establishing paternity or in assisting a child-support enforcement agency will have their family benefits reduced.

size of their block grant reduced by 5%. Subsequent failures will result in a deduction of 2% per year with a maximum deduction of 21%. The bill authorizes further reductions in federal payments to states that fail to comply with federal requirements to establish paternity and enforce child support, or to prosecute those who fail to repay loans in a timely fashion.[7] As we have seen, the Personal Responsibility and Work Opportunity Reconciliation Act (1996) deploys the sovereign power of the national government in ways that extend its regulatory reach, its power to define family responsibilities, its ability to discipline and punish, and its capacity to establish liability.

Not only does the bill establish the two-parent family as a social norm, the working couple as a social ideal, and the state social service agency as a regulatory channel for the administration of child-care services, social security insurance, and medical benefits, this law also privatizes child-care services. Through its various provisions, it redefines child-care services as commodities to be purchased and identifies parental choice as an aim of child-care services.

CHILD-CARE SERVICES AS COMMODITIES

The provisions of Title VI, the Child Care Block Grant Amendments of 1996 (42 U.S.E., § 602, 1110 Stat. 2279), like the regulations governing eligibility for welfare assistance and definitions of family responsibility, also mediate the relationship of the federal government to children through economic rather than protective strategies. The goals of Title VI reflect this new economically driven approach:

1. to allow each state maximum flexibility in developing child care programs and policies that best suit the needs of children and parents within such State;
2. to promote parental choice to empower working parents to make their own decisions on the child care that best suits their family's needs;
3. to encourage States to provide consumer information to help parents make informed choices about child care;
4. to assist States to provide child care to parents trying to achieve independence from public assistance; and
5. to assist States in implementing the health, safety, licensing, and registration standards established in *State* regulations. [italics added]

---

[7]New regulations limit the use of federal funds to provide child-care support or food stamps for periods longer than 3 months unless a parent has worked at least 20 hours per week or participated in a workfare program.

Through its various provisions, Title VI delegates regulatory responsibility for quality control to the states, permits the flow of resources and dollars to previously unregulated providers, and defines no minimum standards of care. In addition, the law eliminates federal guarantees for a minimum standard of living for the nation's children.[8] Altogether, this represents a net loss of 16% in funding for quality child-care services. At the same time, it de-limits the kinds of services for which federal funds can be used. Section 608, for example, prohibits states from allocating block grant funds to support before and after school child-care programs and thus disengages the federal government from efforts to support healthy environments for school-age children while their parents meet work requirements.[9]

On the other hand, the bill permits the use of block grant funds to support private caregivers in an array of unregulated or under-regulated spaces—in churches, home day-care settings, for-profit child-care centers. It grants states authority to make foster care maintenance payments to private child-care institutions, relaxes reporting requirements for child-care centers receiving monies for food supplements, subsidizes training programs for private caregivers, and in a host of other ways provides incentives to private entrepreneurs to establish child-care centers and add to the pool of available services without, it should be added, having to meet federal accountability guidelines or standards of quality care.[10]

CHILD CARE AS DEFICIT REDUCTION

Beyond delegating authority for child-care services to the state, encouraging the flow of dollars and services to private caregivers, and relaxing account-ability requirements, the Personal Responsibility and Work Opportunity Reconciliation Act of 1996 also serves as an instrument of deficit reduction by diminishing the levels of monetary support for children and invoking a

---

[8]Title VI, Section 607 stipulates a reduction from 20% to 4% for the overall minimum amount of certain funds available for state activities to improve the quality of child care, including availability.

[9]Senator Mikulski, in an analysis of the effects of these kinds of regulations, estimated the provisions would leave 4 million children under the age of 6 home alone. Estimates of the number of postkinder-garten school-age children who would become latch-key kids or be left relatively unsupervised are in the tens of millions.

[10]See provisions in Title V, Child Protection, Title VI, Child Care, and Title VII, Nutrition Programs.

rhetoric of parental choice. The bill cuts medical and social benefits, and recalibrates the levels of care to which children are entitled. First, it reduces the size of the block grant allocations being made to the states as it consolidates an array of different federal programs into a single Child Development Block Grant allocation. Second, it offsets increases made in the Head Start and a new Child Care and Development Fund with cuts from other supplementary block grants, such as the Dependent Care and Child Development Block Grants and programs like Healthy Start, Even Start, and so on.[11] Third, it limits eligibility and cuts services for whole classes of previously entitled welfare recipients—for example, recently arrived legal aliens, illegal alien workers, all but the most severely disabled children, and parents under 18 years of age living in adult-supervised settings, among others.[12] The Congressional Budget Office estimates a reduction of 22% in the number of children eligible to receive SSI in 2002.[13]

The Personal Responsibility and Work Opportunity Reconciliation Act, in yet another form of deficit reduction, chips away at the pool of available dollars for food stamps, child nutrition programs, and school lunches, and prohibits the use of federal food dollars for an array of programs and persons. Title VIII expands work requirements and denies access to most legal aliens

---

[11]According to the Department of Health and Human Services, Pub. L. No. 104–193 authorizes an additional $2.9 billion for a child-care development assistance fund, which will help low-income families and those in transition from welfare to work obtain child care. Head Start funding was increased by $446.6 million (12.6%) for FY 1996–1997. However, other child-related spending cuts include $14 million in the Healthy Start program and $300 million (10.7%) in Social Services Block Grants, contributing to a net loss of $16.2 million in both early childhood and child-care funds.

[12]Regulations of Title IV articulate a compelling "government interest" in the enactment of new rules for eligibility and sponsorship agreements that encourage self-reliance and remove public benefits as an incentive for illegal immigration. The title denies an array of benefits to legal aliens who have been in the country for less than 10 years. For example, Subtitle A, Section 402 denies legal immigrants access to food stamps and SSI unless they have worked for 10 years, have been veterans, are on active duty, or are members of such families. Refugees and asylees are also excepted. Children are still eligible to receive benefits of programs such as Head Start, school lunch, child nutrition, foster care and adoption assistance, emergency medical services, disaster relief and public health assistance. Illegal aliens are denied almost all benefits. The law leaves to the states to determine whether children of illegal aliens are permitted to receive subsidized school meals or other child nutrition program benefits.

[13]According to Title II, Subtitle B, for children to deserve SSI funds, their conditions must meet new childhood disability definitions: A child under the age of 18 with an impairment of "comparable severity" to a work disability in an adult will no longer be eligible. Rather, the child must have a "medically determinable physical or mental impairment, which results in market and severe functional limitations" and which is expected to result in death or to last for more than 12 months.

and all illegal aliens. Title IV mandates 3% across-the-board reductions of basic food stamp benefits, limits the availability of food stamps to households with very high shelter expenses, and calculates food stamp benefits strictly in relation to income, without consideration of mitigating circumstances. Title VII, the Child Nutrition Program, standardizes allocations for children with physical or mental impairments, and limits and standardizes food supplement allocations for institutionalized children and for those attending public or nonprofit private high schools. The National School Lunch Act (Subtitles A and B) reduces payment rates for meals in summer camps, school lunch programs, and National Youth Sports programs; prohibits the use of school lunch monies in nutrition projects, food preparation training, or curriculum development; and eliminates cash grants for nutrition education. The new welfare law also reduces federal subsidies for meals and snacks served in family and group day-care centers, middle- or upper-income locations, and summer food service programs. It eliminates special funding for the expansion of the school breakfast and summer food service programs, and reduces the amount of money available for school meals.[14]

In a fourth and last approach to deficit reduction, this act also limits the levels of federal spending by relieving the federal government of the obligation to provide matching grants to states for the support of child-care services, preschool education programs, and an array of other child-friendly services. As a redefinition of the federal obligation, this particular action caps the levels of financial support being made available to the states, reduces the financial obligations of the federal government, and redefines the nature of federal–state partnership.

CONCLUSION

Through the provisions of the Personal Responsibility and Work Opportunity Reconciliation Act of 1996, welfare is defined as a form of family planning, moral reconstruction, and deficit reduction, rather than an approach to child protection, social welfare, or economic insolvency. Its various titles condemn illegitimacy, champion the two-parent family, con-

---

[14]Other welfare limitations with potentially detrimental effects on children are included in many other titles of this law. Title VIII, Section 824 makes nonexempt persons ineligible for benefits if they received food stamps for more than 3 months during the preceding 3-year period without working at least 20 hours per week or participating in a workfare program.

struct economically driven concepts of parent responsibility, and through these means, legitimize the disengagement of federal government support for the family as a site for nurture, education, and love of children.

The bill reflects and sustains what Noam Chomsky (1995) has called a "war against children" (p. 131). It has effectively eliminated the few national entitlements that have historically been available to relieve the costs of childrearing. It has stripped the federal government of sufficient regulatory power to monitor and guarantee children's access to decent health care, housing, education, or learning environments. It has consigned children to the world of privatized, relatively unregulated, and haphazardly available child-care environments while their parents go to work. Children have disappeared as objects of national concern. Their care, as we have seen, has been privatized into invisibility.

REFERENCES

Bremner, R. (1974). *Children and youth in America: A documentary history: Vol. II. 1933–1973.* Cambridge, MA: Harvard University Press.

Burke, L. (1996, December 11). *CRS issue brief: Welfare reform.* Washington, DC: Congressional Research Service.

Child Care and Development Block Grant Amendments of 1996, 42 U.S.E., § 602, 1110 Stat. 2279 (1996).

Chomsky, N. (1995). A dialogue with Noam Chomsky. *Harvard Educational Review, 65*(2), 127–144.

Clinton, W. J. (1996b, July 31). *Statement on welfare reform legislation.*

Clinton, W. J. (1996a, August 22). *Remarks at the signing of the welfare reform bill.*

Finkelstein, B. (1985). Uncle Sam and the children: A history of government involvement in childrearing. In J. M. Hawes & N. R. Hiner (Eds.), *Growing up in America: Children in historical perspective* (pp. 255–269). Champaign-Urbana: University of Illinois Press.

Mikulski, B. (1996, July 25). Congressional Record.

Personal Responsibility and Work Opportunity Reconciliation Act of 1996, Pub. L. No. 44–103, § 110 Stat. 2110 (1996).

Roosevelt, T. (1909). Call for the White House conference on children, 1908. In *Proceedings of the conference on the care of children* (pp. 17–18). Washington, DC.

Winer, L. (1972). *Federal legislation on Indian education, 1819–1970.* Unpublished doctoral dissertation. University of Maryland, College Park.

10

Speaking of and Against Youth

❦ ◆ ❦

Sue Books
State University of New York at New Paltz

Children today, far from holding up the lit lamp of hope like the little girl in Picasso's "Guernica," have become the focus of even greater anxiety and horror than their mothers, than even their single mothers.

—Marina Warner (1994)

We have to see each other with new eyes. We have to come together with warmth.

—Malcolm X[1]

Young people bear the brunt of the anxiety and sometimes hysterical rage of these times, given voice in harsh and very public antiyouth discourses and substantiated in punitive public policies. Discourses rife with distortion, denigration, and fear-mongering have helped create a climate in which policies sure to impoverish more young women and children and to imprison more young men have come to appear necessary, if not inherently desirable. Consider, for example, the public denigration in recent years of young single mothers and their children. "There is a long-term price of illegitimacy," Gibbs (1994), citing no pertinent research, declared in a cover story in *Time* magazine on teenage pregnancy and welfare reform,

> one that resonates at a time when the fear of crime, particularly the crimes committed by a generation of young, pitiless men and boys, has become a national obsession. When people ask where all these 16-year-old predators are coming from, one answer is chilling: from 14-year-old mothers. (pp. 27–28)

---

[1]Quoted in Swadener (1995, p. 32).

In young single mothers "you have a ticking crime bomb," insisted Princeton professor John DiIulio (Gibbs, 1994, p. 28), who sees in the "40 million kids 10 years old and under" now growing up allegedly "fatherless, godless, and jobless," a "coming storm of youth violence" (Butterfield, 1995, p. A18).

In the popular discourse on poverty, for decades the poor have been assigned the roles of "deserving" and "undeserving" in a morality play staged for others (Katz, 1989). In antiyouth discourses, the young, especially the poor and young people of color, are being used in much the same way. Public discourses like those on teenage pregnancy, youth violence, and to some extent educational reform, depict young people in ways that scapegoat them for some of the nation's most serious problems and offer the nation a simplistic picture of itself: one populated by two groups of people–the responsible, respectable (and usually older and White) majority, on one hand, and the irresponsible, dangerous (and often younger and dark) minority, on the other. This social picture comes at a cost—to everyone in the sense that it hinders efforts to gain any real insight into the social challenges of our times, but particularly to the young people stereotyped and caricatured in the popular press and broader political discourse. "Sometimes it feels like we've been buried 6 feet under their perceptions," a 16-year-old girl living in the South Bronx told Jonathan Kozol (1996, p. 40). Cruel stereotypes of predatory young men and promiscuous, calculating young women thrive in perceptions that distort and, as this young person suggests, essentially bury the young.

I attempt to substantiate this argument in what follows after first situating it in a discussion of the social context in which youth bashing has become commonplace.

THE YOUNG, THE POOR, AND THE INCARCERATED

These are dangerous times, especially for the young:

1. Whereas poverty in the United States among adults older than 40 has declined in the last 20 years, poverty among children and young people has risen by 60%.[2] Forty percent of the nation's poor are children and a majority of the poor are younger than 25.[3]

---

[2]Census Bureau data, reported in 1994 and cited in Males (1996, p. 7).

[3]Census Bureau data, cited in Males (1996, p. 265).

2. A study of family homelessness in New York City found not only an increase during the first half of the 1990s, but also that the largest increase—9%—was among children 9 years old and younger (Herbert, 1996, p. A15).
3. The nation now has a "record tens of thousand of its adolescents behind bars under ever-tougher sentencings" (Males, 1996, p. 132).
4. Contrary to popular belief, most of the 1.5 million children and young people who run away from home every year "run away not because they want to but because they have to; because even the streets are safer than where they're running from .... Even so, they are not running to anything but death. Nationwide, more than 5,000 children a year are buried in unmarked graves" (Strauss, 1992, p. 753).

Despite the impoverishment of so many young people and despite what we know about the significance of growing up poor—and therefore often sick, hungry, chronically tired, abused, or homeless—Congress in the summer of 1996 rescinded the nation's 61-year commitment to guaranteeing a federal safety net, however frayed, to the nation's poor. The Personal Responsibility and Work Opportunity Reconciliation Act of 1996 divested the federal government of responsibility for aid to poor children and adults and delegated this work largely to the states, albeit with a $55 billion cut in a broad range of social safety-net programs over the next 6 years. This "freed" the states to do more with less, if they want to and can, or, more likely, to compete to make themselves inhospitable to the poor.

In addition to replacing federal funding with block grants to the states, the welfare legislation provided no new national commitment to or funds for job training or job creation while nevertheless requiring most welfare recipients to find work within 2 years; it set a 60-month lifetime limit on benefits for families, even if parents cannot find stable jobs; it cut food stamp benefits sharply (by $28 billion over the next 6 years); and it made legal immigrants, including children, ineligible for most social service benefits (Children's Defense Fund, 1996d). Whereas legal immigrants represent only about 5% of those on public assistance, they will absorb more than 40% of the cuts (Soros, 1996, p. A23). The welfare legislation was passed at a time when poor children in the United States were already among the poorest in any industrialized country, when 4 million children younger than 12 had already gone hungry during at least part of any year, and when food banks across the country were already struggling to

respond to increasing requests for food unmatched by private contributions.[4]

The Children's Defense Fund (1996d) expects the cuts and structural
changes initiated by the welfare legislation to remove an average of $1,300
a year from the incomes of 8 million of the nation's poorest families and to
impoverish more than 1 million additional children (pp. 1–2). Families with
children will shoulder about 70% of the food-stamp cuts; half of these
families have incomes of less than $6,300 a year ("Excerpts," 1996, p. A10).
About 300,000 legal immigrant children also will lose food-stamp benefits.
And changes to Supplemental Security Income (SSI) will deny help to more
than 300,000 children with such disabilities as autism, tuberculosis, and
mental retardation. Although the legislation increases funds for child care,
the Office of Management and Budget projects a $2.4 billion shortfall if all
states meet their "welfare to work" targets (Children's Defense Fund,
1996e).

Many poor mothers and children almost certainly will resort to prostitution, begging, and drug sales in an economy in which the bottom has been
dropping out for low-skill workers for decades and in which wage cuts for
the young have been particularly severe.[5]

> Median weekly earnings for men younger than 25 who were employed full time
> fell by 31 percent between 1973 and 1994, while those of young women dropped
> by 14 percent. During the late 1960s, the median weekly earnings of young men
> employed full time were equal to nearly three-fourths of those of older men ....
> By 1994, however, ... [they] had fallen to just half those of older men. (Children's
> Defense Fund, 1996a, p. 49)

We can expect "children sleeping on grates" and "an urban crisis unlike
anything we have known since the 1960s," Daniel Patrick Moynihan warned
in the days before President Clinton signed the welfare bill (Pear, 1996, p.
A9).

To what crisis did this devastating legislation respond? From 1980 to
1993, the welfare population grew from 10.6 million to 14.1 million people.
By 1996, it had dropped back to 12.8 million people, including approxi-

---

[4]Findings on the severity of child poverty are from the Luxembourg Income Study of conditions in
18 industrialized countries. Those on child hunger are from a nationwide survey by the Washington,
DC-based Food Research and Action Center. Both findings are reported in Skolnick (1995, p. 783).

[5]Remarks of Hugh Price, president of the National Urban League, published in *The New York Times*
("Some Look," 1996, August 4, p. A26).

mately 9 million children, and federal and state spending for Aid to Families with Dependent Children (AFDC) had stabilized at about $215 billion. To put this in perspective, this sum equaled only about 14% of Medicare spending and 9% of the Pentagon's budget (Kilborn & Verhovek, 1996, pp. A1, A8). Although AFDC benefits varied from state to state, in no state did AFDC and food stamp benefits combined bring family incomes up to the federal poverty line, which in 1996 was $12,980 for a family of three (Children's Defense Fund, 1996b, p. 13). In other words, there had been neither an uncontrolled swelling of the welfare population, almost two-thirds of whom were children, nor vast public giveaways in the form of cash and benefits.

Meanwhile, in the years leading up to welfare repeal, a rash of legislation laid the groundwork for a sharp increase in the number of young people incarcerated and a sharp decrease in the protections they are assured. In what child advocates called a frenzied "adultification" of children, almost all 50 states overhauled their laws in 1995 and 1996 to allow more young people to be tried as adults and to do away with such taken-for-granted protections as the confidentiality of juvenile court proceedings (Butterfield, 1996; Kotlowitz, 1994). "This is no longer a war on crime but a war on children," a lawyer for the American Civil Liberties Union warned about Congressional efforts to undo what has been a core principle of the juvenile justice system for more than 150 years: separation of youths from adults in jails and prisons (Butterfield, 1996, pp. A1, A13).

In the summer of 1996, Congress was working on several bills that together

> would allow more children to be transferred to adult court and adult prisons, make defendants as young as 16 eligible for the death penalty in federal murder cases, and end the critical federal protections for juveniles mandated by the Juvenile Justice and Delinquency Prevention Act. (Children's Defense Fund, 1996c, p. 1)

"We've got to quit coddling these violent kids," said Orrin Hatch, chair of the Senate Judiciary Committee at the time and coauthor of one of the bills. "We'd all like to rehabilitate these kids. But, by gosh, we are in a different age" (Butterfield, 1996b, pp. A1, A13).

Twice as many teenagers were in jail, prison, or other confinement in 1996 as in 1980, and a booming prison-construction industry suggested more of the same in the years ahead. In what may be a worst-case but also prescient example, California prisons held

18,000 guests in 1975, 125,000 in 1994. In the 72-month 1989-1994 period, California added 32,000 new prison spaces—15 every day—at a cost of $2 billion, plus $600 million per year to operate. At triple capacity, they would cage 100,000 .... Not nearly enough, even if adult violence is ignored and adolescent violence becomes the only target. During that same 72-month period, 2.2 million California teenagers were arrested, 865,000 for felonies; 200,000 of the latter violent felonies. (Males, 1996, p. 286)

The situation in Texas was much the same. By mid-1997, Texas expected to have tripled the number of prison spaces it had in 1990 (Males, 1996, p. 131).

SILENCE AND EVASION IN TALK
ABOUT YOUNG MOTHERS

As the nation takes steps that will further impoverish the poor, young single mothers—poor in disproportionate numbers (Polakow, 1993, p. 59)—are being publicly denigrated as "crime bombs" and blamed for "every threat to the fabric of the country—from poverty to crime to homelessness" (Alter, as quoted in Males, 1996, p. 27). It is important to see these accusations for what they are: fear-mongering that has little to do with reality (Books, 1996a). Contrary to suggestions like that in *Time* magazine, the legendary 14-year-old mother is not the typical teenage mother in this country. Two-thirds of all births to teenagers are to 18- and 19-year-olds; mothers under 16 account for only a tiny percentage of these births (Rhode, 1993, p. 313). Also, despite former Surgeon General Joycelyn Elders' assertion in 1994 that 90% of all violent criminals are born to unmarried teenagers, "Even if every single son ever produced by every unwed teenage mother was arrested for a criminal offense every year, at most one-third of the young-male crime volume could be explained" (Males, 1996, pp. 91, 106–107).

Public vilification of 14-year-old girls requires denial of the relevant statistics, denial of the relational dimension of sexuality and childbirth, and dismissal of the social and historical context of present-day concerns about teenage pregnancy. Contrary to popular belief, young women "right now are having babies at about the same rate as they have for most of the century" (Luker, 1996, p. 8). If, as the public discourse suggests, there has been an "epidemic of teenage pregnancy," the epidemic occurred not in the 1980s and 1990s, but rather in the 1950s "when teenagers were having twice as many babies as they had had in previous decades." Then, however, teenage pregnancy was not regarded as a social problem (Luker, 1996, p. 8).

What has changed over time, in addition to public perceptions and judgments, are marriage rates, which have plummeted. And fewer marriages has increased the percentage of unmarried women having babies relative to married women—for adults as well as teenagers. Two-thirds of all single mothers are adults, not teenagers (Children's Defense Fund, 1996a, p. 45; Luker, 1996, p. 8). Long-term patterns of childbirth and marriage show the sexual behavior of young women has mirrored that of older women. "Teen and adult trends are uncannily alike, over decades of turbulent changes in sexual behaviors—the Depression, World War II, the postwar Baby Boom, the 1970's 'Baby Bust,' the legalization of abortion, the recent rise in family poverty" (Males, 1996, p. 61).

Not only do young women tend to live in "the same sexual worlds" as older women, their "partners" tend to be adult men, not their peers. Contrary to the widespread assumption that teenage boys father most of the babies born to teenage girls, men 20 years old and older father two-and-a-half times more babies born to high school girls than high school boys father, and four times more babies born to junior high girls than junior high school boys father (Males, 1996, p. 45). Although 80% of teenage mothers have partners within five years of their own ages—a 17-year-old mother and a 21- or 22-year-old father, for example—records of gonorrhea and syphilis diagnoses going back to the mid-1950s show sexually transmitted diseases (STDs) consistently have been three to four times more prevalent among 10- to 14-year-old girls than among 10- to 14-year-old boys (Males, 1996, p. 49). And comparisons of the hetero-sexual AIDS rate for 19-year-old men and women show the rate for young women is more than ten times higher than the rate for young men (Males, 1996, p. 52).[6]

Clearly, the vast majority of girls and young women with STDs and AIDS are not being infected by their peers, but rather by older men. However, the language of sexual coercion and abuse, including rape, is conspicuously absent from the public discourse on teenage pregnancy

---

[6]In heterosexual sex females are more vulnerable to HIV infection than males, and this explains some—but only some—of the tenfold discrepancy between rates of infection for young adolescent girls and boys. Comparatively, "the AIDS rate among heterosexual adult women is 1.9 times the rate among heterosexual adult men" (Males, 1996, p. 50).

(Males, 1996, p. 16). A 1992 study of 535 teenage mothers in Washington State found two-thirds of the young women had been sexually abused or raped and 70% had been physically abused (Males, 1996, p. 90).

The public discourse on teenage pregnancy has been quiet about the relationship not only between early pregnancy and sexual coercion and abuse, but also between early pregnancy and poverty. Whereas much of the public discourse on teenage pregnancy blames poverty on young single mothers, there has been little acknowledgment of the extent to which poverty precedes young single motherhood. A 2-year study of teenage sexuality by the Alan Guttmacher Institute noted that in 1994, 38% of all 15- to 19-year-olds in the United States lived in families with incomes below or just above the official poverty level. Yet, of the 1 in 10 young people who either became pregnant or impregnated someone else, 73% lived in poverty or near poverty. Of the 1 in 25 who became a parent, 83% lived in poverty or near poverty. And of the 1 in 40 who became a parent while unmarried, 85% lived in poverty or near poverty (Males, 1996, p. 61). Other studies have shown five out of every six teenage mothers were poor *before* they became pregnant (Males, 1996, p. 85).

This suggests that the poverty teenage mothers experience is more an extension of the poverty they knew before having a child than a result of their motherhood itself. "Although it is true that young mothers tend to be poor women, it is much more meaningful to say that poor women tend to become young mothers" (Luker, 1996, p. 12). Poverty causes young single motherhood more than young single motherhood causes poverty. Statistically, there is no evidence that "having a baby as a teenager … inevitably lead[s] to abbreviated schooling and economic hardship, either for the mother or for the child." On the contrary, "students who become pregnant in high school are increasingly likely to graduate and are beginning to do so at rates approaching those of nonpregnant teens" (Luker, 1996, p. 9).

One obviously cannot talk sensibly about pregnancy and childbirth among young women without coming to terms with the significance not only of adult behavior in this "teenage" problem, but also of poverty, rape, and other forms of abuse and exploitation in the lives of millions of young people. These subjects are noticeably absent, however, in most of the public discourse on teenage pregnancy as well as that on school violence—another site of youth bashing taken these days to dangerous extremes.

DANGEROUS DICHOTOMIES IN TALK
ABOUT YOUTH VIOLENCE

The distortion and fury in the public discourse on teenage pregnancy has shaped that on youth and school violence as well. Amidst warnings of the "coming storm of juvenile violence," the national crime rate, including the youth crime rate, appears to be falling (Butterfield, 1995, p. A18). In 1995, violent crime fell more than 9%; the rate of juvenile violent crime declined by just under 3%; and the youth homicide rate, falling for the second consecutive year, dropped more than 15%, and almost 23% since 1993.[7]

These numbers run counter to the discourses of vilification in which the problem of "youth" violence as well as "teenage" pregnancy have been entangled and to the picture we have been invited to imagine of a "storm" of "godless predators" sweeping the county—a depiction of young people generally accompanied by near silence about how "youth" violence compares with "adult" violence and about the degree to which poverty engenders violence. Much has been said about the significant increase in the number of homicide and violent crime arrests among young people in the last decade. Far less has been said about the significance of the 60% increase in child and youth poverty over the last 20 years or about the degree to which trends in youth violence resemble those in adult violence (Males, 1996, p. 7). From 1985 to 1993, youth arrests for violent crime increased by 73% while the adult violent crime arrest rate increased by 41% (Males, 1996, p. 105). However, when violent crime arrest rates for poor male teens and poor adult men in their 20s and 30s are compared, the difference disappears. Statistics for 1993 show "teenagers experienced three murders and 40 violent crime arrests per 1,000 teens living below federal poverty guidelines—the same rate as among similarly impoverished adults in their 20s and 30s" (Males, 1996, p. 19).

In terms of violence as well as sexuality, the behavior of young people mirrors that of adults and reflects the climate of the times.

---

[7]This level of decline in violent crime nationwide was reported by the Department of Justice, based on data from a Census count of people who are victims of violent crime (Butterfield, 1996d, p. A14). The decline in the rate of juvenile violent crime nationwide was reported by the Federal Bureau of Investigation, based on local police reports (Butterfield, 1996c, p. A1).

In the United States of the 1990s, 16 million children and teens live in poverty. Some 350,000 young are confirmed victims of violent and sexual abuse inflicted by caretakers (mostly parents) every year. Given such conditions, teenage violence is not surprising; it is just like the adult violence from which its stems. (Males, 1996, p. 19)

The term "youth violence" misleads in that it suggests something inherent in youth causes, leads to, or invites violent behavior. In fact, it makes no more sense to talk about youth violence than about "'Sagittarian violence' (One in 12 killers! Tripled since 1960!) or 'Smith violence' (The leading name of U. S. murderers!) or 'Brown-eyed violence' (don't even calculate)" (Males, 1996, p. 103).

The charged language and distortion that has shaped the public discourse on youth violence in general has also shaped talk about the violence that occurs in and around schools. Despite claims that school violence has risen drastically in the last few years, that "135,000 kids bring guns to school every day," and that "violence has become commonplace in almost all levels, types, and sizes of schools," a 1993 survey of more than 2,000 public high school seniors found no rising trend (Booth, Bradley, Flick, Keough & Kirk, 1994, p. 33). In 1976, 5% of the White seniors and 6.7% of the Black seniors reported being injured by someone with a weapon at school; in 1993, these figures were 4.3% and 6.4%, respectively (Males, 1996, p. 120). Similarly, 77% of the teachers participating in a 1993 Louis Harris survey said they felt "very safe" in their schools and 22% said they felt "somewhat safe." Only 1% said they felt "not very safe" and less than 1%, "not safe at all" (Elam, Rose, & Gallup, 1995, pp. 42–43).

Even more troubling than the suggestion that violence pervades the schools and therefore threatens all school children is the suggestion that this violence stems from a few, a dangerous and identifiable minority. "Segregating troublemakers is an understandable response of educators who do not want the majority of law-abiding citizens to be tyrannized or physically hurt by a few offenders," The New York Times editorialized ("Segregating," 1994, p. A20). "We cannot let a few children—and frequently it is just a few children—terrorize their teachers and other students," the vice president of the American Federation of Teachers insisted (Cole, 1993/1994, pp. 16–17).

The public discourse on school violence, like that on teenage pregnancy, ignores the relational and contextual nature of violent behavior and the significant role of adults (Males, 1996; Noguera, 1995). Despite the popular view of young people as either harmless or dangerous, either victim or perpetrator (or potential victim or perpetrator), guilt and innocence often are impossible to disentangle. Consider, for example, the story of Napier Traylor:

> You'd probably pick Napier Traylor as a victim, not a perpetrator. And you'd be right. According to his attorney, the 16-year-old was the victim of bullying that went on for many months. A gang of kids from his new school in Boston's Roslindale section harassed Napier, following him to and from school each day, threatening to beat him up, calling his house so often that his mother had the telephone number changed. In February 1988, the gang chased Napier home and again threatened to beat him. Napier and his mother went to the Boston Police Department and complained. The Boston police referred them to the school police. Later that same day the gang members attacked Napier near his house. His mother, standing on the porch, threw a stick to her son, exhorting him to fight. Napier took a knife out of his gym bag. Prosecutors say he stabbed fifteen-year-old Jeffrey Butler in the heart and fled. (Prothrow-Stith, 1991, p.26)

Napier was then charged with manslaughter—a delineation of responsibility that hides the fact that

> in a world full of teachers, principals, clergy, city police, and school police, no one was able or willing to help Napier Traylor find a nonviolent way out of his predicament. No one offered to help .... Bullies tormented him. Professionals failed him. His mother urged him to fight. The streets offered him a weapon. (Prothrow-Stith, 1991, p. 26)

Ignoring the relational dimension of most violence, the public discourse invites a picture of young people as necessarily pitted against each other in a zero-sum contest for educational resources and attention: the promising, good students versus the dangerous, hopeless bad ones. Given who—or what—they are, the question is quietly (and sometimes not so quietly) asked, why bother?

THE PROBLEM WITH SCHOOL IS KIDS

Much of the broader discourse on educational reform affirms this dichoto-mized image of young people: the good versus the bad. We are invited to imagine a group of students able and "ready to learn," but held back, if not actively undermined, by a smaller population of those unable or unwilling to learn. A discourse of contagion suffuses talk about "at risk" children and, more recently, about "bad peer influences" (Swadener, 1995).

Consider, for example, Laurence Steinberg's (1996) widely publicized book *Beyond the Classroom: Why School Reform has Failed and What Parents Need to do*. School reform has failed, Steinberg argues, because reformers have not taken student disengagement into account. This is a dangerous oversight, he suggests in language reminiscent of other antiyouth discourses, because disengagement among students ultimately threatens the broader society. Although "less visible, less dramatic, and less commented upon than other social problems involving youth—crime, pregnancy, violence—student disen-' gagement is more pervasive and in some ways potentially more harmful to the future well-being of American society" (Steinberg, 1996, p. 28).

As in other antiyouth discourses, the alleged danger is attributed not to all young people, but rather to young people raised outside the "authoritative families" that "tend to produce the most well-adjusted children" (Steinberg, 1996, p. 152). Steinberg and his research partners found that Asian students tend to perform better than expected when parenting practices are taken into account whereas Black students tend to perform worse. How to explain this?

> Something in Asian students' lives protects them [from disengagement] even if they are exposed to less than perfect parenting, while something in Black students' lives undermines the positive effects of parental involvement and authoritativeness .... This "something" is the peer group. (Steinberg, 1996, p. 156)

The implications for parents are clear: "Play the percentages" and move to neighborhoods where the threat of bad peer influences is minimized. Parents can "stack the deck" in terms of their child's friends, Steinberg (1996) points out,

> by selecting the setting in which their child will spend time—by living in one neighborhood as opposed to another, by choosing one school over another, and by involving the child in certain types of after-school and weekend activities. This is really a matter of ... trying to maximize the number of "good" peers a child comes into contact with and minimizing the number of "bad" peer influences in the child's environment. (p. 152)

"For many people, there is nothing they can learn that will repay the cost of the teaching," Richard Herrnstein and Charles Murray (1994) proclaimed in *The Bell Curve* (p. 520). Steinberg's far more mainstream book goes the next step: Some kids, the "bad" ones, are not just bad investments in terms of recouping the cost of teaching them, they are significant threats to U.S. society in general and to the "good" kids vulnerable to their influence. Best to keep one's distance.

THE PRACTICE OF YOUTH BASHING

Antiyouth discourses disguise the role of adults in such social problems as apathy and disengagement, violence, the creation of unwanted children, and the inability to sustain long-term loving relationships. Through innuendo, careful selection of statistics, and blatant denigration, these social problems are redefined as youth problems and, more insidiously, as problems of youth of color. The stereotypical teenage mother is a Black 14-year-old; the typical teenage mother, however, is 18 or 19 and White. Similarly, that young Black men in this country now die more often from homicide than from any other cause of death has been widely noted. That the situation differs only nominally for young White men has received far less publicity. In fact, "homicides and suicides leapfrog back and forth [from year to year] as the second and third most common causes of death for young White males," behind auto accidents, their number 1 cause of death (Prothrow-Stith, 1991, p. 14).

There is a danger in not recognizing the poverty suffered disproportionately in communities of color, one index of which is the disproportionate number of young mothers and youth offenders living in these communities. Whereas just under 17% of all White children under 6 are growing up in poverty, almost 44% of all Black children and 41.5% of all Latino children are poor (Children's Defense Fund, 1996a, p. 2). There is also a danger in using this disproportion to suggest that excessive violence and the phenomenon of children whose parents cannot or will not care for them are somehow problems of people of color: something "those people" cause and therefore should solve. Antiyouth discourses do both: they discount the significance of poverty and they invite racist interpretations of its consequences.

Let me clarify: To emphasize the dangers of a public discourse that thrives in fear-mongering and creates a picture of young people as pitted against each other (or, more broadly, against "our" society) is not, of course, to say that violence in the society or its schools should be tolerated. In many neighborhoods, violence endangers everyone who lives and works there, including teachers and students, and this should be stopped. To emphasize the dangers of antiyouth discourses also is not to advocate childbearing among teenagers, disengagement among students, or parental disregard of friends' influence on their children. Justified alarm about these things, however, does not legitimate public vilification of young people, including young people who have broken the law, borne a child, or lost interest in school.

In the words of the poet Adrienne Rich (1994), we need to "listen to the public voice" of these times and "survey our public space" to note and remember

> *who was in charge of definitions*
> *and who stood by receiving them*
> *when the name of compassion*
> *was changed to the name of guilt*
> *when to feel with a human stranger*
> *was declared obsolete. (p. 31)*

The high-pitched and mean-spirited public talk that turns young men into pitiless predators, 14-year-old girls into crime bombs, and 10-year-olds into the unemployed dehumanizes those too young and powerless to challenge other people's definitions of them.

Each child, says the Indian philosopher Rabindranath Tagore, "comes with the message that God is not yet discouraged of man" (Children's Defense Fund, 1996a, p. xi). If the society at large shares this fundamental affirmation of the promise of youth, it rarely shows in our social vocabulary. So what if "many" unwed teenage mothers "have in fact been coerced into sex," a senior editor ranted in a *Newsweek* column. "Every threat to the fabric of this country—from poverty to crime to homelessness—is connected to out-of-wedlock teen pregnancy .... The name of the game is shame."[8]

"Where your treasure is, there will your heart be also" (Matt 6:21). I read these words as a comment on language—a treasure in the sense that language functions as a form of social currency. With respect to public talk about young people, where is our language? How is it used? What does it accomplish? And what does it suggest about our collective heart? How should we regard young people who for whatever reason are not as able or interested in learning as many of their peers? How have these children come to be seen as social albatrosses holding others back? And what ways of thinking about them, and therefore of speaking about them,

---

[8]Alter, J., as quoted in Males (1996, p. 27).

would be better? These questions face all who teach and learn in these difficult times.

Youth bashing diverts attention from a much-needed focus on the suffering of children and young people, makes harsh policies appear justified, and threatens to erode the moral foundations of public schooling and social supports for the young. Why support crime bombs? Why not enact "tough on crime" measures in the face of a "coming storm of youth violence"? And why not ensure that schools are safe for—that is, are *for*—those who want to learn? Youth bashing also gives credence to a particular social vision—namely, one of "us" against "them." The good kids versus the bad ones or, more broadly, the good society versus its nemesis, portrayed as the young, dark, and deviant. Along with whatever else youth bashing accomplishes, it invites us to see the world as a given: The die has been cast and the forces of good and evil identified. All that's left is to quash the threat to the cherished "American way of life"—contingent, it's understood, upon married, financially secure parents encouraging their children to follow in their footsteps.

Reflecting on the moral or ideological dimension of antiyouth discourses, I am aware that this world of "us" and "them" in which good and evil are clear and distinct differs sharply from the world I learned to imagine in the mainstream Protestant churches my White middle-class parents took me to in the 1950s and 1960s. In those places where order and tradition were revered, I was taught to value and have faith in a world in which everything is always possible (the moral of the story of the Resurrection), in which every child is infinitely precious in God's eyes (and therefore ought to be in mine too), and in which "the least" get whatever they need, not because they are better or more deserving, but because they do not have what they need. It's one thing to acknowledge the complexity and political difficulty of making this world real. It's quite another to dismiss the vision entirely, as the antiyouth discourses implicitly do. Youth bashing not only denigrates the young, it also mocks and undermines what have been some of the most important hopes and dreams of the generation now denigrating the young.

The older generation—my generation—owes the young something much better than this. We owe them not only the social supports they need to grow and to prosper, but also inspiring visions in which they themselves figure prominently as bearers of hope and creators of an always new and always potentially better world. Holding the public discourse to a higher standard of responsible truth telling would be a small but important step in this direction.

REFERENCES

Books, S. (1996). Fear and loathing: The moral dimensions of the politicization of teen pregnancy. *Journal of Thought, 31*(1), 9–24.

Boothe, J., Bradley, L., Flick, T. M., Keough, K., & Kirk, S. (1994, January). America's schools confront violence. *USA TODAY Magazine,* 33–35.

Butterfield, F. (1995, November 19). Crime continues to decline, but experts warn of coming 'storm' of juvenile violence. *The New York Times,* p. A18.

Butterfield, F. (1996a, May 12). States revamping laws on juveniles as felonies soar. *The New York Times,* pp. A1, A24.

Butterfield, F. (1996b, June 24). Republicans challenge notion of separate jails for juveniles. *The New York Times,* pp. A1, A13.

Butterfield, F. (1996c, August 9). After 10 years, juvenile crime begins to drop. *The New York Times,* p. A1.

Butterfield, F. (1996d, September 18). A large drop in crime is reported. *The New York Times,* p. A14.

Children's Defense Fund. (1996a). *The state of America's children: Yearbook 1996.* Washington, DC: Author.

Children's Defense Fund. (1996b, May). Federal poverty guidelines. *CDF Reports,* Vol.17(6), p. 13.

Children's Defense Fund. (1996c, August). Congress considers "predator" bills. *CDF Reports,* Vol. 17(9), pp. 1–2, 4.

Children's Defense Fund. (1996d, September). New welfare law: Need for state advocacy intensifies. *CDF Reports,* Vol. 17(10), pp. 1–2, 9.

Children's Defense Fund. (1996e, September). Welfare Law: How the welfare act will work. *CDF Reports,* Vol. 17(10), pp. 5–9.

Cole, J. (1993/1994, Winter). Moynihan is right: We must draw the line. *American Educator,* Vol. 17(4), 16–17.

Elam, S., Rose, L., & Gallup, A. (1994). The 26th annual Phi Delta Kappa/Gallup poll of the public's attitudes toward the public schools. *Phi Delta Kappan, 76*(1), 41–56.

Excerpts from debate in the Senate on the welfare measure. (1996, August 2). *The New York Times,* p. A10.

Gibbs, N. (1994, June 20). When young, single women have children, it almost guarantees they will be poor: Can welfare reform break the pattern? *Time,* Vol. 143(25), pp. 27–28.

Herbert, B. (1996, September 23). Families on the edge. *The New York Times,* p. A15.

Herrnstein, R. J., & Murray, C. (1994). *The bell curve: Intelligence and class structure in American life.* New York: Free Press.

Katz, M. (1989). *The undeserving poor.* New York: Pantheon.

Kilborn, P. T., & Verhovek, S. H. (1996, August 2). Clinton's welfare shift reflects new Democrat. *The New York Times,* pp. A1, A8.

Kotlowitz, A. (1994, February 13). Their crimes don't make them adults. *The New York Times Magazine,* pp. 40–41.

Kozol, J. (1996). *Amazing grace: The lives of children and the conscience of a nation.* New York: Crown.

Luker, K. (1996). *Dubious conceptions: The politics of teenage pregnancy.* Cambridge, MA: Harvard University Press.

Males, M. A. (1996). *The scapegoat generation: America's war on adolescents.* Monroe, ME: Common Courage Press.

Noguera, P. (1995). Preventing and producing violence: A critical analysis of responses to school violence. *Harvard Educational Review, 65*(2), 189–212.

Pear, R. (1996, July 20). Senate votes to deny most federal benefits to legal immigrants who are not citizens. *The New York Times*, p. A9.

Polakow, V. (1993). *Lives on the edge: Single mothers and their children in the other America.* Chicago: University of Chicago Press.

Prothrow-Stith, D. (1991). *Deadly consequences.* New York: HarperCollins.

Rhode, D. (1993). Adolescent pregnancy and public policy. In D. Rhode & A. Lawson (Eds.), *The politics of pregnancy: Adolescent sexuality and public policy* (pp. 301–335). New Haven, CT: Yale University Press.

Rich, A. (1995). *Dark fields of the republic.* New York: Norton.

Segregating student troublemakers. (1994, October 11). *The New York Times*, p. A20.

Skolnick, A. A. (1995, September 13). "More!" cry children as Congress shakes its head. *Journal of the American Medical Association, 274*(10), 783.

Some look at the welfare plan with hope, but others are fearful. (1996, August 4). *The New York Times*, p. A26.

Soros, G. (1996, October 2). Immigrants' burden. *The New York Times*, p. A23.

Steinberg, L. (1996). *Beyond the classroom: Why school reform has failed and what parents need to do.* New York: Simon & Schuster.

Strauss, D. L. (1992, June 1). A threnody for street kids. *The Nation*, p. 752.

Swadener, B. (1995). Children and families "at promise": Deconstructing the discourse of risk. In B. Swadener & S. Lubeck (Eds.), *Children and families "at promise"* (pp. 17–49). Albany: SUNY Press.

Warner, M. (1994). *Six myths of our time.* New York: Vintage Books.

Author Index

❧ ◆ ❧

A

Ada. A. F., 69
Adnopoz, J., 51, 52, 53
Afulayan, J., 41
Alcoff, L., 111, 112
Almeida, C., 14
Anderson, G., 41, 55, 56
Anderson, J. D., 160
Andiman, W., 47, 48, 49, 50, 51, 52
Apfel, R., 51, 54, 55
Arbitell, M., 42
Arnot, M., 24
Arnow, H., 93, 94
Austin, R., 125

B

Babad, E., 138
Baldwin, J., 42
Barad, S., 41
Bassuk, E. L., 5, 9, 13
Bauman, L., 48, 50, 53
Belluck, P., xxii
Belton, D., 25
Benne, K., 138
Bennett, K. P., 100, 101
Berck, J., 14
Berliner, D. C., xxii
Bey, M., 49

B

Bhabha, H. K., 122, 123
Biddle, B. J., xxii
Biklen, S. K., 24, 112
Birnbaum, M., 138
Black, S., 48
Boker, L., 42
Books, S., 188
Boothe, J., 192
Borman, K. M., 93, 97, 106, 107
Boxer, A., 141, 152, 153
Bradley, L., 192
Bradsher, K., xxi
Bremner, R., 171
Brink, J., 41
Britzman, D. P., 112
Brodkey, L., 117
Brown, G., 56
Buchmann, M., 127, 134
Buehler, J., 49
Bumiller, E., xxiii, xxiv
Burke, L., 174
Butterfield, F., 184, 187, 191

C

Campbell, J. C., 90
Cartoof, V. G., 125
Chmiel, J. S., 49
Chomsky, N., 182
Chu, S., 49
Clausen, J., 56
Clinton, W. J., 171, 172

Cohen, F., 55
Cole, J., 192
Comstock, G. D., 150, 158
Conkle, L., 42
Conner, E. M., 49
Conway, G. A., 50
Coontz, S., 112
Cummins, J., 69

D

Dane, B., 48
D'Angelo, L. J., 50
Dash, L., 124
Deisher, R. W., 151
deMarrais, K., 99
Demos, E. V., 55
Dennis, D. I., 154
DePaola, L., 41
Detels, R., 49
DiLapi, E. M., 146
Dobash, R., 24, 40
Doctorow, E. L., 3
Dohoney, J. M., 15
Dondero, T. J., 50
Dorning, M., 161
Draimin, B., 53, 54, 56
Dubrow, N., 8
Dunn, J., 56

E

Eckert, P., 24
Edelson, J., 41
Ehrenreich, B., 4
Ehrhardt, A., 54, 55
Eisenhart, M., 24
Eisenstein, Z. R., 121, 133, 134
Elam, S., 192
Elkind, P., 41
Ellison, R., xx, 20
Enger, C., 49
Evans, N. J., 161
Everhart, R., 25

F

Fagan, J., 42
Fanos, J., 47, 48, 51, 54, 55, 62

Fantuzzo, J., 41
Farrow, J. A., 151
Fernandez, R., 129
Fine, M., 25, 27, 112, 117, 118, 132
Finkelstein, B., 169
Flick, T. M., 192
Forrest, J. D., 129, 131
Forsyth, B., 51, 52, 53
Foucault, M., 125
Fraser, N., 121
Freire, P., 160
Friend, R., 139, 140, 141, 142, 143, 153, 155, 159, 162
Furman, E., 56

G

Gallup, A., 192
Garbarino, J., 8
Garmezy, N., 55
Geary, P. A., 129
Geballe, S., 47, 48, 50, 51, 52, 56, 59, 61
Gelber, R., 49
Gibbs, N., 183, 184
Gibson, P., 151
Ginchild, R., 56, 59
Giroux, H., 134
Goldberg, G. S., 4
Goldman, N., 129, 131
Gonsiorek, J. C., 153
Gonzalez, C. T., 153
Gordon, L., 4, 121, 148
Gorey, E., 51, 52, 53, 55, 57, 58
Gould, R., 47, 48, 50, 51, 52, 60, 62
Gover, J., 150, 153
Graff, H. J., 123, 126
Graham, N., 49
Greenhouse, S., xxi
Griffin, M. L., xxii
Griffin, P., 144, 145
Groce, N., 52, 53
Gruendel, J., 47, 48, 50, 51, 52, 55, 56
Grusznski, R., 41
Gwinn, M., 49

H

Haberman, M., 17
Hall, P. L., 13
Hansen, K., 42

Harlow, R. E., 154
Harrington, M., xx
Harris, T., 56
Harrison, D., 17
Hayman, C. R., 50
Henshaw, S., 129, 131
Herbert, B., 16, 185
Herdt, G., 141, 152, 153
Herek, G. M., 141, 150, 153
Herrnstein, R. J., 194
Hetrick, E. S., 153
Hoff, L., 24, 40
Holland, D., 24
Holland, P., 128
Holmes, S. A., xxi
Holquist, M., 125
hooks, b., 133, 160
Howell, J., 27
Hudis, J., 54, 55
Hughes, H., 41, 42
Hunter, J., 150

I

Igoa, C., 69, 74

J

Jacobs, F. H., 14
Jacobson, R. L., 49
Jaffe, P., 41, 42
James, A., 126
Jennings, K., 159, 162
Jones, E. F., 129, 131
Jones, L., 92
Jouriles, E., 41

K

Karon, J. M., 49
Kastenbaum, R., 51
Katz, M., 184
Kaufman, T., 5
Kavanaugh, 42
Kelly, G., 24
Keough, K., 192
Khare, M., 49
Kilborn, P. T., 187
Kincaid, J. R., 125

King, C. R., xxii
Kingsley, L. A., 49
Kirk, S., 192
Kiselev, P., 49
Klein, H. A., 98
Klein, J., 112
Kotlowitz, A., 187
Kozol, J., xxii, xxiii, 107, 184
Kremen, E., 4
Kroger, J. A., 106, 107
Krysial, G. J., 150
Kunen, J. S., xxiii
Kunzel, R. G., 121

L

Lade, D., 58
Lambert, L., 41
Lawson, A. 124
Lazere, E., 5
LeCompte, M. D., 99
Lenzer, J., 133
Lesko, N., 121, 123, 125, 129, 132
Levine, C., 48
Lewis, M., 54, 55
Lincoln, R., 129, 131
Linehan, M. F., 17
Lipkin, A., 147, 149, 162
Lipson, M., 52, 53
Little, P., 14
Lorde, A., 139
Lubeck, S., xx
Luker, K., 121, 188, 189, 190
Luthar, S., 55, 56

M

Males, M. A., 184, 185, 188, 189, 190, 191, 192, 193, 196
Maloney, M. E., 92, 93, 96, 97, 100
Mandelbaum, R., 56, 59
Mann, C., 6, 7
Martin, D. A., 153
Martin, H., 41, 42
Martino, T., 41
Mathis, J. C., 119
Maza, J. A., 13
McChesney, K. Y., 13
McCoy, C. B., 89, 91, 98
McCoy, H. V., 98

McDonald, G. J., 153
McFerron, J., 42
McLaren, P., 138
McQuillan, G., 49
McRobbie, A., 24
Mellins, C., 54, 55
Michaels, D., 48
Mikulski, B., 172, 179
Miller, C., 50
Miller, D., 97
Miller, S., 48
Minton, H. L., 153
Mullen, F., 56
Munoz, A., 49
Murcott, A., 121
Murray, C., 194

N

Nagler, S., 51, 52, 53
Neisen, J., 139, 140
Nelson, H. L., 118, 119
Nicarthy, G., 24
Nihlen, A., 24
Noguera, P., 192
Norwood, W., 41
Novick, A., 53, 62

O

Obermiller, P. J., 92, 93, 96, 97, 100, 106,
    107
Oldendick, R. W., 97
Orenstein, P.
O'Sullivan, M. T., 49

P

Parrot, S., 6, 7
Patterson, C., 147
Pear, R., 186
Pearce, D., 4
Pellegrini, D., 56
Peng, Y., 49
Perez-Porter, M., 56, 59
Petersen, L. R., 49, 50
Pharr, S., 142
Philliber, W. W., 89, 91
Pipher, M., 114, 116
Piven, F. F., 4
Plomin, R., 56

Polakow, V., 4, 14, 15, 188
Pollard, D., 24
Prince, T., 143
Prothrow-Stith, D., 193, 195
Prout, A., 126
Purcell-Gates, V., 102
Purpel, D. E., xxiv

Q

Quint, S., 18
Quinton, D., 56

R

Rafferty, Y., 11, 12, 13, 14
Rains, P. M., 131
Raitz, K. B., 89, 90
Randolph, M., 42
Reid, J., 42
Reiling, D., 15
Remafedi, G., 151, 153
Rhode, D., 188
Rich, A., 140, 196
Rodway, M., 41
Rofes, E., 153
Rogers, M., 49
Rollins, N., 13
Roosevelt, T., 170
Rose, L., 192
Rosenberg, L., 13
Rosenberg, P. S., 49
Rosoff, J. E., 129, 131
Ross, D., 124
Roth, J., 48
Rotheram-Borus, M. J., 54
Rubin, G., 138
Rubin, L., 25
Ruddick, S., 125
Rutter, M., 55, 56
Rutter, R. A., 129

S

Sander, J., 124
Savin-Williams, R. C., 155
Schaecher, R., 150
Schechter, S., 24
Schneider, M., 153, 154
Schodolski, V., 113
Scott, G., 49

Sedgwick, E. K., 127
Segura, J., 54
Selik, R., 49
Shapiro, S., xxiv
Shear, M., xxiii
Shearer, W., 49
Shin, M., 13
Siegel, R., 48, 51, 52, 53, 55, 57, 58
Silverman, J., 129, 131
Simons, R., 49
Sivertsen, W., 138
Skolnick, A. A., 186
Smith, A. J., 150
Smith, G. A., 129
Smith, R., 55
Solberg, A., 131
Solinger, R., 121
Soros, G., 185
Sperling, R. S., 49
St. Louis, M., 50
Starnes, B., 98
Stein, G., 48
Steinberg, L., 194
Steinbock, M., 5, 14
Steinmetz, S., 6, 7, 24, 40
Stewart, J., 42
Strauss, D. L., 185
Strauss, M., 24, 40
Sullivan, J., xxiii
Sullivan, M., 97
Super, D. A., 6
Sutton, S., 41
Swadener, B. B., xx, 183, 193

T

Telingator, C., 51, 54, 55
Thames, T., 138
Thompson, S., 112, 118
Tickamyer, A. R., 90
Tickamyer, C., 90
Torres, A., 129, 131
Treadway, L., 154, 160
Treichler, P., 121
Tremble, B., 153, 154
Trenchard, L., 147
Trevino, D. G., 98
Trinh, T. M., 112
Troiden, R. R., 153, 154
Turner, R. L., 105

U

Ulack, R., 89, 90

V

Valli, L., 24, 25
Van Dyke, R., 49
Verhovek, S. H., 187

W

Wagar, J., 41
Walker, L., 24, 40, 41
Wallace, C., 24
Walling, D. R., 153, 160
Warner, M., 183
Washington, J., 161
Weatherley, R. A., 125
Weber, B., xxiii
Wehlage, G. G., 129
Weinberg, G. H., 141
Weis, L., 25, 27, 112
Weller, J., 100
Werner, R., 55
Westoff, C. F., 129, 131
Westra, B., 42
White, E., 24
White, J. E., xxiii
Whitlock, K., 146, 154
Wiener, L., 50, 51, 53, 54, 55, 62
Wilgoren, D., xxiii
Willis, P., 25
Wilson, J. C., 157
Wilson, S., 41, 42
Wilson, W. J., 7
Winer, L., 170
Wolfe, D., 41, 42
Woods, C., 17
Woog, D., 155, 156
Wrigley, J., 24
Wulf, D., 129, 131

Y

Yoakam, J., 154, 160

Z

Zak, L., 42
Zigler, E., 55, 56

Subject Index

❦ • ❦

A

Abuse, sexual, *see* Sexual abuse
Acquired Immunodeficiency Syndrome
        (AIDS), 47–62, 133, 146, 189
    populations affected by, 48–50
    prevalence, 48–50
Adolescence, 123–126, 132, 134
Aid to Families with Dependent Children
        (AFDC), 6, 19, 59, 171, 174, 187
AIDS-affected children and youth, xxvi,
        47–62
    barriers to a caring response, 57–60
    and invisibility, 48–50, 55, 57, 60, 62
    and resilience, 55–57
    and schooling, 60–62
    and stigma, 52, 58
    vulnerability of, 48, 50–53
Appalachia, 89–90
Appalachian children, urban, xxvii–xxviii,
        89–109
    history of migration, 93–94
    and invisibility, 91, 108–109
    and poverty, 90, 98–100
    and schooling, 91, 94–109
    stereotypes of, 97–98, 107
    values of, 92–93
Art as a second language, xxvii, 73–87

B

Baldwin, James, 143, 148

B

Benjamin Franklin Day Elementary
        School, 18–19
Bright Prospects Alternative School,
        128–130, 132

C

Children of the Rainbow Curriculum, 147
Civilizing Act, 169–170
Concealment, culture of, 38–39
Contract with America, 16
Critical rationality, xii–xiii

D

Dollmaker, The, 93–96
Domestic violence, *see* Violence, domestic

E

Earned Income Tax Credit Bill, 171
Education, *see* Schools and schooling
    social foundations of, xvi

F

Family Leave Act, 171

G

Gay and lesbian youth, *see* Lesbian, gay, bi-
     sexual, and transgendered youth
Gide, Andre, xii
Girls, *see also* School-aged mothers
     in an alternative school for adjudicated
          teens, xxviii, 111–119
     and invisibility, 111–114, 117–119
     as performers: 113–118
     and public schooling, 119
     and sex, 114–118
     and sex education, 118
     and sexual abuse, 112–113, 116–117
     in an alternative school for young
          mothers, 128–132
White working-class, 33–39

H

Harvey Milk School, 154
Heterosexism, 138–160
     systemic maintenance of, 143–152
     and tolerance of harassment and
          violence, 138, 148–152
HIV disease, *see* AIDS and AIDS-affected
     children
Homeless children, xxv, 3–20
     and advocacy, 16–20
     increase in number of, 4–6, 185
     invisibility of, 3–4, 16, 20
     and the McKinney Act, 11–13
     Michael's story, 8–10, 15
     Monika's story, 1–11, 14
     and the Personal Responsibility and
          Work Opportunity Act, 6–7
     and schooling, 11–19
     stigmatization of, 14–16
Homelessness, xxi, 3–6, 8–20
Homophobia, 141–159

I

Immigrant children, xxvi–xxvii, 67–87
     and art, 73–87
     loss and isolation, 68–72
     messages to teachers, 72–73
     and religion, 83–84
     and schooling, xxvii, 68–86
     and visibility and invisibility, 67–70,
          73–76, 78–79, 83–84
Improving America's Schools Act, 12–13
Invisibility, ix–xi, xix–xxi, xxiv–xxv
     of AIDS-affected children and youth,
          48–50, 55, 57, 60, 62
     of children in the Personal Responsibil-
          ity and Work Opportunity
          Reconciliation Act, 182
     of girls in an alternative school for adju-
          dicated teens, 111–114,
          117–119
     of homeless children, 3–4, 16, 20
     of immigrant children, 67–70, 75
     of school-aged mothers, 121–122, 126,
          134–135
     and sexual abuse, 112–113, 117–118
     of sexual minority youth, 137–141,
          146, 148, 151–152
     of urban Appalachian children, 91,
          108–109

L

Lesbian, gay, bisexual, and transgendered
     youth, xxi, 137–163
     and the culture of schooling, 139–152
     and heterosexism, 139–159
     and homophobia, 141–159
     invisibility of, 137–141, 146, 151–152
     responses to homophobia and het-
          erosexism, 152–157
     and suicide, 138, 151–152
     violence against and harassment of,
          138, 148–152, 155, 158
Love, xiii, 146, 182
Lower Price Hill Community School,
     106–107

M

McKinney Act and Amendments, 9, 11–13
Meier, Deborah, 105
Mothers, school-aged, xxviii–xxix,
     121–135
     and normative age chronologies,
          122–128, 133–134
     representations of, in the public dis-
          course, 121, 124, 134,
          183–184, 188–191

N

Nabozny, Jamie, 150

P

Personal Responsibility and Work Opportunity Reconciliation Act of 1996, xxv, xxix–xxx, 6–7, 16, 26, 59, 169–182, 185–187
and commodification of child care, 178–179
and deficit reduction, 179–181
and invisibility of children, 182
and state-constructed norms, 173–175
and view of family, 175–178
Poverty, see also Personal Responsibility and Work Opportunity Reconciliation Act
among Appalachians, 90, 98–100
in communities of color, 195
and teenage pregnancy, 190
of women and children, 3–20, 184–188
and youth violence, 191
Public policy and child welfare, 169–173, 183

R

Reproductive rights, 133–135

S

Sampier, Florence, 62
Schmitz, Jonathan, 149
School-aged mothers, see Mothers, school–aged
Schools and schooling, x–xi, xvi, xxii–xxiv
and AIDS-affected youth, 60–62
in an alternative school for young mothers, 128–132
and Appalachian children, xxvii–xxviii, 91, 94–109
Benjamin Franklin Day Elementary School, 18–19
Bright Prospects Alternative School, 128–130, 132
and discourse on educational reform, 193–195
and domestic violence, xxvi, 37–43
Harvey Milk School, 154
heterosexist and homophobic culture of, xxix, 137–163
and homeless children, xxv, 11–19
and immigrant children, xxvii, 68–86
Lower Price Hill Community School, 106–107
as models of inclusion, 157–163
and the needs of girls, 119
and school-aged mothers, 128–132
segregation in, xxiii
Thomas J. Pappas Regional Education Center, 17, 19
Sex education, 118, 122, 131–134, 146–147, 158
and homosexuality, 146–147, 158
Sex and sexual abuse, xxviii, 32–33, 112–118, 125, 146, 174, 189–190
and invisibility, 112–113, 117–118
Sheldon, Lou, 144
Social Security Act, 171
Stereotyping of Appalachians, 93, 97–98, 107
Stigmatization, x, xii
of homeless children, 12, 14–16,
of people affected by AIDS, 52, 58
of young people, 183–184, 188, 191, 195–197

T

Teenage mothers, see School-aged mothers
Teenage pregnancy, see School-age mothers
Temporary Assistance to Needy Families (TANF), 6, 59, 174, 176
Thomas J. Pappas Regional Education Center, 17, 19

and reproductive rights, 133–135
and schooling, 128–132
and social age, 122, 129–132, 134–135
and visibility and invisibility, 121–122, 126, 134–135

V

Violence
    antigay and antilesbian, 138, 148–152,
        155, 158
    domestic, xxv–xxvi, 5, 9, 23–44
        and African American women, 28
        and concealment, culture of, 38–39
        effects on children, 40–42
        and homeless women and children,
            9
        and literature on schooling, 24–25
        and schooling, 37–43
        and White working-class girls,
            33–39
        and White working-class women,
            26–33
    youth, 184, 187–188, 191–193
        representation of, in the public dis-
            course, 191–193

W

Waterworks, The, 3
Welfare law, *see* Personal Responsibility
        and Work Opportunity Recon-
        ciliation Act
Women
    African-American and domestic vio-
        lence, 28
    and AIDS, 49
    and poverty, 4–5
    White working-class and domestic vio-
        lence, 26–33

Y

Yesterday's People, 100
Youth bashing, xxx, 183–197
    and educational reform, 193–194
Youth, sexual minority, *see* Lesbian, gay, bi-
        sexual, and transgendered youth
Youth violence, *see* Violence, youth

About the Authors

❈ ◆ ❈

Sue Books, a former journalist, is now an assistant professor in the Department of Educational Studies at the State University of New York at New Paltz where she teaches graduate and undergraduate courses in the social and philosophical foundations of education. She has published articles on issues related to education and poverty, education and work, and the public stigmatization of young people.

Kathleen Bennett deMarrais is an associate professor at Northern Arizona University's Center for Excellence in Education. Previously, she was a member of the faculty at the University of Tennessee, Knoxville, where she taught social foundations courses, established a qualitative research program, and developed the Urban/Multicultural Teacher Education Program. She also has worked at the University of Alaska, Fairbanks, as a field-coordinator in Bethel for a teacher education program for Native Alaskans. She is concerned with equity issues in schooling, particularly as related to gender and diversity. She has published numerous articles and is co-author of *The Way Schools Work: A Sociological Analysis of Education.*

Elyssa Doner is a doctoral candidate in the Department of Education Policy, Planning, and Administration at the University of Maryland, College Park. A recipient of a Maryland Graduate School Fellowship, she is currently exploring federal education policies with a focus on the ways in which budget processes inform the character and implementation of education policies.

Barbara Finkelstein is professor of education history in the Department of Education Policy, Planning, and Administration, University of Maryland, College Park. Her books, monographs, and articles focus on the historical and cultural dimensions of childhood policies, teacher roles, classroom practices, and curriculum policies in the United States and other nations. She has received many awards for published work in the history of childhood and education, and received a Senior Research Fellowship from the Japan Society for the Promotion of Sciences where, as a visiting scholar at the University of Tokyo, she studied childhood education and diversity policies and practices in Japan.

Richard A. Friend has worked as an educator and trainer for nearly 20 years. He is currently on the faculty of the University of Pennsylvania's Graduate School of Education in the Human Sexuality Education Program and works actively as a consultant and trainer in the areas of diversity, leadership, team building, and training of trainers. In addition, he conducts training and research on homophobia issues and their costs, undoing homophobia and heterosexism in organizations and in schooling, helping youth move from surviving to thriving, and understanding homophobia and heterosexism across the life span.

Shelley Geballe is co-director of Citizen's for Connecticut's Children and Youth and a lecturer in health policy at the Yale School of Public Health. For 10 years she was associate legal director of the Connecticut Civil Liberties Union Foundation, where she brought class action litigation on behalf of foster children, children living with AIDS, and other disenfranchised citizens. She co-edited *Forgotten Children of the AIDS Epidemic* (Yale University Press, 1995), co-produced a public television special on the same topic, "Mommy, Who'll Take Care of Me?" and speaks frequently on issues confronting children who are losing their parents to AIDS.

Janice Gruendel is executive director of Citizens for Connecticut's Children and Youth. She served as the deputy commissioner of three Connecticut agencies (Department of Children and Youth Services, Department of Health, and Department of Mental Retardation) and also as director of health services for the Department of Correction. She was vice president for the Education Group at Rabbit Ears Productions, developing quality multimedia educational products. She co-edited *Forgotten Children of the AIDS Epidemic* (Yale University Press, 1995) and co-produced the public television special on the same topic, "Mommy, Who'll Take Care of Me?"

Cristina Igoa, born in the Philippines, experienced life an as immigrant child in Colombia and later in the United States. Currently, she teaches immigrant students in a sheltered ESL program in the Hayward (California) Unified School District. She also teaches at the School of Education, College of Notre Dame, in Belmont. In 1975, she co-founded the Mission Reading Clinic in San Francisco. In 1980, she established a language center for immigrant children, which won the J. Russell Kent Award for exemplary programs in San Mateo County, and in 1994 she was awarded the University of San Francisco Educational Alumni's Outstanding Teacher Award.

Nancy Lesko is an associate professor in the Department of Curriculum and Instruction and an adjunct in Women's Studies at Indiana University-Bloomington. She teaches in the areas of curriculum, multiculturalism, and feminism, and has a strong interest in social theories and education. She is at work on a sociological examination of knowledges about adolescence, *Act Your Age! Developing the Modern Scientific Adolescent.*

Julia Marusza recently completed her dissertation entitled "Canal Town Youth: Constructing Poor White Identities in the Spaces of a Postindustrial Urban Community" at the State University of New York at Buffalo. In this project, the intersections of race, class, and gender are explored among a group of impoverished White middle school girls and boys as they spend time in the local bilingual school and historically White community center.

Reem Mourad is a master's degree candidate in the Department of Education Policy, Planning, and Administration at the University of Maryland, College Park. Formerly a teacher and a journalist who attended schools in Lebanon, he is currently pursuing graduate study that focuses on the historical and intercultural dimensions of education among indigenous peoples in the United States and other nations.

Valerie Polakow is a professor of education at Eastern Michigan University. She is the author of *The Erosion of Childhood* (University of Chicago Press, 1982) and *Lives on the Edge: Single Mothers and Their Children in the Other America* (University of Chicago Press, 1993), which won the Phi Delta Kappan Book of the Year Award in 1994. She has written numerous articles about women and children in poverty, welfare policies, homelessness, child care policy, and educational advocacy. During 1995 she was a Fulbright scholar in Denmark, researching family and child care policies. She has been active in local, state, and national advocacy organizations.

Linda Steet is an assistant professor of social foundations of education and women's studies at The University of Michigan–Flint. Her specializations are the historical sociology of education, multicultural education, and popular culture and education. Steet is currently working on a history of girls' public reform schools and examining present cultural practices regarding the identification and treatment of delinquent girls. She also has a forthcoming book being published by the State University of New York Press, *Imaginative Geography: Teaching Orientalism in American Popular Education Through National Geographic, 1888–1988.*

Lois Weis is professor of sociology of education at the State University of New York at Buffalo. She is the author and/or editor of numerous books and essays on social class, race, and gender, including, most recently, *Off White* (Routledge, 1997), *Beyond Silenced Voices* (State University of New York Press, 1994), and *Beyond Black and White* (State University of New York Press, 1997). Her upcoming book (with Michelle Fine), *The Unknown City,* is based on 3 years of fieldwork funded by the Spencer Foundation. Beacon Press will publish the volume in 1998.

Please remember that this is a library book,
and that it belongs only temporarily to each
person who uses it. Be considerate. Do
not write in this, or any, library book.

DATE DUE

JE 12 '04			
DE 7 04			
AP 30 05			
MR 12 '06			
MR 13 '06			
MY 18 '06			
AG 23 '06			
AP 12 '07			
MR 10 08			
SEP 01 2010			

DEMCO 38-296